# The History of the
## WORLD CUP

Brian Glanville

# The History of the
# WORLD CUP

**Faber & Faber**
London Boston

*First published as* The Sunday Times History
of the World Cup *in 1973*
*by Times Newspapers Limited*
*This revised edition published in 1980*
*by Faber and Faber Limited*
*3 Queen Square London WC1N 3AU*
*Filmset by Latimer Trend & Company Ltd Plymouth*
*Printed in Great Britain by*
*Redwood Burn & Co Ltd, Trowbridge and Esher*
*All rights reserved*

*British Library Cataloguing in Publication Data*

Glanville, Brian
   The history of the World Cup.—Revised ed.
   1. World Cup (Soccer)—History
   I. Title   II. 'Sunday times' history of
   the World Cup
   796.33'466      GV943.49

   ISBN 0–571–11498–9

# Contents

# List of Illustrations

*between pages 96 and 97*

The author and publishers are glad to acknowledge the following copyright-holders of illustrations reproduced in this book:

Colorsport, 25
Keystone Press Agency, 1–17, 19, 20
S & G Press Agency, 22, 24
Syndication International, 18, 21, 23, 26–28

# Foreword

Interest in international football began in 1872, when the first match between any two countries was played. This was Scotland v. England in Glasgow. Fifty-eight years later, in 1930, Uruguay staged the first World Cup tournament in which thirteen countries took part, only three being from Europe, presumably because in those days a two to three week sea voyage was involved.

As a member of the FIFA World Cup Organising Committee since 1950, when the first post-war competition was staged in Brazil, and as President during four tournaments, I feel qualified to write a foreword to this history of the greatest sports event in the world, second only to the Olympic Games. I am pleased to do so because in this ever-changing world of sport the history of international events becomes lost unless it is recorded. Not only the statistics, but the atmosphere in which the games were played; outstanding players, referees, administrators should be remembered. So, too, should the interest which the resident ambassadors and their respective staffs show in their team's participation. On no-match days receptions, invitations to visit other sports clubs and sometimes to private homes are arranged; these breaks from training and the constant togetherness are generally regarded as of great benefit to the team.

In this volume, Brian Glanville has sought to revive the memories of old times and provide interesting information for all those who will want to have details of all previous competitions at the time of the World Cup to be staged in Spain in 1982.

In this book the reader will learn of the changes in the competition from those early days. He will recall the great players who have taken part, the exciting matches, one of the most skilful being between Brazil and Sweden in Stockholm in 1958 when Pelé, an unknown player, was in devastating form; of the enlarged and splendidly equipped stadia built to house the ever-increasing number of spectators wishing to witness the matches.

From 1974 the World Cup trophy was named simply 'The FIFA World Cup'. I was asked by Brazil to allow them to present a gold cup to be called the 'Stanley Rous Cup' but although I was grateful for the gesture I asked the Executive Committee to refuse the generous offer because I have always been averse to trophies bearing names of persons. Invariably, a trophy with a name attached is referred to with a shortened title such as 'The World Cup' and that is what the cup is now styled. That does not mean that Jules Rimet and his fellow pioneers have been forgotten. They would certainly have been surprised at the development of the competition they founded, considering the number of countries involved and the changes in the regulations in the present competition.

It is important that enthusiasts for the game should know and under-stand how the World Cup is organised in other countries and conti-nents. As Honorary President of an international federation I am sure that this history of the World Cup will enlighten the readers about football as it is played in all parts of the world. The information about the world's greatest football tournament as set out in the pages of this book is welcome and I recommend it to be widely read and as a useful addition to the bookshelf and library of all those who are interested in the game of soccer.

STANLEY ROUS

# Uruguay

## 1930

## Background to 1930

Like so many of the best ideas in football, that of the World Cup was conceived in France. Its true parents were, indeed, two Frenchmen: Jules Rimet, after whom it was eventually named, and Henri Delaunay. Rimet was President of the French Federation, FFF, for thirty years from its beginning in 1919, and President of FIFA, the Fédération Internationale des Football Associations, from 1920 to 1954; an extraordinary record. Delaunay, who had been concerned with running French football from 1908, was officially Secretary from 1919 till his death in 1956, a little before the death of the 83-year-old Rimet.

These two men complemented each other: Rimet the persuader, the diplomat, sometimes intransigent, always devoted to the game; Delaunay the worker, visionary and energetic. Sometimes they quarrelled, but they were the pioneers of French football, European football—and the World Cup.

The very first meeting of FIFA took place in Paris in 1904—without the benefit of British attendance—and decided rather grandly that it alone had the right to organise a world championship. This right was not to be exercised for twenty-six years. In 1920, at FIFA's Antwerp congress, concurrent with the Olympic Games, the idea of a World Cup, previously much debated, was accepted in principle. In 1924, at the Paris Olympics, the FIFA meeting discussed it in more serious detail, while a dazzling and hitherto obscure Uruguayan side walked off with the soccer tournament.

Two years later, at FIFA's congress, Delaunay proclaimed: 'Today international football can no longer be held within the confines of the Olympics; and many countries where professionalism is now recognised and organised cannot any longer be represented there by their best players.'

This had always been true of Britain, which even before the war had been represented by genuine amateurs and which in a couple of years would withdraw from FIFA over the question of broken time payments. Now, it was keeping out such rising countries as Austria and Hungary, while many of those which competed were professionals in all but name. In 1928, in Amsterdam, where Uruguay retained their title against a strong challenge from Argentina, Delaunay's resolution that the World Cup be set on foot at once was adopted. But where should it be played?

There were five aspirants: Italy, Holland, Spain, Sweden and Uruguay. Tiny Uruguay, with its proud footballing tradition—'Other countries have their history,' their team manager, Viera, would say at

the 1966 World Cup, 'Uruguay has its football'—made an offer extraordinary for a country of merely two million people. They would pay
all travelling and hotel expenses for the visiting teams, and they would
build a new stadium for the tournament. It would be in central Montevideo, and would be called the Centenary Stadium, for Uruguay in
1930 would be celebrating a hundred years of independence. It would
be built in only eight months, three of which included the rainy season.

Faced by such transcendent enthusiasm, what could the European
countries do but withdraw—altogether? None of the four disappointed
hosts made the trip to Uruguay, which in those days took a wearying
three weeks.

## The Contenders

Allotted the World Cup at FIFA's 1929 congress in Barcelona, Uruguay
found themselves, two months before it was due to kick off, without a
single European entrant. In addition to the four we have mentioned,
the Austrians, Hungarians, Germans, Swiss and Czechs said no; the
British were out of FIFA. Belgium, Romania and Yugoslavia vacillated,
as did France, though after Rimet's appointment to the FIFA presi-
dency, and Uruguay's 1924 appearance in Paris, the moral imperatives
were strong.

Embittered, insulted, the Latin American federations threatened to
withdraw from FIFA; a threat they would be making many times in the
years to come. Belgium and Romania at last adhered—Belgium under
the pressure of the veteran FIFA Vice-President, Rodolphe William
Seeldrayers, Romania under that of King Carol himself. Though the
German-speaking king was never popular in Romania, he had always
had much to do with Romanian sport. One of his first acts, on coming
to the throne, was to grant an amnesty to all suspended Romanian
footballers. Now he picked the Romanian team himself and brought
pressure on the companies which employed them to give them time
off for Uruguay. Yugoslavia also agreed to go, so there would be four
European entrants; but not even by the greatest feat of imagination
could they be ranked among the élite. The bitterness in Montevideo
was scarcely assuaged.

In the 1924 Olympics Uruguay had thrashed Yugoslavia 7–0 and
France 5–1. In 1928, Belgium had been beaten by Argentina 6–3; and
now they were travelling without three of their best players, including
Bastin.

Argentina, traditional rivals of Uruguay in the Lipton Cup, would
be there, however, and would be doughty rivals. In 1928, it had taken
a replay before they succumbed 2–1 in the Olympic Final.

The United States would be there too; moreover, they were one of the teams seeded in the four qualifying pools, which had been set up only when it was realised there wouldn't be enough countries to make a knock-out competition possible. At this time there was still professional football of a sort in the States, the rump of the attempt by such as Bethlehem Steel to put the sport on its feet in the 1920s. The American team, managed by Jack Coll of Brooklyn Wanderers, was made up largely of British and Scots pros: Alec Wood, James Gallacher, Andrew Auld, James Brown and Bart McGhee from Scotland, George Moorhouse from England. They were powerfully-built men whom the French players nicknamed 'the shot-putters'.

Brazil were present, but it was not long since the gates had been opened to the black player and the game there was still somewhat in a condition of inspired anarchy. Chile and Mexico, who made up Pool I with Argentina and France; Bolivia, in Pool II with Brazil and Yugoslavia; Peru, in Pool III with Uruguay and Romania; Paraguay, in Pool IV with the USA and Belgium completed the entry of thirteen. The four Pool winners would go into the semi-finals.

Uruguay were unquestionably the favourites, though their fine team of the 1924 and 1928 Olympics was fractionally past its peak; in the image of its famous centre-forward, Pedro Petrone. Nevertheless, it had home advantage and its still abundant talent in its favour, and it is arguable that it would have won the tournament whatever European teams had come, even England, Scotland and the formidable Austrian Wunderteam.

## The Earlier Matches

The four European teams, whose boat had picked up the Brazilians en route, were tumultuously welcomed in Montevideo, though none had been seeded head of a group; a distinction reserved for Uruguay, Argentina, Brazil and the USA. The Centenary Stadium was, alas, still unfinished, thanks to heavy rain; early matches had to be played on the grounds of the Penarol and Nacional clubs, Pocito and Central Park. On Sunday afternoon, July 13, France opened the tournament against Mexico with a 4–1 win; although their admirable and unspectacular goalkeeper, Alex Thépot, was kicked on the jaw after ten minutes, giving way to his left-half, Chantrel. (There would be no substitutes for another forty years.) The French team was a good and lively one, with Etienne Mattler, who would play so well for France for so long, at right-back, Pinel as pivot, and a captain, Alex Villaplane, the right-half, who would ultimately be shot by the French Resistance for collaborating with the Nazis.

Two days later, France faced the gifted Argentinians—and were most unlucky to go down by 1–0. Monti was at his most ferocious, hurting the ankle of Lucien Laurent, France's inside-left, early in the game, and giving Pinel, who largely overplayed him, some kind of a knock every time they met. Monti it was who scored the goal, nine minutes from time. Argentina were given a free kick, twenty yards out. As Monti took it, Pinel stepped to his right, unsighting the excellent Thépot—and the shot flashed into the net.

Three minutes later, with Maschinot, the centre-forward limping after another tackle by Monti, Marcel Langiller raced the length of the field. It might have been the equaliser, but Almeida Rego, the Brazilian referee, suddenly blew for time. Instant chaos. While Argentina's fans invaded the field of Central Park, the French players assailed the referee, insisting there were six minutes left. Mounted police galloped on to the field, Senhor Rego consulted his watch and his linesmen, and at last, raising his arms, cried to the heavens that he had erred in good faith. Cierro, the Argentinian inside-left, fainted, and the game resumed, and the remaining minutes petered uneventfully away.

Afterwards, Uruguay's watching players declared that France deserved to win, Thépot and Pinel were carried off shoulder high, and the Argentinians complained accordingly to the Organising Committee, threatening to go home; thus sounding what would become another tediously familiar note.

In their next match, against Mexico, deprived of Manuel Ferreira, taking a university exam, they brought in young Guillermo Stabile, *El Infiltrador*, destined to become the competition's leading scorer and eventually his country's team manager.

This was a match in which the Bolivian referee, Ulysses Saucedo, gave no fewer than five penalties—Monti was not playing!—of which perhaps two were justified.

Stabile, who had scored three goals against Mexico, kept his place for a tempestuous game against Chile, Ferreira coming in as inside-left. Two minutes from half-time Monti, back again, kicked at Torres, Chile's left-half, as he jumped to head the ball. Torries retaliated, and both teams indulged in a protracted brawl, broken up with great difficulty by the police.

Argentina, Stabile scoring twice more, won 3–1 and advanced to the semi-finals. A tired France had anti-climactically gone down 1–0 to Chile, managed by the old Hungarian star, George Orth.

Uruguay did not enter the fray till July 18, when the Centenary Stadium was at last ready to receive them. Not unexpectedly, perhaps, the game against Peru was a disappointment. Peru's defence held out well, and where Romania had scored three against them, Uruguay could manage only one; a late one by Castro—a player who had lost the lower part of one arm.

For their next match, against Romania, Uruguay brought in

Scarone and their new star, Pelegrin Anselmo, for Castro and Petrone, respectively, winning 4–0 in a canter to qualify.

In Group II, Yugoslavia unexpectedly toppled Brazil 2–1 in their first game. Brazil were individually cleverer, collectively inferior. Two of the Yugoslav team, Beck and Stefanovic, had just helped Sète win the French Cup. Tirnanic and Beck scored in the first half-hour, another goal was disallowed for offside, and Brazil could muster but one reply through their captain, Neto. Each team then beat Bolivia 4–0, and the Yugoslavs went through.

So did the United States, their strong defence and breakaway attacks routing Belgium and Paraguay in turn by 3–0. In the semi-final, alas, the much greater pace and sophistication of the Argentinians simply overwhelmed them and they crashed 6–1; precisely the score by which Uruguay trounced Yugoslavia. The half-time score was only 1–0, a goal credited to Monti, but in the second half the Americans simply fell apart, conceding five more, the last three within nine minutes, two to the swift right-winger, Peucelle. Brown, their own outside-right, got their only goal.

Eighty thousand spectators watched Uruguay despatch Yugoslavia after sustaining the shock of a fourth-minute goal by Seculic. Cea and Anselmo made it 2–1 by the interval, and Yugoslavia were then refused, on a controversial offside decision, what would have been their equaliser.

So, in the second half, Uruguay scored four. Fernandez caught the Yugoslav defence off guard with a cleverly lobbed free kick which Iriarte converted, then Cea, the inside-left, scored two more, the first after a mistake by Yugoslavia's captain and right-back, Ivkovic. Next day, Argentina joined them in a Final which would be a repetition of the Olympic Final of 1928.

## The Final   Uruguay v. Argentina

In Buenos Aires the excitement was phenomenal. Ten packet-boats were chartered to take fans across the River Plate to Montevideo, but they were insufficient; thousands of desperate supporters thronged the centre of Buenos Aires, clamouring for more boats. When they eventually sailed, at ten o'clock on the eve of the Final, a great crowd thronged the quayside to see them off, letting off fireworks and chanting, '*Argentina si, Uruguay no!* Victory or death!' Arriving in Montevideo, the Argentinians were searched for revolvers by customs and police; and searched again at the entrance to the Centenary Stadium. The kick-off was scheduled for two o'clock; the gates were opened at eight in the morning, and by noon the ground was packed. Though it could take 100,000, the attendance was limited to 90,000—with memories of an inaugural day when the police had been overwhelmed by the crowds and the ticket offices, now closed with metal grilles, were assailed.

John Langenus, chosen, as had been expected, to referee the match, demanded that the safety of himself and his linesmen be guaranteed, and only a few hours before kick-off did his fellow referees authorise him to preside. The Argentinian players had been under a police guard day and night, mounted police escorting their coach to and from each training session. Around the stadium, soldiers with fixed bayonets kept the crowds moving; and after all this there was still the question of the match ball.

Each team insisted on a ball of native manufacture; a point which had not been covered in the regulations. It was finally decided that Langenus should toss up on the field. To a fusillade of firecrackers, he did. Argentina won.

Though Uruguay clearly had to be favoured on their own stadium, before their own crowd, the team had not played with the assurance of its predecessors. Moreover, Pelegrin Anselmo was unfit and was replaced at centre-forward by Castro; Petrone's sun had definitely set. Argentina might have missed Orsi, but they had found Stabile, and their forward play had been excellent; full of fast, sweeping, intelligent movements, the traditionally fine ball control allied to subtle positioning. In goal, however, there was a manifest weakness. Angelo Bossio's flashy, unreliable play had led to his being dropped from the semi-final, but his replacement, Juan Botasso, was no great improvement.

The first half was pregnant with surprises. After only twelve minutes, Pablo Dorado, the Uruguayan right-winger, gave his country the lead, but Peucelle, his opposite number, equalised, and ten minutes from half-time John Langenus boldly sanctioned a goal by Stabile which Nasazzi, Uruguay's captain, fiercely insisted was offside. Crowds being unpredictable organisms, there was no attempt to invade the pitch this time, merely a stunned acceptance.

The crowds came to life again ten minutes after the interval, when Pedro Cea capped an insidious dribble with the equalising goal. Uruguay had broken the spell. Ten minutes more and the young Uruguayan outside-left, Santos Iriarte, put them ahead, and finally Castro, Anselmo's understudy, smashed the ball into the roof of the net in the concluding seconds. Uruguay had won an exciting and surprisingly good-tempered game.

Motor horns blared in triumph, ships blew their sirens in the port, flags and banners flew, the next day was proclaimed a national holiday. The golden, 50,000-franc Cup, designed by a French sculptor, Abel Lafleur, was consigned to Nasazzi by Jules Rimet.

In Buenos Aires, the Uruguayan Consulate was stoned by an infuriated mob until the police dispersed it by opening fire. The World Cup was well and truly launched.

# RESULTS: Uruguay 1930

## Pool I

France 4, Mexico 1 (HT 3/0)
Argentina 1, France 0 (HT 0/0)
Chile 3, Mexico 0 (HT 1/0)
Chile 1, France 0 (HT 0/0)
Argentina 6, Mexico 3 (HT 3/0)
Argentina 3, Chile 1 (HT 2/1)

|           | P | W | D | L | GOALS F | A | Pts |
|-----------|---|---|---|---|---------|---|-----|
| Argentina | 3 | 3 | 0 | 0 | 10      | 4 | 6   |
| Chile     | 3 | 2 | 0 | 1 | 5       | 3 | 4   |
| France    | 3 | 1 | 0 | 2 | 4       | 3 | 2   |
| Mexico    | 3 | 0 | 0 | 3 | 4       | 13| 0   |

## Pool II

Yugoslavia 2, Brazil 1 (HT 2/0)
Yugoslavia 4, Bolivia 0 (HT 0/0)
Brazil 4, Bolivia 0 (HT 1/0)

|            | P | W | D | L | GOALS F | A | Pts |
|------------|---|---|---|---|---------|---|-----|
| Yugoslavia | 2 | 2 | 0 | 0 | 6       | 1 | 4   |
| Brazil     | 2 | 1 | 0 | 1 | 5       | 2 | 2   |
| Bolivia    | 2 | 0 | 0 | 2 | 0       | 8 | 0   |

## Pool III

Romania 3, Peru 1 (HT 1/0)
Uruguay 1, Peru 0 (HT 0/0)
Uruguay 4, Romania 0 (HT 4/0)

|         | P | W | D | L | GOALS F | A | Pts |
|---------|---|---|---|---|---------|---|-----|
| Uruguay | 2 | 2 | 0 | 0 | 5       | 0 | 4   |
| Romania | 2 | 1 | 0 | 1 | 3       | 5 | 2   |
| Peru    | 2 | 0 | 0 | 2 | 1       | 4 | 0   |

## Pool IV

United States 3, Belgium 0 (HT 2/0)
United States 3, Paraguay 0 (HT 2/0)
Paraguay 1, Belgium 0 (HT 1/0)

|               | P | W | D | L | GOALS F | A | Pts |
|---------------|---|---|---|---|---------|---|-----|
| United States | 2 | 2 | 0 | 0 | 6       | 0 | 4   |
| Paraguay      | 2 | 1 | 0 | 1 | 1       | 3 | 2   |
| Belgium       | 2 | 0 | 0 | 2 | 0       | 4 | 0   |

## Semi-finals

**Argentina 6**    **United States 1**

Botasso; Della Torre, Paternoster; Evaristo, J., Monti, Orlandini; Peucelle, Scopelli, Stabile, Ferreira (capt.), Evaristo, M.

Douglas; Wood, Moorhouse; Gallacher, Tracey, Auld; Brown, Gonsalvez, Patenaude, Florie (capt.), McGhee

SCORERS
Monti, Scopelli, Stabile (2), Peucelle (2), for Argentina
Brown for United States
HT 1/0

**Uruguay 6**    **Yugoslavia 1**

Ballesteros; Nasazzi (capt.), Mascheroni; Andrade, Fernandez, Gestido; Dorado, Scarone, Anselmo, Cea, Iriarte.

Yavocic; Ivkovic (capt.); Milhailovic; Arsenievic, Stefanovic, Djokic; Tirnanic, Marianovic, Beck, Vujadinovic, Seculic.

SCORERS
Cea (3), Anselmo (2), Iriarte for Uruguay
Seculic for Yugoslavia
HT 3/1

## Final

**Uruguay 4**    **Argentina 2**

Ballesteros; Nasazzi (capt.), Mascheroni; Andrade, Fernandez, Gestido; Dorado, Scarone, Castro, Cea, Iriarte.

Botasso; Della Torre, Paternoster; Evaristo, J., Monti, Suarez; Peucelle Varallo, Stabile, Ferreira (capt.), Evaristo, M.

SCORERS
Dorado, Cea, Iriarte, Castro for Uruguay
Peucelle, Stabile for Argentina
HT 1/2

# Italy
## 1934

## Background to Italy

It would be twenty years before the World Cup returned to South America—and to Uruguay. The 1934 tournament was altogether more high-powered and highly competitive, though for the first and only time so far the holders did not defend. Uruguay, still piqued by the defection of the European 'powers' in 1930, plagued, too, by one of those periodic players' strikes which would still torment them over forty years later, stayed at home. Italy organised it, Italy won, prompting the reflection of John Langenus: 'In the majority of countries, the World Championship was called a sporting fiasco, because beside the desire to win all other sporting considerations were non-existent, and because, moreover, a certain spirit brooded over the whole Championship. Italy wanted to win, it was natural, but they allowed it to be seen too clearly.'

Given the Fascist climate of the times, it was perhaps inevitable. The Italian team, the *azzurri* (blues) were 'Mussolini's *azzurri*', the Duce himself would appear, heavy-chinned and smirking under a yachting cap, at Rome's Stadio Torino. Vittorio Pozzo, the Italian *Commissario Tecnico*, a great anglophile but a great authoritarian, unquestionably used the inflated spirit of the times to promote an atmosphere, a discipline, which subsequent Italian managers have envied, and which would never have been possible without it; any more than Pozzo himself, the revered father figure.

He and the equally authoritarian anglophile Hugo Meisl of Austria, were the dominant figures in European football between the wars, sharing the friendship of Herbert Chapman, the remarkable Yorkshireman who built up Arsenal. The 'natural' final would have been between Italy and Meisl's so-called Wunderteam, fractionally past its peak but still a fine side, which had whacked Italy 4–2 in Turin only months before the World Cup began. They would meet in the semifinal.

This time, it would be a knock-out competition with sixteen teams in the first round; a dispensation which meant that Brazil and Argentina came some eight thousand miles to play just one game. There had been, besides, a qualifying competition, in which, curiously, even the Italians were obliged to take part. They beat Greece in Milan, a match in which Nereo Rocco of Triestina, later the outstanding manager of Milan, played his only (half) game for his country.

The tournament had been assigned to Italy at the Stockholm congress of 1932. It was realised that it could no longer be confined to a single city, nor to a country without huge resources. Uruguay had in fact paid everyone's expenses and still made a comfortable profit in 1930, but the scale was growing. 'The Italian Federation', promised its delegate, *Avvocato* Mauro, 'is capable of sustaining these burdens, and even in the case of an adverse balance wants to hold the entire final stages of the tournament, using as its theatre the numerous and flourishing Italian cities, all provided with magnificent stadiums.' Behind the hard-working Mauro and his pleasant energetic colleague, Engineer Barassi, the Fascist government stood ready to pick up the cheque.

## The Opening Games

There was still, curiously, an eliminating match to play before the tournament proper could begin; curiously because it took place in Rome between two countries as distant as Mexico and the United States. The Americans, with only two survivors from their 1930 semi-final team, won, but were thrashed 7–1 in the same Stadio Torino by Italy in the following game. Thirty-two teams had entered the qualifying tournament; twenty-two from Europe, eight from the Americas, one each from Asia and Africa—none from Britain.

Both South American teams went out at once. In Genoa, Spain were 3–1 up against Brazil at half-time, a score which did not change. Argentina went down 3–2 to Sweden, their team including not a single member of the 1930 side.

In Turin, France provided the chief surprise of the round, doing far better than had been expected against the Austrians, who had most of the luck that was going. Austria won only in extra time with a most dubious goal.

The Germans, who had prepared thoroughly, were startled by Belgium in Florence, but recovered strongly. The Belgians scored twice in the first half to give them a 2–1 lead; then the team blew up. Conen, Germany's centre-forward, completed a hat trick, and his side won 5–2.

In Trieste the fancied Czechs were troubled by the Romanians. Dobai scored for Romania after eleven minutes, but Puc, the thrustful Czech left-winger, and Nejedly, their dangerous, graceful inside-left, replied in the second half. The winner was rather a lucky goal, for Nejedly received the ball after Sobotka won it in a bounce-up.

Hungary were given a surprisingly hard time of it by Egypt in Naples, winning only 4–2. Switzerland beat the Dutch 3–2 in Milan; one of their goals, by the bespectacled centre-forward Kielholz, came from a shot which hit a bump in the ground and was crazily diverted.

**The Second Round**

The second round included two fascinating pairings: Italy would play Spain in Florence; Austria and Hungary, those old foes, would meet at Bologna.

Italy were rough, the referee weak. Spain took the lead with a goal which might have demoralised a less resilient team than Italy. When Langara, the centre-forward, took a free kick, Regueiro—whose son would play for Mexico in the 1968 Olympics—swung at the ball, miskicked it utterly, and in miskicking beat the wrong-footed Combi. A minute after the interval, Italy were lucky to equalise when Pizziolo, the right-half, took another free kick. Zamora, obstructed by Schiavio, could only push the ball out, and Ferrari drove it home.

In extra time, Pozzo switched Schiavio and Guaita, as he would in the Final, but now it was unproductive. After the game he called each of his players, one by one, into the salon of the hotel where they were staying on the Lungarno. For the replay the following day he wanted only volunteers, and there were three changes. Pizziolo had broken his leg—another blow Italy had ridden with aplomb—and gave way to Ferraris IV, while de Maria and Borel had their only game of the competition, in attack. Spain by contrast were able to use only four of their previous team. Noguet, a young reserve, stood in for Zamora, and Bosch, the left-winger, was hurt as early as the fourth minute. Eight minutes later Meazza, always dangerous in the air, rose gracefully to Orsi's corner and headed Italy into the semi-finals.

In Bologna, Hugo Meisl picked the busy little inside-forward Horwarth and he, though no Sindelar, gave the team fresh drive in what Meisl described as 'a brawl, not an exhibition of football'. After only seven minutes, Horwarth raced in to convert Zischek's cross, and with Sarosi well under form Hungary found it hard to get back into the game.

Six minutes after half-time, Zischek, in the centre, drove in Bican's pass to make it 2–0, and the match began to get rough. Sarosi reduced the lead from a penalty, things grew rougher still, and Markos, Hungary's right-winger, foolishly got himself sent off just when his team threatened to equalise. As it was, they pressed gamely on till the end, though the most dangerous shot was Sindelar's, gloriously saved by Szabo. Austria, calmer and better together, had deserved their win, and had found new life.

In Milan, heavy rain did not prevent a large crowd, mushroomed with umbrellas and chequered with swastika flags, from attending the Germany–Sweden game. Germany, with one inside-forward lying deep, the other upfield, met in Sweden a team of similar Nordic propensities, solid rather than skilful, and had slightly the better of the first half.

Twelve minutes after the break, Rosen, the Swedish centre-half, found Kroon, his left-winger, unmarked ten yards from goal. Kroon shot wide, and Sweden's chance had gone. Three minutes later, when Rydberg, who had made two fine saves in the first half, could only push a ball out, Hohmann, Germany's inside-right, scored. Another three minutes and he got a far more spectacular goal, beating both Swedish backs and drawing Rydberg out of goal before placing his shot coolly past him.

Sweden soon afterwards lost their left-half, E. Andersson, who was hurt, but they kept on gamely and Dunker scored them a consoling if irrelevant goal.

At Turin, the Czechs won the best match of the round against the combative Swiss. The game swung and swayed, but the Czechs always seemed to have the resources of skill, stamina and confidence to regain the lead, running out winners by 3–2.

### The Semi-Finals   Italy v. Austria

The semi-finals now brought together Italy and Austria in Milan, and Germany and the Czechs in Rome. By all rights, the Italians should have been tired, the Austrians favoured, but Hugo Meisl would have none of it. Italy, he said, had better reserves that Austria, were better prepared and would be better supported. Perhaps his pessimism would have been confounded again had not Horwarth, the lively catalyst, been injured, his place going to Schall; and had it not been for a deluge creating just the heavy surface which the Vienna school found anathema.

Zischek and Sindelar—sternly guarded by Monti—were particularly disadvantaged in the heavy conditions, but Smistik had a magnificent game at centre-half. The only goal was scored by the Argentinian right-winger Guaita after eighteen minutes, in a clever move that followed a corner. Later, he missed another chance to score, and Austria, who looked much more tired than the surprisingly lively Italians, did not have a shot at goal until the forty-second minute. Ferraris was in dominant form, which was as well for Italy when the Austrians turned on pressure for a quarter of an hour after the interval. In the last minute, with Italy again calling the tune, Zischek picked up a clearance by his goalkeeper, Peter Platzer, and tore through Italy's defence while the crowd watched, silent and aghast. But he shot wide, and Italy had reached the Final.

### Czechoslovakia v. Germany

So did the Czechs, who beat Germany in Rome, showing clearly that
the W formation, like patriotism, was not enough. They frolicked
round the muscular, well-organised but uninspired Germans like
Lilliputians round a Gulliver, while a curious weakness of the Germans
was poor finishing. Rahn, Seeler and Muller were far away. The
Germans, moreover, began the game most cautiously, both inside-
forwards, rather than just one, lying deep; Hohmann, their talented
inside-right, was seriously missed.

The crowd, including Mussolini in his yachting cap, was neutral
and restrained as the Czechs gladly took up the initiative the Germans
gave them. After twenty-one minutes Junek, the right-winger, concluded an attack which swept all the way across the forward-line with
a shot which Kress could only beat out. Nejedly scored; and Czechoslovakia became a little complacent.

The second half, however, saw them regain their grip, and victory
seemed inevitable—when Planicka made one of those errors which
remind one of Disraeli's epigram that the defects of great men are the
consolation of dunces. He simply stood and watched as a long shot by
Noack, Germany's inside-left, sailed over him into goal. 1–1.

Germany, thus reprieved, pressed fiercely, and Ctyroky almost put
through his own goal. Ten minutes after the equaliser, however, the
forceful Puc belted a free kick from just outside the area against the bar.
Krcil, the left-half, sent it back into the net. Germany collapsed, and
Nejedly, taking Cambal's pass, dribbled fluently through to add the
third.

Three days before the Final, Germany consoled themselves with
victory in the third place match in Naples against a dejected Austria.
Both teams made several changes, and Germany scored after only
twenty-four seconds; another save-rebound-shoot affair, scored by
Lehner. Conen got a second, Horwarth, fit again, made it 1–2, and
for a while Austria made the Germans look ploddingly inadequate.
But Lehner eventually scored again for Germany, and the only goal
of the second half came from the Austrian left-back Seszta's thirty-yard
free kick. Play became rough, but Germany survived.

### The Final    Italy v. Czechoslovakia

Rome had been curiously phlegmatic about the tournament, and even
for the Final there were surprising gaps on the terraces. It was perhaps
a pity the game was not played in the north, for the Stadio Torino,

with its pitch of less than regulation size, its less than 'capacity' crowd, was hardly an ideal arena.

It was known that Italy had the stamina and the power, not to mention home advantage and support, but the Czechs had wonderful skill and subtlety. The Czechs, indeed, began with some splendid, characteristically short-passing 'Danubian school' football, with Cambal, the centre-half, everywhere, Puc a great trial to the Italian right flank, Svoboda a clever inside-right. Planicka, though fate would be cruel to him again, looked authoritative in goal, ably abetted by his right-back, Zenisek. Pozzo felt that both teams were keyed up, not least his goalkeeper, Combi, and that the game was a disappointing one in consequence.

There was no goal till twenty minutes from the end. Then Puc, who had been off the field with cramp, returned to take a corner. When the ball finally came back to him, he struck a long shot to Combi's right, the goalkeeper dived late—and Italy were one down. How near the Czechs then came to making the game sure! Sobotka missed a fine chance, Svoboda banged a shot against the post. The Italian attack was stuttering: Schiavio looked tired, Guaita moved into the middle to confuse matters.

Things looked black for Italy till eight minutes from the end, when a goal dropped out of the blue. Raimondo Orsi, the Argentinian left-winger, received the ball from Guaita, ran through the Czech defence, feinted with his left foot and shot with his right. The ball, swerving crazily, brushed Planicka's desperate fingers and curled freakishly into the net. Next day, Orsi tried twenty times to repeat the shot for the benefit of photographers, with no goalkeeper in goal; and failed!

So there was extra time. Pozzo decided he wanted Schiavio and Guaita to keep switching, but such was the tumult of the ecstatic Italian fans that he was unable to make himself heard. At last he rushed around the pitch and managed to tell Guaita. The second time the switch was made it produced a goal.

Ninety-seven minutes had been played when a limping Meazza got the ball on the right wing, where the Czechs had tended to neglect him. He crossed to Guaita, who made ground and in turn found Schiavio. He, with a final effort, beat Ctyroky and shot past Planicka. When asked afterwards what strength he had called on, he said wryly, 'The strength of desperation'.

Italy had not only won the World Cup; they had made a profit of a million lire in the process. The more sceptical wondered if they would have won anywhere else. Four years later, they would get their answer.

# RESULTS: Italy 1934

## First round

Italy 7, United States 1 (HT 3/0)
Czechoslovakia 2, Romania 1 (HT 0/1)
Germany 5, Belgium 2 (HT 1/2)
Austria 3, France 2 (HT 1/1, 1/1) after extra time
Spain 3, Brazil 1 (HT 3/1)
Switzerland 3, Holland 2 (HT 2/1)
Sweden 3, Argentina 2 (HT 1/1)
Hungary 4, Egypt 2 (HT 2/1)

## Second round

Germany 2, Sweden 1 (HT 1/0)
Austria 2, Hungary 1 (HT 1/0)
Italy 1, Spain 1 (HT 1/0, 1/1) after extra time
Italy 1, Spain 0 (HT 1/0) Replay
Czechoslovakia 3, Switzerland 2 (HT 1/1)

## Semi-finals

*Rome*

| **Czechoslovakia 3** | **Germany 1** |
|---|---|
| Planicka (capt.); | Kress; Haringer, Busch; |
| Burger, Ctyroky; | Zielinski, Szepan |
| Kostalek, Cambal, | (capt.), Bender; |
| Krcil; Junek, Svoboda, | Lehner, Siffling, Conen, |
| Sobotka, Nejedly, Puc. | Noack, Kobierski. |

SCORERS
Nejedly (2), Krcil for Czechoslovakia
Noack for Germany
HT 1/0

*Milan*

| **Italy 1** | **Austria 0** |
|---|---|
| Combi (capt.); | Platzer; Cisar, Seszta; |
| Monzeglio, Allemandi; | Wagner, Smistik (capt.), |
| Ferraris IV, Monti, | Urbanek; Zischek, |
| Bertolini; Guaita, | Bican, Sindelar, |
| Meazza, Schiavio, | Schall, Viertel. |
| Ferrari, Orsi. | |

SCORER
Guaita for Italy
HT 1/0

## Third place match

*Naples*

| **Germany 3** | **Austria 2** |
|---|---|
| Jakob; Janes, Busch; | Platzer; Cisar, Seszta, |
| Zielinski, | Wagner, Smistik |
| Muenzenberg, Bender; | (capt.), Urbanek; |
| Lehner, Siffling, | Zischek, Braun, Bican, |
| Conen, Szepan (capt.), | Horwath, Viertel. |
| Heidemann. | |

SCORERS
Lehner (2), Conen for Germany
Seszta for Austria
HT 3/1

## Final

*Rome*

| **Italy 2** | **Czechoslovakia 1** |
|---|---|
| (after extra time) | |
| Combi (capt.); | Planicka (capt.); |
| Monzeglio, | Zenisek, Ctyroky; |
| Allemandi; | Kostalek, Cambal, |
| Ferraris IV, Monti, | Krcil; Junek, |
| Bertolini; Guaita, | Svoboda, Sobotka, |
| Meazza, Schiavio, | Nejedly, Puc. |
| Ferrari, Orsi. | |

SCORERS
Orsi, Schiavio for Italy
Puc for Czechoslovakia
HT 0/0

# France
## 1938

## Background to France

By 1938 and the third World Cup, Europe was in turmoil. The *anschluss* had swallowed up Austria, whose best players had been greedily snatched by the German national team, while Spain was in the throes of civil war. From South America, meanwhile, Uruguay, still piqued by the refusals of 1930 and troubled by a continuing crisis of professionalism, declined to come to France; as did Argentina. The Argentinians were still sulking because France's candidature for the World Cup had been preferred to their own at FIFA's 1936 Congress at the Opera Kroll, Berlin. After coquetting with the organisers for months, they at length decided to stay at home; a decision which provoked a riot outside their federation's offices in Buenos Aires that the police had to quell.

The tournament included—for the first and only time to date—the Cubans, Poles and Dutch East Indies, while the Swedes, Romanians and Swiss were again present. The Czechs, runners-up in 1934, still had Planicka in goal, the classic Nejedly at inside-left and Kostalek at right-half. Otherwise they, like Italy, had rebuilt. Once more, despite distances and early eliminations, the competition was to follow a knock-out pattern.

## The First Round

Italy were very nearly knocked out at once: in Marseilles, by the Norwegians, who had given their Olympic team an arduous run for their money. Norway, playing with six of the team which had lost only 2–1 to Italy in the Olympic semi-final, were a goal down in only the second minute. Piola found Ferrari, whose shot was dropped by the Norwegian goalkeeper. Ferraris II, the left winger, shot the ball home. R. Johansen, the Norwegian right-back, now indicated Piola to his centre-half, Eriksen, who nodded and dropped back to dedicate himself successfully to the big centre-forward, Henriksen, the little right-half, taking his place in midfield. The pendulum swung.

Brunyldsen, the mighty centre-forward, now began to set dreadful problems for the Italian defence. He was well abetted by his fast, direct left-winger, Brustad, and Kwammen, a composed inside-right. Three times post and bar were hit, and finally Brustad, in the second half, received from Brunyldsen, cut inside Monzeglio, and equalised. Soon afterwards, Brustad had the ball in the net again, to be given offside; and just before time, Olivieri made his famous save from Brunyldsen.

Five minutes into extra time, Piola at last evaded the Norwegian defence, when Paserati shot. Again H. Johansen could only block, and the centre-forward scored. Italy had survived their hardest match of the tournament.

The Brazilians were drawn against Poland, in Strasbourg. The game turned out to be an extraordinary one, with extra time, eleven goals, and infinite swings of the pendulum. Brazil had the classic, coloured full-back, Domingas Da Guia and the wonderfully elastic black centre-forward, Leonidas, scorer of four goals; the Poles had their blond inside-left Willimowski, himself the scorer of four.

At Strasbourg it was wet and muddy, but Leonidas was as dangerous as ever. In the second half, he once took off his boots and threw them dramatically to his trainer, but the Swedish referee, Eklind, made him put them on again.

Surprisingly, the Brazilians chose no fewer than six debutants in their team, but by half-time Leonidas already had a hat trick, and his team were leading, 3–1. After this, the Polish half-backs took hold of the game, and it was Willimowski who ran riot. He scored twice, forcing extra time. Willimowski got another in the supplementary period, but goals by Leonidas and Romeo, a coruscating inside-right, took Brazil narrowly through.

In Paris, at the Parc des Princes, it took a replay before the brave Swiss put out the Germans. In the first half, Gauchel gave Germany the lead, but Trello Abegglen, a popular figure in France after much success with Sochaux, headed in Wallaschek's centre. The second half and extra time produced no more goals.

Five days later—World Cups moved at a more leisurely pace in those days—the Swiss fielded an unchanged team. The Germans now picked three Austrians.

There were now six goals. Germany were actually 2–0 up by half-time, Hahnemann, their Austrian centre-forward, and Loertscher, with an unfortunate own goal, having scored. Wallaschek made it 2–1, and when Aebi, the Swiss left-winger, temporarily went off injured, his team increased rather than relaxed their pressure. Aebi came back, Bickel equalised, and the splendid Abegglen scored twice more to give Switzerland victory.

In Toulouse, Cuba, who were only there because Mexico had withdrawn, astonished the Romanians, who still had three members of their 1930 team. The result was an exciting 3–3 draw and the Cubans, unimpressed by fervent praise for their fine goalkeeper, Carvajales, dropped him from the replay. Undaunted, Carvajales called a Press conference of his own at which he promised that Cuba would win the replay: 'The Romanian game has no more secrets for us. We shall score twice, they will only score once. *Adios, caballeros.*' He proved right, though some, including the linesman and Final referee, Georges Capdeville, thought the Cuban winner was offside.

Stalemates, indeed, proliferated. There was another at Le Havre between Czechs and Dutch; this was, however, resolved in extra time, when the loss through injury of van der Veen finally proved too much for Holland.

France, the hosts, were another team with plenty of experienced World Cup men. Thépot—who, with Delfour and Aston, had been 'chaired' by the crowd at the Gare de Lyon on his return from the 1934 World Cup—had gone. But a superb new goalkeeper had emerged in Laurent di Lorto, who had played brilliantly against the Italians earlier that season at the Parc des Princes. Delfour and Aston were still there; so was Etienne Mattler. Alfred Aston, indeed, was recalled to the right wing when Roger Courtois dropped out ill, and had a magnificent game against Belgium at Colombes. So did Jean Bastien of Marseilles, a young right-half making his debut in place of the injured Bourbotte.

France scored against their old foes in forty seconds when Badjou, Belgium's surprisingly recalled 1930 World Cup keeper, could only parry Jean Nicolas' shot, and Veinante, yet another 1930 veteran, shot home. After ten minutes, Nicolas slipped through for a second, but Isemborghs scored for Belgium in a breakaway, and it was twenty-five minutes into the second half before France made the game sure, Aston taking out two defenders and making a second goal for Nicolas.

At Reims, Hungary brushed aside the Dutch East Indies 6–0, Sarosi and Zsengeller scoring a couple each.


## The Second Round

Now Italy, the holders, met their French hosts in Paris. Pozzo brought in Foni for Monzeglio, and Amedeo Biavati and Gino Colaussi on the wings, but he kept Serantoni, who had had a dreadful game in Marseilles. His confidence was rewarded, for Serantoni played with robust aplomb for the rest of the World Cup, an inspiring figure to the team.

Played at the enlarged Colombes Stadium before 58,000 fans, the match at first found both teams uneasy, remembering perhaps the 0–0 draw of the previous December. It was Piola who turned the tide. He not only threatened the French goal, but distributed the ball superbly with head and both feet, and moved cleverly to the flanks, lithe and explosive. When his opponent, the naturalised Austrian Gusti Jordan, was presumptuous enough to leave him in the second half, it proved disastrous.

Colaussi put Italy ahead after only six minutes, swerving round

Bastien and sending over a cross-ball which made its way through Di Lorto's hands and into the net. But within less than a minute Delfour found Veinante with a delightful pass, praised by Pozzo as the best of the tournament. Aston cunningly let the centre run, and Oscar Heisserer, the Alsatian inside-right, equalised.

In the second half, Piola settled matters. When Jordan and Diagne unwisely went upfield together, Biavati robbed Diagne and sent a long deep pass to Piola, who ran on to score. Next, Piola sent Colaussi down the left, a long crossfield ball found Biavati, the right-winger drew Mattler and flicked it to Piola, who headed it in.

The Swedes, managed by Joseph Nagy, a Hungarian, now annihilated the weary and inept Cubans by 8–0. Torre Keller, captain and inside-right, a survivor of the 1924 Olympic team and now aged thirty-five, made and scored a goal, while Gustav Wetterstroem, the 'bombardier of Nörrkoping', forerunner of the great Gunnar Nordahl, scored four, his flaxen hair flying.

At 5–0 the French journalist, Emmanuel Gambardella, shut his typewriter. 'Up to five goals,' he announced, 'is journalism. After that, it becomes statistics.'

At Bordeaux, where Brazil played the Czechs, there was carnage. The final toll was one broken leg—alas, the dazzling Nejedly's—one broken right arm, Planicka's, a bad stomach injury for Kostalek, lesser injuries for Peracio and Leonidas, and three expulsions, for Machados and Zeze of Brazil, and Riha, the Czech outside-right.

Soon after the start Zeze, Brazil's right-half, inexplicably and brutally kicked Nejedly, to be sent off by Hertzka, the Hungarian referee. Despite this, Brazil scored after half an hour through Leonidas. A minute from half-time, off went Riha and Machados for exchanging punches.

Fifteen minutes after the interval, Domingas Da Guia, so elegant yet so unpredictable, so opposed to what he called 'shock football' yet at times so violent, handled the ball and Nejedly, then still in one piece, scored the penalty. There were no goals in extra time, and Brazil's impertinent appeal against the result of the match was rejected.

The replay, a strange study in group psychology, was as proper and placid as the first match was violent. Georges Capdeville of France succeeded Hertzka as referee; the atmosphere might also have been helped by the fact that the Czechs chose six new players and the Brazilians nine.

So confident were the Brazilians of victory that the main party left for Marseilles, and the semi-final against Italy, before the game began! They were taken aback when Kopecky—a fine, attacking left-half, moved to inside-left to replace the irreplaceable Nejedly—scored. In the second half, however, Brazil got into their stride, played much exquisite football, and should have had many more than the two goals they scored. Leonidas, splendid again, equalised after an hour, beating Planicka's deputy, Burkert. What looked like a good goal by Senecky was not awarded when Walter, Brazil's keeper, seemed to pull the ball back from behind his goal line, and Roberto was thus able to volley the winner.

## The Semi-Finals   Italy v. Brazil

Now, however, Brazil's self-assurance would undo them. Eight changes were made, the revenants including Zeze and Machados, the man sent off in Bordeaux, who would later, but only later, be punished.

It was a sad, bad day for the Olympian Domingas Da Guia, whose son, Ademir Da Guia, would himself play for Brazil some thirty years later. Piola, big and physical, was just the kind of player to unsettle and annoy him, while to make matters worse the fleet Colaussi streaked past him to score the first goal. For Domingas the game plainly reduced itself to a personal duel with Piola, and, when, after fourteen minutes, Piola went past him again, he chopped him down. Piola made a histrionic meal of it; up came the cool Meazza, captain of the side, to convert the penalty an instant before his ripped shorts fell down.

That was the end of Brazil, whose two best chances went to and were missed by Peracio, standing in for Leonidas. Their one goal came, meaninglessly, from Romeo after eighty-seven minutes, at a time when the *azzurri* had relaxed.

## Hungary v. Sweden

Sweden, christened 'the team of steel', now played Hungary at Colombes on the eightieth birthday of their monarch, Gustav v. It was of no help. Hungary, undeterred when Nyberg scored in a mere thirty-five seconds, majestically walked over them. By half-time Zsengeller had scored twice, Titkos once, and the Hungarians were so dominant that the second half was a formality. Sarosi headed a fourth, Zsengeller got the fifth; there could have been ten. 'An excellent training match for the Hungarians', remarked Rudi Hiden, now keeping goal for the Racing Club de Paris.

Three days before the Final, Sweden, without the veteran draughts-playing Keller, still held a 2–1 lead against Brazil at half-time in the third-place match at Bordeaux. In the second half Leonidas, appropriately captain for the day, scored twice, bringing his personal total to eight, the highest of the tournament. Patesko missed a penalty and Brazil won, 4–2.

### The Final  Italy v. Hungary

On June 19, fifteen days after the opening match, Italy defended their Cup against Hungary at Colombes. Pozzo had chosen a pleasant retreat in St Germain-en-Laye, where all passed placidly; the team was composed and confident.

The Hungarians were at Vesinst. It was agreed that Sarosi himself had still to show his true form; but if he showed it in the Final that would be good enough. On the other hand, his one failing was a lack of devil, a distaste for physical contact, which was hardly a quality to bring success against the ever-robust Italians. Still, half a dozen of the Hungarians had World Cup experience from 1934, Zsengeller had been scoring freely, and the level of individual skill was as always exceptionally high. The players were however, inclined, to be static; nor had they the tremendous finishing power of their successors in the fifties. In the event, it was Italy's greater drive and commitment which would prevail.

Six minutes into the match, Serantoni cleared to the deep-lying Biavati, who raced almost the length of the field, employing his celebrated foot-over-the-ball feint, before finding Meazza, from whom the ball went swiftly on for Colaussi to dash in and score. There was a sweep and scope about the move which was beyond the powers of the Hungarians.

In less than a minute, however, Sarosi had touched Sas's cross to the unmarked Titkos, and it was 1–1.

But Meazza and Ferrari, Italy's inside-forwards, were still being given far too much leeway, and after fifteen minutes Meazza nonchalantly made the chance for Piola to restore Italy's lead. From this point, the more dynamic, modern Italians never lost their hold. Ten minutes from half-time the balding Ferrari, with an imperious gesture, pointed out the unmarked Colaussi to Meazza. Straight to the winger went the ball, and Colaussi sped past Polgar to get his second goal.

Twenty minutes into the second half, after a goalmouth mêlée, Sarosi unexpectedly reduced the lead, but Vincze, Locatelli and Sarosi himself were well mastered by the Italian defence, and only the left-winger Titkos gave any real trouble. Meazza and Ferrari quickly recovered their grip on midfield, Colaussi, the master of Polgar, was given plenty of the ball, and the Hungarian right flank tottered.

It was from the Italian right, however, that the last goal came, ten minutes from the end, Biavati interpassing with Piola and finally backheeling him a pass which the centre-forward smashed into goal.

Italy, most deservedly, had kept the Cup. At the end of the game Meazza wept; Monzeglio, the reluctant reserve, wept; Biavati put his head in his hands; Andreolo went round embracing everybody; and Pozzo stood uncaring while water poured from the trainer's bucket into his shoes.

There would be no more World Cups for a dozen years.

# RESULTS: France 1938

## First round

Switzerland 1, Germany 1 (HT 1/1, 1/1) after extra time
Switzerland 4, Germany 2 (HT 0/2) replay
Cuba 3, Romania 3 (HT 0/1, 3/3) after extra time
Cuba 2, Romania 1 (HT 0/1) replay
Hungary 6, Dutch East Indies 0 (HT 4/0)
France 3, Belgium 1 (HT 2/1)
Czechoslovakia 3, Holland 0 (HT 0/0, 0/0) after extra time
Brazil 6, Poland 5 (HT 3/1, 4/4) after extra time
Italy 2, Norway 1 (HT 1/0, 1/1) after extra time

## Second round

Sweden 8, Cuba 0 (HT 4/0)
Hungary 2, Switzerland 0 (HT 1/0)
Italy 3, France 1 (HT 1/1)
Brazil 1, Czechoslovakia 1 (HT 1/1, 1/1) after extra time
Brazil 2, Czechoslovakia 1 (HT 0/1) replay

## Semi-finals

*Marseilles*

| **Italy 2** | **Brazil 1** |
|---|---|
| Olivieri; Foni, Rava; Serantoni, Andreolo, Locatelli; Biavati, Meazza (capt.), Piola, Ferrari, Colaussi. | Walter; Domingas Da Guia, Machados; Zeze, Martin (capt.), Alfonsinho; Lopez, Luisinho, Peracio, Romeo, Patesko. |

SCORERS
Colaussi, Meazza (penalty) for Italy
Romeo for Brazil
HT 2/0

*Paris*

| **Hungary 5** | **Sweden 1** |
|---|---|
| Szabo; Koranyi, Biro; Szalay, Turai, Lazar; Sas, Szengeller, Sarosi (capt.), Toldi, Titkos. | Abrahamson; Eriksson, Kjellgren; Almgren, Jacobsson, Svanstroem, Wetterstroem, Keller (capt.), Andersson, H., Jonasson, Nyberg. |

SCORERS
Szengeller (3), Titkos, Sarosi for Hungary
Nyberg for Sweden
HT 3/1

## Third place match

*Bordeaux*

| **Brazil 4** | **Sweden 2** |
|---|---|
| Batatoes; Domingas Da Guia, Machados; Zeze, Brandao, Alfonsinho; Roberto, Romeo, Leonidas (capt.), Peracio, Patesko. | Abrahamson; Eriksson Nilssen; Almgren, Linderholm, Svanstroem (capt.), Berssen, Andersson, H. Jonasson, Andersson, A Nyberg. |

SCORERS
Romeo, Leonidas (2), Peracio for Brazil
Jonasson, Nyberg for Sweden
HT 1/2

## Final

*Paris*

| **Italy 4** | **Hungary 2** |
|---|---|
| Olivieri; Foni, Rava, Serantoni, Andreolo, Locatelli; Biavati, Meazza (capt.), Piola, Ferrari, Colaussi. | Szabo; Polgar, Biro; Szalay, Szucs, Lazar; Sas, Vincze, Sarosi (capt.), Szengeller, Titkos. |

SCORERS
Colaussi (2), Piola (2) for Italy
Titkos, Sarosi for Hungary
HT 3/1

# Brazil
## 1950

## Background to Rio

The 1950 World Cup, now known officially as the Jules Rimet Trophy, was dubiously organised, ludicrously unbalanced, and produced one of the finest climaxes, as well as one of the greatest shocks, of any World Cup yet.

Hurdling the world war, it took place for the second time in South America, and for the second time there were defections and withdrawals. England at last competed.

Brazil had approached the competition with great ambitions, buoyant zeal and intensive effort—even if this was not quite intensive enough to complete in time the building of the immense three-tiered Maracanà Stadium by the banks of the little Maracanà river. This colossal edifice, with room for 200,000 spectators—the largest in the world—was still in the process of completion when the teams arrived. The very soldiers were called in, in a desperate attempt to finish it in time, but on the day of the Final itself, when 200,000 people did throng the Maracanà, its approaches still resembled a vast builder's yard.

Enthusiasm for the game in Brazil, already huge before a war in which they had been only tangentially concerned, was by now fanatical. For the poor, it was the way out of the dreadful slums of the *favelhas* which tumbled down the hills of Rio, of the remote hovels of a vast state-like Minas Gerais. Black players had long since transformed and dominated Brazilian football. Their extraordinary reflexes, at once balletic and gymnastic, their conception of the game, so radically new, so explosively effective, at one point in the tournament caused a Roman newspaper to cry: '*Come resistere?*'—How to resist?

The four British Associations had returned to FIFA in 1946, and the World Cup Committee had indulgently designated the British Championship a qualifying zone— for *two* teams. Scotland rewarded their courtesy by sullenly and indefensibly announcing that unless they won the British title they would not compete. All thus turned on their traditional meeting with England at Hampden Park in April. England won streakily with a goal by Chelsea's Roy Bentley. Bauld's shot hit the English bar, and the Scottish FA refused to change its mind. Billy Wright, the England captain, pleaded with the Scottish captain, George Young, to appeal, insisting that Scotland's presence in Brazil would make a great difference to England, but Young got nowhere.

Not that Scotland were the only team to withdraw. The Argentinians, having squabbled with the Brazilian Federation, repeated their peevish behaviour of 1938 and sourly pulled out of a tournament that this time took place on their doorstep. Czechoslovakia, too, who

took a long time after the war to regain their powers, opted out in a
flurry of spiteful criticism.

The case of France was rather more complex. They did not qualify,
for Yugoslavia won their group, but when Turkey refused to come,
after beating Syria 7–0 to gain a place, the French were invited. After
all, the idea of the World Cup had been nurtured in Paris, where Jules
Rimet had kept the trophy under his bed throughout the war; even if
no less a pioneer than Henri Delaunay had resigned from the World
Cup Committee in protest against the decision to play the tournament
in pools rather than on the previous knock-out basis which had been
intended.

Delaunay, as we shall see, did have a point.

France at first agreed to come, then sent an experimental team to
Belgium which was whipped 4–1, lost at home to Scotland, and had
second thoughts. These were exacerbated when they heard what their
programme would be. Drawn in the same group as Uruguay and
Bolivia, they would have to play one game at Porto Alegre, the next
two thousand miles away at Recife. They sent a cable threatening to
stay at home if the arrangements were not changed. The Brazilian
Federation refused and, to their immense chagrin, France withdrew.

There is no doubt that the arrangement of the tournament greatly
and grossly favoured Brazil, who played every one of their six matches
but the second in Rio, while the other teams were obliged to traipse
exhaustingly around the whole of this huge country. The idea seems
to have escaped everybody that if there were groups, these should
logically be centred on one place. Moreover, the muggy, humid,
debilitating climate of Rio was certainly a handicap to visiting teams.

Since Portugal refused to take Scotland's place, the World Cup was
left with a miserable complement of only thirteen teams; leaving the
Uruguayans with merely feeble Bolivia to beat. It was extraordinary
that another team could not have been moved into their pool from one
of the two pools which had four; the more so as the groups had no
geographical basis.

There were other, distinguished, absentees. Germany were still
excluded from FIFA as a result of the war. Austria, beaten 3–0 by
Sweden in the first round of the 1948 Olympiad, had limply decided
that their team was too young; though it gave them the lie by beating
Italy on Prater just before the competition started. By 1954, it would
be too old.

Hungary, like Russia, was for the moment lurking behind the Iron
Curtain.

**The Contenders** Italy

Italy, the holders of the Cup, would compete even though the terrible disaster of the Superga air crash in May 1949 had largely destroyed their chances. That day the aeroplane carrying the brilliant Torino team, returning from a friendly in Lisbon on their way to a fifth consecutive Championship, crashed into the wall of a hillside monastery. Every player was killed, including eight of the current Italian national side. Among them were the splendid captain and inside-left Valentino Mazzola, whose son would be a star in the 1970 World Cup Final.

Pozzo had gone that very year, disappointed by the flight to *sistema*, the third back game, from his beloved *metodo* tactics, and disgusted by the galloping commercialisation of Italian football. In his place reigned Ferruccio Novo, the President of Torino; and, surprisingly, a Tuscan journalist, Aldo Bardelli. Bardelli, together with a number of the Italian players, refused to travel by air, and the protracted sea voyage played havoc with the condition of a team which had insufficient time to get fit again. Moreover, Bardelli and Novo quarrelled like cat and dog, and before the competition even began Bardelli had been relieved of his powers. There was talent in the team, but the auguries were bad.

Sweden

Italy played in the same group as Paraguay and Sweden. The Swedish team had been pillaged by Italian clubs after its fine Olympic victory in 1948, when four of the splendid forward-line had decamped. The team manager, an ebullient little Yorkshireman called George Raynor, had put together, with astonishing speed, a new side good enough to qualify for Brazil. A splendid guerrilla-general of a tactician—whose 1953 Swedish team, depleted again, was good enough to draw 2–2 with Hungary in Budapest mere weeks before they thrashed England at Wembley—Raynor was also much loved by his men. He had been a moderate outside-right with clubs like Rotherham and Aldershot, but the war had dramatically changed his career. Posted as a physical training instructor to the Staff College at Baghdad, he had organised an international football team with such rapid success that Stanley Rous, the progressive and internationally-minded Secretary of the English FA, had taken notice. Like good fairies, the FA whisked him in 1946 from reserve team trainer of Aldershot to the team managership of Sweden.

With his coaches' conventions—'a stewpot of brains'—his camps for 'tomorrow's men' and his devoted coaching of individual players, he

made Sweden into a real power. Hans Jeppson, the imminent scourge
of the Italians, was one of his protégés; Raynor had marked him early
on as a potential international centre-forward and had spent hours in
pressure-training on his kicking.

'Nacka' Skoglund, a Stockholmer, only just twenty years old, had
emerged propitiously just in time for the World Cup. He joined AIK
Stockholm from a Third Division club, playing splendidly on their tour
of England; little, very blond, he was a delightful ball player with a
very good left foot. Kalle Palmer, whose shooting, unexpectedly strong
for one so slight, had toppled Eire in Dublin, complemented him well.

### England

England's team manager, the first they had ever appointed on a full-
time contract, was a very different figure. Walter Winterbottom, who
took office in 1946, was a Lancashire man from Oldham; a tall,
pleasant, pedagogic figure who had paid his way through Carnegie
College of Physical Education by playing centre-half for Manchester
United, and had reached high rank in the Royal Air Force during the
war.

Fluent and dedicated, he combined with his managership the job
of director of coaching, which he pursued with almost religious
application, never disguising the significant fact that he considered it
the more important of his tasks. Perhaps it was, for he and his followers
ultimately changed the reactionary face of British football, but this
was not really an attitude to go with winning World Cups. The hardened England professionals at first received Winterbottom with
immense scepticism, insisting, as Stanley Matthews did in print, that
an international player should be let alone to play his own game. In
fact one of the chief charges against Winterbottom is precisely that he
did *not* impose and apply sufficiently stringent tactics. But with all his
virtues, he was never a players' man, could never bridge the gap left by
his complete lack of experience of club management. Moreover, as a
team manager he was responsible to a bumbling selection committee
of club directors, and in a position paralleling that of a permanent
civil servant who stays in office while governments fall. Sir Stanley
Rous was unquestionably his mentor, and there was something a little
hierarchical about the situation, a sort of officers-and-men, gentlemen-
and-players, aspect which would change radically with the appointment of Alf Ramsey.

The England team he brought to Brazil was among the favourites,
and was full of talent. There were Wright and Ramsey, Finney and
Mortensen, Mannion and Matthews. Yes, Matthews; held in deep
suspicion by the English selectors as too brilliant, too agelessly in-

destructible an outside-right to trust. He had been playing for England
since 1934, was now thirty-five years old and as embarrassingly
effective as ever. The marvellous swerve which, as he said, 'came out
of him under pressure', was intact. Tom Finney, a wonderful two-
footed winger in his own right, had provided the excuse for dropping
him, but when Finney was chosen on the left and Matthews on the
right there had been ten goals in Lisbon, four in Turin. Now grudgingly
and belatedly, Matthews was recalled from the Football Association
eleven's tour of North America, where they had played and beaten the
USA World Cup eleven despite an exhausting train journey.

Bert Williams, the Wolverhampton goalkeeper, blond and resilient,
was a splendid athlete who had ably succeeded the famous Frank
Swift. Billy Wright, the fair-haired wing-half and captain, had a
boyishly loyal personality that made him a perfect third man in the
chain of command which devolved from Rous to Winterbottom.
Ultimately winner of 105 international caps, he was not a great player
but he was a very fine one, above all in defence, where he would eventually settle down as a centre-half despite his lack of height.

The inside-forwards, Stanley Mortensen and Wilf Mannion, were
both possibly a little past their peak, but still players of exceptional
quality. Mortensen, a north-easterner who had turned himself from a
slow player into a thrillingly fast one and had survived an aeroplane
crash during the war, was a fearless and prolific scorer and Matthews'
partner at Blackpool. Mannion, from Middlesbrough, spanned the
war with his career; a quick, inventive player who had been the best
man on the field when Britain beat 'The Rest of Europe' team 6–1 in
Glasgow three years earlier in the match which celebrated Britain's
return to FIFA. At centre-half the big, young Laurie Hughes of
Liverpool succeeded Franklin.

The other teams in the group were Spain, with fine wingers in
Basora and Gainza; Chile, with George Robledo of Newcastle to lead
them; and the United States.

### Brazil

The new, saturnine, moustached coach of the Brazilian team, Flavio
Costa, who was said to earn £1,000 a month, clearly meant there to be
no repetition of 1938 and its vagaries. His team was cloistered for four
months in a house just outside Rio with veranda and swimming pool,
lavishly furnished from top to bottom with the gifts of Rio firms.
Married men were forbidden to see their wives, bedtime was ten
o'clock sharp and before it each player had to swallow a vitamin drink.

## The Opening Games

The competition was given a spectacular start at the Maracanà, where the traffic jam was such that hundreds of motorists had to leave their cars and walk to the stadium. Many entrances were still not ready, others were blocked by the crowds, swarming over rubble and smashed scaffolding. When Brazil came on to the field in their white shirts with blue facings they were greeted by a twenty-one gun salute and a cacophony of fireworks let off by the crowd. Toy balloons floated into the air, Brazilian troops released 5,000 pigeons and a cascade of leaflets dropped from an aeroplane on to the pitch. The Mexicans, with a sharp sense either of self-preservation or of *comme il faut*, did not enter this maelstrom till fifteen minutes later.

The game itself was a dull one, in which Brazil scored four goals while scarcely forcing themselves at all. The powerful black Baltazar was Brazil's centre-forward for the moment, with the graceful, incisive Ademir and Jair on either side of him, and these three divided the goals, Ademir getting two.

In São Paulo, Sweden toppled Italy. The Italians were accomplices of their own defeat, for Novo picked an almost perversely unbalanced team. True, he was without the vivacious Benito ('Poison') Lorenzi, his best inside-forward, who was injured, but to replace him with a veteran left-half in Aldo Campatelli, a pre-war survivor playing out of position, was ludicrous.

Italy began well enough in front of an Italo-Brazilian crowd which was loudly behind them. Riccardo Carapellese, their clever outside-left and captain, gave them the lead after seven minutes, but by half-time Jeppson and Sune Andersson, the right-half, had scored, Jeppson got another midway through the second half. Muccinelli, the little Italian right-winger, replied and Carapellese hit the bar, but Italy were beaten. Their 'revenge' was oblique but comprehensive; eight of that Swedish side would join Italian clubs.

Now Sweden had only to draw with Paraguay at Curitiba, which they did. Italy, in São Paulo, beat Paraguay 2–0, but it was to no avail. Pool III was Sweden's.

In Pool II, England and Spain began with unexceptional victories. At the Maracanà England found breathing difficult but beat Chile 2–0, with goals from Mortensen in the first half and Mannion in the second. England omitted Matthews, playing Finney on the right and Jimmy Mullen, the tall, fast Wolves winger, a prodigy before the war, on the left. The attack was led by Roy Bentley, a Bristolian. He was perhaps a little too far ahead of his time for the team's good, for when playing for Chelsea he rejoiced in wandering and falling deep. England, used to a Dean or a Lawton—who had played his last international a couple of years before—were not quite geared to such subtleties.

Spain won 3–0 at Curitiba against the United States, who were captained from right-half by Eddie McIlvenny, a Scot who only eighteen months earlier had been given a free transfer by Wrexham, of the Football League's Third Division; and emigrated. Maca, the left-back, was a Belgian; Larry Gaetjens, the centre-forward, a Haitian who would disappear sadly and mysteriously in that sinister island some twenty years later.

Four of the 1948 Olympic team, which playing with a roving centre-half had lost 9–0 to Italy, were present. Now they had a good stopper in Colombo, and they astonished Spain when their clever inside-forward, John Souza, scored after seventeen minutes, a lead they held gallantly till the last ten minutes. Then Spain scored twice in two minutes through the dashing Basora, and the robust centre-forward, Zarra, so powerful in the air, made it 3–1.

Bill Jeffrey, the dedicated Scot who managed the American team, had every reason to feel proud of it. He had emigrated to the United States thirty years earlier, played for a railway works team and was then persuaded to join Penn State College as coach after playing against them. It was a temporary appointment which had lasted ever since. Combining his coaching with teaching in the machine shop, he had produced an unending series of successful teams; but none as remarkable as this World Cup side.

In Pool IV Uruguay had nothing to do but beat Bolivia, which they did 9–0 at Recife. Four goals were by Juan Schiaffino, a tall, pale, slender inside-left of great elusiveness and consummate strategic skill. Schiaffino and the right-wing pair, Alcide (Chico) Ghiggia and Julio Perez, had been members of the previous year's 'amateur' team which took part in the South American Championship, during yet another of Uruguay's endemic strikes. 'Amateur' Uruguay had lost 5–1 to Brazil, but did discover three stars. Perez was little behind Schiaffino in craft, while the hunched, thin, moustached, sunken-cheeked Ghiggia, a personification of the anti-athlete, had an acceleration, a control at speed and a right-foot shot that made him formidable.

### England v. U.S.A.

For their ill-starred second match against the United States, the formality that turned out a fiasco, England travelled to Belo Horizonte. Though the little stadium, with its bumpy surface and inadequate changing facilities, was primitive—the great 100,000-stadium of today lay far in the future—England seemed otherwise to be in clover. The mountain air, by contrast with that of Rio, was invigorating, and the party stayed happily as guests of the Morro Velho gold mine, English-owned and employing 2,000 British workers. Mr Arthur Drewry, acting as sole selector, clearly had two possibilities: to regard the match as a practice run for the team which had beaten Chile, or to rest them and make use of his reserves. He chose the first alternative; and who could blame him? Subsequent criticism, the argument that he should have picked Matthews, was pure wisdom after the event. Even Bill Jeffrey admitted that the United States had no chance. Several of his players stayed up into the small hours the night before.

But for England the game would turn into the waking equivalent of an anxiety dream, in which it was impossible to do the one essential thing, the thing which should have been so farcically easy—score goals.

The day was heavy with cloud, through which the sun broke only fitfully. The England attack quickly set up camp in the American half, hit the post, shot over the bar, and all in all they seemed to be comfortably adjusting their sights. In the meantime the excellence of Borghi in goal and the resilience of the half-back line of McIlvenny, Colombo and Bahr, kept them at bay.

Then, eight minutes from half-time, the incredible happened. Bahr shot from the left, Williams seemed to have the ball covered, when in went Gaetjens with his head to deflect it out of his reach. Did he head it, or did it hit him? There were supporters of both views, but the question was irrelevant; the goal was valid. England, keeping the ball too close, shooting wide or not at all, scored none, while the clever distribution of John Souza saw to it that the defence could not relax. Once, from Ramsey's typically immaculate free kick, Mullen's header seemed to have crossed the line before it was kicked clear, but England —with Mortensen now at centre, Finney at inside-right—gained only a corner.

At the final whistle, newspapers burned on the terraces, a funeral pyre for England, and spectators rushed on to the pitch to carry the brave American team out shoulder-high.

## The Pool Winners

England went back to Rio, to try their last throw against Spain. Reports had told them that the Spanish backs played square and were vulnerable to the through pass. Milburn, the perfect centre-forward to exploit this, with his marvellous sprinting was preferred to Bentley, Matthews was brought in on the right and Finney moved to the left. After fourteen minutes, Milburn headed Finney's centre past the otherwise unbeatable Spanish reserve goalkeeper Ramallets, but the goal was disallowed for offside by Italy's Signor Galeati. Newsreel photographs would show a Spanish defender putting Milburn onside, but as it was Zarra headed in Basora's centre for the winner, five minutes after half-time. So Spain won Pool III.

In Pool I there was a closer finish than had been expected. The Brazilians were pushed very hard by a Yugoslav team light years ahead of the 1930 World Cup side. Above all it possessed the essential for a W formation team, a magnificent 'quadrilateral' of wing-halves and inside-forwards: Zlatko, Cjaicowski I and Djajic; Rajko Mitic and Stefan Bobek.

They had no trouble in mopping up the Swiss 3–0 in Belo Horizonte, Tomasevic scoring twice from centre; and the Mexicans 4–1 at Porto Alegre, where Cjaicowski's younger brother got two from left-wing. But these were long journeys they were making and, worse still, just before they were due to take the field in their decisive match against Brazil in Rio, Mitic cut his head on a girder.

It was decisive because Brazil, against all expectations, had slipped, dropping a point to Switzerland at São Paulo, which meant that a draw would see Yugoslavia through.

The Swiss, playing their recently adopted *verrou* formation, the forerunner of *catenaccio*, had made only three changes from the team defeated by Yugoslavia, but it was enough to work wonders. Antenen, later a distinguished outside-right, moved from inside-right to centre; Bickel, the veteran skipper, to the right-wing, while in Jacky Fatton they had a fast, insidious left-winger. The Brazilians—faint echoes here of the 1938 semi-final—had picked something of a political team to please São Paulo, between which city and Rio their football was at that time polarised. The half-back line was completely changed to *paulistas*, of whom the strong, immaculate right-half Carlos Bauer would keep his place, Jair was hurt and Alfredo, a wing-half, played outside-right, with Maneca moving inside.

Against the rugged Swiss *verrou*, with the blond Neury a great barrier in the middle, it wasn't good enough. True, Alfredo put Brazil ahead, but Fatton met one of Bickel's strong, accurate crosses to equalise. Baltazar scored a spectacular goal to restore Brazil's advantage before half-time, but two minutes from the end, after the *verrou* had absorbed much punishment, Switzerland broke, for Tamini to make it 2–2.

For the Yugoslav match, Flavio Costa now chose the remarkable Zizinho-Ademir-Jair inside-forward trio, and chose Chico for the left-wing. Yugoslavia came out without Mitic, waited while the Mayor of Rio exhorted the teams, then turned straight round and went back to the dressing-rooms. They were pursued by Mervyn Griffiths of Wales, the referee, who ordered them back and refused to postpone the kick-off while Mitic was treated. So the unlucky Slavs began reluctantly and anxiously with ten men, and had lost a goal traumatically within three minutes, when Ademir received from Bauer and scored. When

Rajko Mitic—team manager of their fine 1968 side—finally came on, wearing a huge white bandage, his subtle skills and clever probing, his fine understanding with Bobek, transformed his team, and by half-time Brazil looked a troubled side. Perhaps if Cjaicowski ii had taken a marvellous chance to equalise, things might have been different, but he missed it. Within minutes Bauer had found Zizinho, who dribbled his sinuous, irresistible way through Yugoslavia's defence to make it 2–0.

The following day, Uruguay and Spain came through; these three and Sweden would make up the final pool.

The idea of having a final pool was a strange one which has never since been adopted. The trouble with a World Cup is that it is precisely that; a *cup* competition, greatly restricted in duration, in which luck and injuries have little time to level out, however you arrange things. Sometimes, as in the three pre-war World Cups, the three won by Brazil, and perhaps that won in 1966 by England, the strongest team prevails. But on other occasions, as in 1950 and again in 1954, there were dramatic upheavals.

## Final Pool Matches   Brazil v Sweden; Brazil v. Spain

Sweden were Brazil's first victims. George Raynor's plan was to seek an early goal—the goal he and Sweden would get in the 1958 World Cup Final—and 'We had two chances before they even moved.' But both were missed, and in the nineteenth minute a hopeful shot by Ademir beat Svensson, after which—the deluge.

Brazil now played the football of the future, an almost surrealist game, tactically unexceptional but technically superb, in which ball players of genius, while abrogating none of their own right to virtuosity and spectacle, found an exhilarating *modus vivendi*.

Before half-time, Ademir had scored his second goal, while Chico added the third. The second half was sheer exhibition: Ademir brought his total to four, Chico his to two, while Maneca's goal made seven. All Sweden could muster was a penalty by Sune Andersson, their right-half.

Spain were next on the chopping block, tired after their fine, close match against Uruguay. Brazil thrashed them, with Eizaguirre back in goal for splendid Ramallets, 6–1; 3–0 at half-time. Jair and Chico scored a couple each, Zizinho one, Parra an own goal, Ademir none at all.

That meant four points to Brazil, while Uruguay had with difficulty amassed three; a draw would thus give Brazil a Cup which seemed as good as theirs.

### Uruguay v. Spain; Uruguay v. Sweden; Spain v. Sweden

On July 9, while Brazil were annihilating Sweden, Uruguay were just holding out in a dramatic match against Spain in São Paulo. It was a rough game, full of the Spanish temper, but kept under control and saved as an admirable match by the refereeing of Mervyn Griffiths.

Uruguay, whose swift, skilled forwards always troubled the rather heavy, third back Spanish defence, took the lead through Ghiggia. But with Igoa and Molowny a fine, foraging pair of inside-forwards in the best W formation manner, Basora setting Andrade problems on the wing, Spain were 2–1 ahead by half-time; both goals Basora's. Meanwhile, the two Gonzalvos and the gymnastic Ramallets were keeping Uruguay's attack at bay.

In the second half, the inspiring Varela drove the Uruguayans forward, just as he would against Brazil, and eighteen minutes from the end he himself thundered into the Spanish penalty area to equalise.

In their second game, once more at São Paulo, Uruguay were lucky to get the better of Sweden, who also held a 2–1 lead against them at half-time. The determining factor was probably the weariness of Skoglund, who made little contribution; nor were Sweden helped when a bad foul by Matthias Gonzales put Johnsson, their right-winger, off the field for an extended period.

Though the Uruguayans were both immeasurably fresher and technically much superior to the Swedes, they never dominated them. Kalle Palmer even gave his team the lead after five minutes for Ghiggia to equalise, but Sundqvist, the fast Swedish left-winger—who, like Ghiggia, would play for Roma—made it 2–1. Sweden, however, had shot their bolt, and two goals in the second half by Miguez, the Uruguayan centre-forward, gave them a bare 3–2 win.

For their last match, against Spain, Raynor switched his team's wingers, brought in Rydell for Skoglund, while Bror Mellberg, already standing in for Jeppson, moved to inside-right. The result, again in São Paulo, was a splendid 3–1 win over Spain.

### Brazil v. Uruguay

If you are going to have a cup at all, you had better have a Cup Final. The odd thing was that in 1950, though no provision was made for one, the Brazil-Uruguay match which decided things was such a thriller, such a glorious climax, that no official Final could have done its job better. Indeed, people still talk about it, erroneously if understandably, as the Final.

Though Flavio Costa showed anything but over-confidence, the mood in Brazil before the decisive match with Uruguay was one of bounding euphoria. How could they lose? How, indeed, could they do anything but win? The intricate, galvanic combination of their inside-forward trio, Zizinho, Ademir and Jair, was devastating. One move, which Raynor had particularly admired, was especially unusual and effective. To vary the normal method of attack—short passes alternating with deeper, sharply-angled balls to the wings, sometimes over twenty yards—Ademir would pass back to the dominating Bauer. Bauer would wait, foot on the ball, while Zizinho in his relaxed, loping way would trot back like an obedient dog to take it from him.

'The Uruguayan team,' warned Costa presciently, 'has always disturbed the slumbers of Brazilian footballers. I'm afraid that my players will take the field on Sunday as though they already had the Championship shield sewn on their jerseys. It isn't an exhibition game. It is a match like any other, only harder than the others.'

Colonel Volpe of the Uruguayan delegation remained sturdily sanguine, reminding those who spoke to him that Uruguay had already beaten Brazil once that year.

Vittorio Pozzo, present this time not as a combatant but as a journalist, was staggered by the address made by the Governor of the state of Rio at the Maracanà, immediately before the game.

'You Brazilians, whom I consider victors of the tournament . . . you players who in less than a few hours will be acclaimed champions by millions of your compatriots . . . you who have no equals in the terrestrial hemisphere . . . you who are so superior to every other competitor . . . you whom I already salute as conquerors.' The Uruguayans, long before the eulogy had ended, were clearly fretting. Finally, the teams lined up; and Brazil attacked.

With most of the immense crowd roaring them forward, they beat against a Uruguayan defence in which, for the moment, the huge Varela played a wholly destructive part. If he was marvellously resilient, the little, black Andrade was no less stalwart, while Maspoli performed acrobatic prodigies in goal. Time and again, Zizinho, Ademir and Jair, that terrifying trio, worked their sinuous way through the blue walls of Uruguay's defence. Time and again, a last-ditch tackle by Andrade or Varela, an interception by the flying Maspoli, frustrated them. In the sixteenth minute there was a tremendous mêlée in the Uruguayan area, but Andrade strode into the middle of it and cleared. Seven minutes later Jair let fly a tremendous shot, only for Maspoli to leap across his goal and deflect it for a corner. There was another massed onslaught on the Uruguayan goal, this time thwarted at last by Varela, glad to kick upfield.

The respite was short. Soon Friaça was taking Brazil's third corner of the match and shooting when the ball came back to him out of the vortex, only for Maspoli to hurl himself among the lunging legs and turn it for another corner. Next minute Ademir, deadliest shot of the competition, was left alone in front of goal; the shot was powerful and well placed, but again Maspoli somehow reached it.

It was just about now that Uruguay, shaking themselves like a great dog, began at last to come into the game. Barbosa, the agile black Brazilian goalkeeper who had virtually been watching the game, now found himself in sudden, desperate movement as Ghiggia and Miguez broke to make a chance for Schiaffino, whose raking shot forced Barbosa to leap mightily.

Brazil retaliated at once, forcing another corner, at which Jair banged a shot against the post. Now Maspoli performed new heroics, saving from Ademir, diving wonderfully to a low shot by Zizinho.

The last seven minutes of the half saw a relaxing of the Brazilian pressure, a time out of war for Uruguay's defence. Three times their attack got away for a shot and there were substantial straws in the wind by half-time.

But they were forgotten two minutes after the restart when the Uruguayan citadel fell at last. Ademir and Zizinho, working the ball quickly and cleverly, drew Uruguay's defence left, switched it right, and there was Friaça, running in to shoot in full stride—and score.

The goal had come too late to demoralise Uruguay. They had held out long enough, ultimately launched sufficient attacks, to be quite sure the Brazilians were mortal. Their response to the blow was not to crumble but to hit back vigorously, and while the crowd was distracted by the grim sight of a corpse being taken away on a stretcher, the Uruguayan forwards set about Brazil's defence. After two raids had been beaten off, Schiaffino's typically precise through pass sent Perez away for a rocketing shot which Barbosa reached only with his finger-tips. Now Varela had definitively committed himself to attack. Brazil's wingers, thus given more space, enjoyed it briefly, Andrade having to recover superbly to tackle the galloping Friaça. But Ademir, waving his arms urgently to encourage his colleagues, seemed to realise something was amiss.

After twenty minutes Uruguay struck again; and scored a goal which had long been in the wind. Varela trundled the ball into the Brazilian half before sending little Ghiggia flying down the right, where he was now the master of inadequately covered Bigode. The winger's centre reached a totally unmarked Schiaffino who, after four strides, let fly a shot Barbosa had no hope of saving.

Brazil kicked off; but the virtue, the *brio*, had gone out of them. It was Varela who bestrode the field, nonchalant and indomitable, masterfully breaking up and launching attacks, the old-school centre-half *par excellence*.

After thirty-four minutes of the half Ghiggia received a pass and found Perez, who shook off Jair, made ground, and returned the ball to Ghiggia. Once more Brazil's left flank was turned. Ghiggia ran on to the ball, shot—and it was in the net again. Uruguay led, 2–1.

Moments later, by some trick of the sun, Maspoli's goal was bathed in light, as if to symbolise the victory. In the last minute even Augusto, Brazil's captain and right-back, was in the Uruguayan penalty area, but there was no breaching that defence. Mr Reader, the referee and consummate master of the occasion, blew his whistle; and the World Cup, after twenty years, had returned to Montevideo.

## Pools I, II, III, IV

Brazil 4, Mexico 0 (HT 1/0)
Yugoslavia 3, Switzerland 0 (HT 3/0)
Yugoslavia 4, Mexico 1 (HT 2/0)
Brazil 2, Switzerland 2 (HT 2/1)
Brazil 2, Yugoslavia 0 (HT 1/0)
Switzerland 2, Mexico 1 (HT 2/0)

|  | P | W | D | L | GOALS F | A | Pts |
|---|---|---|---|---|---|---|---|
| Brazil | 3 | 2 | 1 | 0 | **8** | **2** | 5 |
| Yugoslavia | 3 | 2 | 0 | 1 | **7** | **3** | 4 |
| Switzerland | 3 | 1 | 1 | 1 | **4** | **6** | 3 |
| Mexico | 3 | 0 | 0 | 3 | **2** | **10** | 0 |

Spain 3, United States 1 (HT 0/1)
England 2, Chile 0 (HT 1/0)
United States 1, England 0 (HT 1/0)
Spain 2, Chile 0 (HT 2/0)
Spain 1, England 0 (HT 0/0)
Chile 5, United States 2 (HT 2/0)

|  | P | W | D | L | GOALS F | A | Pts |
|---|---|---|---|---|---|---|---|
| Spain | 3 | 3 | 0 | 0 | **6** | **1** | 6 |
| England | 3 | 1 | 0 | 2 | **2** | **2** | 2 |
| Chile | 3 | 1 | 0 | 2 | **5** | **6** | 2 |
| United States | 3 | 1 | 0 | 2 | **4** | **8** | 2 |

Sweden 3, Italy 2 (HT 2/1)
Sweden 2, Paraguay 2 (HT 2/1)
Italy 2, Paraguay 0 (HT 1/0)

|  | P | W | D | L | GOALS F | A | Pts |
|---|---|---|---|---|---|---|---|
| Sweden | 2 | 1 | 1 | 0 | **5** | **4** | 3 |
| Italy | 2 | 1 | 0 | 1 | **4** | **3** | 2 |
| Paraguay | 2 | 0 | 1 | 1 | **2** | **4** | 1 |

Uruguay 8, Bolivia 0 (HT 4/0)

|  | P | W | D | L | GOALS F | A | Pts |
|---|---|---|---|---|---|---|---|
| Uruguay | 1 | 1 | 0 | 0 | **8** | **0** | 2 |
| Bolivia | 1 | 0 | 0 | 1 | **0** | **8** | 0 |

## Final pool matches

*São Paulo*

**Uruguay 2** — **Spain 2**

Maspoli; Gonzales, M., Ramallets; Alonzo,
Tejera; Gonzales, W., Gonzalo II; Gonzalo
Varela (capt.), III, Parra, Puchades;
Andrade; Ghiggia, Basora, Igoa, Zarra,
Perez, Miguez, Molowny, Gainza.
Schiaffino, Vidal.

SCORERS
Ghiggia, Varela for Uruguay
Basora (2) for Spain
HT 1/2

*Rio*

**Brazil 7** — **Sweden 1**

Barbosa; Augusto Svensson; Samuelsson,
(capt.), Juvenal; Nilsson, E.; Andersson
Bauer, Danilo, Bigode; Nordahl, K., Gard;
Maneca, Zizinho, Sundqvist, Palmer,
Ademir, Jair, Chico. Jeppson, Skoglund,
Nilsson, S.

SCORERS
Ademir (4), Chico (2), Maneca for Brazil
Andersson (penalty) for Sweden
HT 3/0

*São Paulo*

**Uruguay 3** — **Sweden 2**

Paz; Gonzales, M., Svensson; Samuelsson,
Tejera; Gambetta, Nilsson, E.; Andersson
Varela (capt.), Johansson, Gard,
Andrade; Ghiggia, Johnsson, Palmer,
Perez, Miguez, Mellberg, Skoglund,
Schiaffino, Vidal. Sundqvist.

SCORERS
Ghiggia, Miguez (2) for Uruguay
Palmer, Sundqvist for Sweden
HT 1/2

*Rio*

**Brazil 6** — **Spain 1**

Barbosa; Augusto Eizaguirre; Alonzo,
(capt.), Juvenal; Gonzalvo II; Gonzalvo
Bauer, Danilo, III, Parra, Puchades;
Bigode; Friaça, Basora, Igoa, Zarra,
Zizinho, Ademir, Panizo, Gainza.
Jair, Chico.

SCORERS
Jair (2), Chico (2), Zizinho, Parra (own goal)
for Brazil
Igoa for Spain
HT 3/0

*São Paulo*

**Sweden 3** — **Spain 1**

Svensson; Samuelsson, Eizaguirre; Asensi,
Nilsson, E., Andersson, Alonzo; Silva, Parra,
Johansson, Gard; Puchades; Basora,
Sundqvist, Mellberg, Fernandez, Zarra,
Rydell, Palmer Panizo, Juncosa.
Johnsson.

SCORERS
Johansson, Mellberg, Palmer for Sweden
Zarra for Spain
HT 2/0

**Uruguay 2**          **Brazil 1**
Maspoli; Gonzales,    Barbosa; Augusto
M., Tejera;           (capt.), Juvenal;
Gambetta, Varela      Bauer, Danilo, Bigode;
(capt.), Andrade;     Friaça, Zizinho,
Ghiggia, Perez,       Ademir, Jair, Chico.
Miguez, Schiaffino,
Moran.

SCORERS
Schiaffino, Ghiggia for Uruguay
Friaça for Brazil
HT 0/0

## Final positions

|         | P | W | D | L | GOALS F | A | Pts |
|---------|---|---|---|---|---------|---|-----|
| Uruguay | 3 | 2 | 1 | 0 | 7 | 5 | 5 |
| Brazil | 3 | 2 | 0 | 1 | 14 | 4 | 4 |
| Sweden | 3 | 1 | 0 | 2 | 6 | 11 | 2 |
| Spain | 3 | 0 | 1 | 2 | 4 | 11 | 1 |

# Switzerland

## 1954

## Background to Switzerland

If the result of the 1950 World Cup was a shock, that of the 1954 World Cup was a cataclysm. Never had there been so hot, so inevitable, a favourite as Hungary; the team which had brought new dimensions and horizons to the game. For the past few years, since they had ended a long sojourn behind the Iron Curtain by coming out to win the 1952 Helsinki Olympic title, they had been, quite simply, unbeatable. They had squared the circle, solved football's equivalent of the riddle of the Sphinx: how to reconcile the traditional skills, the supreme technique, of Continental football with the strength and shooting power of the British.

Since Poland had scratched, the Hungarians had not even been obliged to win a match to qualify. They were grouped with the West Germans—now readmitted to the World Cup, still under the shrewd command of little Sepp Herberger—and the Turks.

The World Cup Committee, in its doubtful wisdom, had devised a new eliminating scheme whose complexity was rivalled only by its illogicality. Instead of putting a total of four countries in four groups and getting each group to play the others, it seeded two teams in each group and kept them apart, each being thus obliged to play only the two unseeded teams. Since equality on points became highly probable it was laid down, first, that teams level at full-time would play extra time, and second, that if at the end of the group two teams were still level, they would play-off. It was this tortuous, fatuous arrangement which produced the ultimate anomaly of Germany winning the Final against a Hungarian team that had previously beaten them 8–3.

Switzerland itself was a curious choice for the staging of a World Cup, and in the event the task was too great. Though the crowds were encouragingly large, thanks no doubt to Switzerland's accessibility, organisation was haphazard and the excesses of the Swiss police sometimes unpleasant.

## The Contenders   Germany

At the start, Germany were not much fancied. Their team had qualified with some ease against Norway and the Saar, and was built round players from Kaiserslautern. Above all there was the thirty-three-year-old captain and inside-forward, Fritz Walter, an admirable player, not quite presaging the extraordinary, more spectacular Netzer, but certainly a very skilled ball player and a fine, economical, strategist, with an excellent shot besides. Otmar Walter, his brother, played at centre-forward, while Horst Eckel, the versatile right-half, was another Kaiserslautern man.

## Uruguay

Uruguay, the Cup holders, had another strong team, though now they were no longer an unknown quantity. There were a couple of splendid new wingers in Julio Abbadie, succeeding the frail Alcide Ghiggia, and Carlo Borges, while even the excellent Julio Perez had been surpassed and replaced, at inside-right, by Xavier Ambrois. The massive Varela was still there, fourteen years after his first cap, as were Andrade, Maspoli, Miguez and the incomparable Schiaffino.

The Uruguayans were seeded in Pool III with Austria, Scotland and the Czechs making up the number. The Czechs, who had qualified against Bulgaria and Romania, were still far from regaining their pre-war stature.

## Austria

Austria—such seemed to be their fate in World Cups—were marginally over the crest. Three years before, they had had what was probably the best team in Europe, playing the old *metodo* game, pivoting in the classical way round a marvellous, attacking centre-half in Ernst Ocwirk, who was still their captain. Ocwirk, tall, muscular and dark, the possessor of a wonderfully strong and accurate left foot and impeccable technique, was ironically a supporter of the third back game. Now he had had his wish fulfilled; Austria had espoused it at last. Uruguay still hadn't, but Brazil had.

## Scotland

Scotland, having finished second to England in a British championship which doubled as a World Cup qualifying group, this time deigned to compete. They also broke with custom by appointing Andrew Beattie, their former celebrated left-back and manager of Huddersfield Town, as team manager. Unfortunately, the players themselves were a poor lot. Lawrie Reilly, the lively Hibernian forward, was ill, and there was no obvious goalkeeper, the job going to Fred Martin of Aberdeen. Willie Fernie, the Celtic inside-right, was a player of undoubted technical gifts but most doubtful consistency; his club colleague, Neil Mochan, was a centre-forward who had returned to Scotland after failing in English football.

Tommy Docherty, the fair-haired, powerful Preston North End wing-half, was a footballer of bite and intelligence, deeply interested in foreign football, who would afterwards praise Schiaffino as the finest inside-forward he had ever met. But even in prospect the general impression was one of honest mediocrity.

### England

England were grouped with Belgium and Switzerland, with Italy the other seeded team. Their selectors chose a ridiculous team in which two men—Peter Harris, outside-right, and Bedford Jezzard, centre-forward—were winning their first caps.

Matthews, now aged thirty-nine, and still good enough to shame the selectors with his untarnished excellence, had again been grudgingly recalled to the colours at the last moment. There was no successor at centre-half to Neil Franklin, after four uneasy years; if the backs had been defenestrated, Gil Merrick had been retained as goal-keeper.

Tom Finney was still about; Nat Lofthouse, the squat, strong Bolton centre-forward, with bags of courage and a fierce left foot in addition to his ability in the air, would lead the line. Ivor Broadis, a Londoner who had begun with Spurs and then made a name as the clever player-manager of Carlisle before joining Sunderland and other leading clubs, was at inside-forward; a neat prompter with a good shot. Once again the captain was Billy Wright, who would gain new fame in a new position.

### Brazil, Yugoslavia and France

Brazil, with Pinheiro as a third back and Zeze Moreira as their sternly dedicated manager, came without their marvellous 1950 trio, Zizinho, Ademir and Jair. Of these only Zizinho was a possible choice, but he had been rigorously passed over in favour of less exotic players. One of these was the black Didì, master of the swerving free kick. Baltazar, another negro, was back again at centre-forward, and there was a formidable new outside-right in Julinho.

At full-back the two Santoses—stalwart, black Djalma and tall, strong, stylish Nilton—would play, while Bauer, a hero of 1950, would captain the team from wing-half. Yugoslavia and feeble Mexico would make up the pool, the fourth team being France.

The Yugoslavs, who had given Brazil such a run for their money in Rio, had taken full points in a qualifying group with Israel and Greece, but scored a mere four goals. They had developed a spectacular new goalkeeper called Vladimir Beara, who had once briefly studied ballet, and had all the associated attributes. Zlatko Cjaicowski was captain again, Mitic and Bobek resumed at inside-forward, while there was a resourceful new left-half in Boskov and a superb left-winger in the versatile Branko Zebec.

The French team had a talented half-back line in Penverne, Jonquet and Marcel, the young, emerging Raymond Kopa at outside-right, Jean Vincent on the left wing. They too had taken maximum qualifying points, against Eire and Luxembourg.

### Italy

Italy arrived in some turmoil. All had gone right, now all had suddenly been going wrong.

Lajor Czeizler, an elderly, *rusé* Hungarian, had built his qualifying team on the so called *blocco viola*; that is on the Fiorentina defence. This had not pleased the Milanese fans, and Czeizler abandoned his previous attacking principles, recalling the vulpine, veteran Capello and making the slim Carlo Galli of Roma his centre-forward. Though Italian football had not yet succumbed to the dreadful dead hand of *catenaccio*, with its manic defensive posture, pressures were enormous, economics arcane.

Still, there was Benito 'Poison' Lorenzi, the Tuscan with the forked tongue, whose control, imagination and finishing power had been so valuable to Inter. There was the handsome, blond, olive-skinned, blue-eyed *jeune premier* Giampiero Boniperti of Juventus, whom the Agnelli—of Fiat—would later make into a millionaire and who, captaining club and country, would later become Juventus' very President. Giorgio Ghezzi, nicknamed 'Kamikhaze', was a brave and elastic goalkeeper; and surely Switzerland and Belgium formed no great obstacle?

Unfortunately Czeizler, despite his outward appearance of middle European aplomb and sophistication, simply lost control in Switzerland, picking ridiculous teams—or allowing them to be picked for him—and letting discipline go to the winds. By the time the team was ensconced in its picturesque *ritiro* outside Basel for the play-off, anarchy reigned.

### Hungary

Puskas, Kocsis, Hidegkuti, Bozsik; these were the names, the men, around whom the extraordinary Hungarian team was built. Ferenc Puskas, nicknamed the 'Galloping Major' in England for his army rank, was the captain, the star of stars, a squat little Budapest urchin-figure, plastered hair parted down the middle, with superb control, supreme strategy, and above all a left-footed shot which was unrivalled in the world, dangerous from any distance up to thirty-five yards.

Sandor Kocsis—'Golden Head'—a smaller and more delicate player than Puskas, was just as formidable when the ball was in the air; another accomplishment in which foreign footballers could previously never match the British, with their Lawtons, Deans and Lofthouses.

Nandor Hidegkuti had perfected a quite new concept of centre-forward play. His secret was that he not only lay deep much of the time, allowing Kocsis and Puskas to work as a double spearhead and to ply them with clever passes; he was also deadly when he broke upfield, to make use of his own tremendous right-foot shot.

In midfield—a term which then still lay in the future—Hidegkuti had the vigorous assistance of the team's right-half, Josef Bozsik, a driving, attacking player, with strength, confidence and, of course, superb control; his side's chief dynamo.

On the wings there were excellent players, little behind these three, in Budai II on the right, and the fast and incisive Zoltan Czibor on the left.

Gyula Grosics, the goalkeeper, was a player of particular importance, not only because he was an excellent and supple performer beneath the bar, good with crosses, but because he was so ready to tear out of his penalty area to kick clear as an extra back.

Though nobody applied the term at the time, it can be seen with hindsight that Hungary's tactics were an early version of 4-2-4. Zakarias, the left-half, was always tucked in beside his burly centre-half Lorant, leaving Bozsik to roam the area of mid-field. The tendency of Hidegkuti to go up as well as back, however, was a major variant.

The Hungarian backs, Buzansky and Lantos, were big, muscular players who did not stand on ceremony. The tendency was to say that Hungary's attack carried its defence, but if the record were analysed the 'goals against' were relatively few.

Over this remarkable team presided the Deputy Minister of Sport, Gustav Sebes, and under him a coach, Gyula Mandi. Training was varied and inventive, and the players were encouraged to practise athletics, even mountaineering. Needless to say there was great emphasis on training with the ball—still, amazingly, a rare thing in bizarrely conservative Britain—and 'match situations' were re-created in practice.

It seemed as if, having harnessed finishing power to their new Sarosis, Orths, and Konrads, Hungary had produced a type of super-footballer, had found a way of preparation which was ideal. Yet when the smoke cleared, when Puskas and Kocsis decamped a couple of years later, it became perfectly clear that all we had been seeing was an illustration of Walter Winterbottom's dictum that every great team is built round a core of great players. While Kocsis and company were present, every man looked a giant, Sebes was a wizard, Mandi an inspired manager. When they went, the fabulous structure of Hungarian football proved to be nothing of the sort; the lean years began.

## The Opening Matches

The Hungarians began by scoring seventeen goals in their first two games. Ultimately more significant was the fact that in the second, against West Germany, they lost Puskas, kicked by the big, blond German centre-half, Werner Liebrich. In retrospect, it was the kick that won the World Cup. Puskas would later vow it was deliberate. Observers felt that the tackle was at least harsh.

Hungary found no great difficulty in scoring nine goals against South Korea in Zurich. Kocsis and Puskas scored five between them and Lantos, the burly left-back, belted a free kick through the Korean wall.

West Germany, having easily beaten Turkey 4–1 in Berne, virtually threw away the Hungarian match in Basel. All the German forwards but Fritz Walter scored for Germany, the first goal going to Berni Klodt, for the moment their right-winger. In the wings lurked the brawny, dark-haired Helmut Rahn, belatedly recalled in the nick of time from Montevideo, where he had played superbly for his club, Rot Weiss Essen, when they beat Penarol—who had offered him a prodigious contract.

The team annihilated 8–3 by Hungary at Basel was not quite the scratch side some later called it. For one thing, it included Rahn himself, scorer of the third German goal; an augury to which few can have paid attention. For another, it introduced at centre-half Liebrich, who would regain his place in the quarter-final. But it cannot be pretended that Germany played flat out. Even with Puskas off the field for an hour with his injured ankle, it was a Hungarian picnic; especially for Kocsis, who scored four. The Germans then made seven changes of personnel and thrashed Turkey 7–1 in Zurich, with Morlock, the strongly-built inside-right, scoring three. Clearly their Hungarian experience had left no trauma.

England began with a curious game against Belgium in Basel; one awash with goals. The Belgians had eliminated Sweden, hopelessly denuded of their stars by Italian clubs, and had beaten Yugoslavia in Zagreb. They had two admirable centre-forwards in Anderlecht's great-hearted Jef Mermans, who now played on the right wing, and Rik Coppens, the well-sprung Beerschot leader, famous for the skill he showed with his back to the goal.

This game, like many others, was televised. Television would now become a potent reality in the World Cup; not always, as we shall see, for the better. The beginnings, in 1954, were modestly substantial; by

1970 the television audience for the Final had built up to a stupendous 800 million.

For the English television audience at least, the game was a disappointment, even though there was consolation in the splendour of Matthews, sinuously beating opponents, cleverly making openings, a complete forward and footballer whose suggestions were all too often spurned.

The English team, lamented *The Times*, were 'like those rare children of light who can pass through any experience protected by a sheath of impenetrable innocence'. The blond, versatile Pol Anoul shot Belgium into the lead from the irrepressible Coppens' pass after only five minutes. England responded with three goals. After twenty-five minutes an admirable through pass from Billy Wright sent Broadis through to equalise. Nat Lofthouse, with a spectacular diving header, gave them the lead and in the second half, after Taylor of Manchester United should have had a penalty, Broadis made it 3–1 with a deflected shot.

The match looked signed, sealed and delivered; but then the English defence, in which Luton's Sid Owen was a shaky centre half and Merrick a porous goalkeeper, collapsed twice, allowing first Anoul and then Coppens to make it 3–3. Another remarkable burst by Matthews, finishing this time with the untypical crescendo of a fine shot, almost restored the lead, but Gernaey seized the ball under the crossbar.

So there was extra time, and a very quick goal for England; a dummy by Taylor, a square pass by Broadis, a strong, high shot by Lofthouse. The crowd, steadily pro-British throughout the series, seemed relieved; but then Jimmy Dickinson, the quiet, consistent Portsmouth left-half, headed Dries' long free kick into his own goal. 4–4. Billy Wright, significantly, spent the closing minutes at centre-half, with Owen limping on a wing with cramp. Wright would stay there for five distinguished years.

The previous day, a Scottish team showing plenty of fight had lost 1–0 to Austria in Zurich. The defence played strongly and well; the forwards might have had two goals: once when Ernst Happel flung Mochan to the ground in the penalty area—but the kick was given outside it—and once in the very last minute. Willie Ormond, the clever Hibernian left-winger, crossed the ball, Alan Brown backheeled, Neil Mochan shot through a crowd of players. The ball struck Happel, and as Schmied, Austria's goalkeeper, plunged, it hit his hand, rolled up his arm: he finally seized it just the right side of the line.

So the goal which Probst had coolly scored, taking a return pass from Alfred Koerner to beat Martin after thirty-three minutes, won the game.

What Scotland had lacked in finesse they had largely made up in spirit, but now came disaster. Andy Beattie resigned. He would go, he said, immediately after the second game, which was to take place in Basel against the champions, Uruguay. The implication was that the Scottish officials, having gone as far as appointing a team manager, could not bring themselves far enough to let him manage. The immediate consequences would be atrocious.

Uruguay had not begun well. In Berne, they had beaten the Czechs 2–0 on an unfamiliar, muddy pitch, presenting Abbadie, Borges and Ambrois in attack, and the powerful, fair-haired José Santamaria as stopper. So far, indeed, did he sometimes fall behind the rest of his defence that he virtually became a sweeper. The champions did not score till Miguez headed in Ambrois' centre twenty minutes from time. Schiaffino adding a second with a thundering free kick; one of those shots which belied the slenderness of his limbs.

In Basel, the Uruguayans simply cut the Scots to pieces; ridiculed them, toyed with them, humiliated them. The 'vulnerable' defence contained Scotland's plodding forwards without difficulty, while Scotland's own defenders, in the words of an English critic, 'stood around like Highland cattle'.

'They will die in the sun,' predicted Vittorio Pozzo before the kick-off—and, metaphorically at least, he was right. Schiaffino quite simply bestrode the field, his swerve and footwork baffling Scotland's defence, his passes splitting it time and again. To such delectable promptings Abbadie and Borges responded with glee, running the Scottish backs ragged. Obdulio Varela, huge-thighed and ubiquitous, made nonsense of the fact that, at thirty-nine, he was a few months older even than Stanley Matthews. Rodriguez Andrade, on the right flank now, distributed the ball immaculately and controlled it effortlessly. Again one was told that the defensive system 'left gaps', though a more obvious inference was that the system as a whole was flexible, and would open or close, oyster-like, according to the circumstances.

Not one of Uruguay's seven goals was headed. Borges and Miguez scored in the first half, while in the second Borges and Abbadie got a couple each, Miguez another. The last of all, ten minutes from time, saw Abbadie dribble round both Scottish backs and then Martin, the goalkeeper. With their glorious technique, their bewildering changes of pace—an ability they shared with the Hungarians—Uruguay had taken Scotland back to school. Most ironically, it was in Scotland itself that such football had been conceived.

Italy, meanwhile, were having vertiginous ups and downs. Their first game, held in Lausanne, was narrowly lost to Switzerland when it might have been won. The Swiss, who had drawn 3–3 with Uruguay a month before the tournament, had less of the play, but prevailed through enthusiasm, while the erratic refereeing of Brazil's Viana led to chaos. 'An English or Scottish referee,' wrote the doyen of French critics, Gabriel Hanot, 'would have given two or three penalties in the first half against the Swiss, and would have sent the two Italian backs Vincenzi and Giacomazzi off in the second.' Galli and Boniperti were dumped or obstructed time and time again without let or hindrance, till the Italians decided on lynch-law, Fatton being kicked in the stomach and Flueckiger in the back.

Twenty-four minutes into the second half, when Benito Lorenzi scored a goal which would have made it 2–1 for Italy but was given by Viana as offside, there was pandemonium.

The goal looked a perfectly good one to most people, and there were those who thought Viana's decision had been influenced by the way Lorenzi had been chiding him throughout the game. After a limpid movement, Galli drove Pandolfini's pass against a post, and Lorenzi finished the job; only for the goal to be denied.

One then, as the *Corriere della Sera* put it, 'witnessed one of those scenes which often occur on our grounds, the players swarming round the referee, some tearing their hair, some eating the grass in their desperation. Boniperti was the fiercest towards Viana, who in his turn vigorously shoved the *azzurri* away until the little storm had blown over.'

So, some twelve minutes from time, when Giacomazzi missed a pass by Jacky Fatton, Hugi was able to beat Ghezzi for the winner.

The Italians now made three changes and, on the familiar territory of Lugano, thrashed a wearied Belgian team 4–1, to force a play-off with Switzerland. The star of the Italian attack was the vivacious Lorenzi, switched to the centre from the right wing after thirty-five minutes. This time when he scored, in the second half, the goal was allowed, and he might have had several more, in a dazzling performance.

Switzerland, meanwhile, lost 2–0 to a far from exceptional English team on a boiling hot afternoon in Berne. England made a number of changes, the most significant of which was the moving of Billy Wright to centre-half, where he had a dominating game. Matthews and Lofthouse were unfit, so the Wolverhampton left-wing pair of Dennis Wilshaw and the veteran Jimmy Mullen, in his fifteenth year as a professional, played. Tommy Taylor, who would die so wretchedly at Munich four years later, led the attack, while Bill McGarry (Huddersfield) was successfully capped at right-half. Merrick, encouragingly but, as it proved, deceptively, had a much better game in goal.

The most distinguished feature of the match were the goals scored by Wolves' left wing. Mullen, receiving Taylor's flick three minutes from half-time, went round Parlier, the goalkeeper, for the first.

Midway through the second half, Dennis Wilshaw calmly and cleverly evaded Eggimann, Bocquet and Neury, before beating Parlier, too. So much, it seemed, for the Swiss *catenaccio*; Italy must surely win the play-off in Basel.

But in their castellar retreat the Italians were in a state of turmoil and anarchy. 'Open acts of indiscipline' were spoken of, and when Czeizler announced his team it was a weird one. Cappello was out, Galli was out and Segato, the Fiorentina left-half, an essentially defensive player, was at inside-left. The formation never began to get together. 'It was not a defeat,' observed the *Corriere della Sera*, 'it was a disaster. . . . We left the stadium in a state of authentic prostration, unable to look the Swiss in the face.'

At half-time the Italians were but one goal behind—scored by Josef Hugi after thirteen minutes. But a couple of minutes into the second half the lively Ballaman headed in a corner he himself had forced, and Italy cracked. Though Nesti did head a goal some twenty minutes later, the Swiss were constantly on top, Hugi and Jacky Fatton adding goals in the last five minutes. Switzerland were triumphantly through to the quarter-finals against Austria.

Having squeezed through against Scotland, the Austrians had had no trouble with the Czechs, whom they despatched 5 0 in Zurich; two for Stojaspal, three to Probst, all but one in the first half.

The best of all these group games was unquestionably that drawn 1–1 by Brazil and Yugoslavia in the exquisite setting of Lausanne's Olympic Stadium, with Lake Geneva lambently below and the misted Savoy Alps above. The teams provided football of a purity worthy of the setting, though it was a pity that the tournament's silly rules should automatically oblige them to play extra time when there was no question of a deadlock on points.

Yugoslavia were an impressive blend of youth and experience, their 1950 stars now being supported by such players as Bernard Vukas, the wiry, blond centre-forward, and Milos Milutinovic, a fair-haired, skilful outside-right. Zeze Moreira had justified the 'new order' in Brazilian football on the grounds that 1950's was a fair-weather attack, capable of scoring goals only when it did not matter; yet now his team played some beguiling football.

At first, the supple Vladimir Beara had much to do in goal, but then Yugoslavia, strong in their formidable 'quadrilateral', took hold of the midfield and might have scored, were their finishing only better. The Brazilians entertained with the wizardries of Didì and the tight, fast dribbling of Julinho, his face as impassive as an Aztec god's, his right foot a mighty hammer.

Three minutes from half-time, Vukas and Mitic made an opening for Branko Zebec which the left-winger exploited. From that point,

Brazil controlled the game. Didì hit a post, Julinho put in three deadly shots and at last Didì, with a cannonade on the turn, got the equaliser. Neither team over-exerted itself in extra time.

The draw meant that France were eliminated. Narrowly defeated by Yugoslavia in their opening game, they had a most impoverished 3–2 win over Mexico, secured with a late penalty by Raymond Kopa, which prompted several enraged Mexicans to attack the referee.

### The Quarter-Finals    Brazil v. Hungary (Battle of Berne)

The quarter-finals pitted Hungary against Brazil at Berne, in a match which was destined to become notorious; England against Uruguay in Basel; Germany against Yugoslavia, in Geneva; Austria against Switzerland, in Lausanne.

The Battle of Berne, as it has come to be known, has in retrospect been blamed chiefly on Brazil. Theirs were the first and greater excesses on the field, theirs the shameful, brutal invasion of the Hungarian dressing-room after the game. Yet there was provocation. The World Cup Disciplinary Committee would, Pilate-like, wash its hands of the horrid affair; Brazil and Hungary themselves would lamentably refuse to punish their players. Indeed, when Arthur Ellis, the game's one hero, later asked the expelled Josef Bozsik whether he had been suspended, Bozsik haughtily replied: 'In Hungary, we don't suspend Deputies.'

What remains a matter for contention is the exact part played in the fracas by the injured Ferenc Puskas, who watched the match from the touchline. At the end of the game, according to the *Corriere della Sera*, he 'struck the Brazilian centre-half Pinheiro in the face with a bottle as he was entering the dressing-rooms, causing a wound eight centimetres long.' The same report quoted Ernst Thommen, the Swiss President of the World Cup Committee, as saying that he had seen Puskas' attack on Pinheiro, that he had been present at the battle in the dressing-rooms which followed, and that he would be making a full report. Subsequently, however, doubt was cast on Puskas' alleged aggression; though there is no doubt that Pinheiro left the stadium heavily bandaged. Some accounts later made the assailant 'a spectator'; but which?

In the event, it was only the superb refereeing of Arthur Ellis that enabled the match to be completed at all; and even then he was obliged to send off three players. In England his refereeing was eulogised, in Brazil it was excoriated—but neutral critics agreed that it deserved the warmest praise. An Italian journalist called it 'magisterial', adding that if it was severe, then 'severity was legitimate and necessary'.

Without Puskas—at least *on* the field—Hungary moved Czibor to inside-left, and used the Toths on the wings. Brazil made three changes in attack, keeping only their formidable right-wing pair of Didì and Julinho. Within eight minutes, under pelting rain, they found themselves two goals down; the Hungarians had made their familiar galloping start.

Hidegkuti's was the first goal, coming after only three minutes. He drove the ball home after Castilho had blocked shots by Czibor and Kocsis, having his shorts ripped off him in the process. Then he was involved in the second goal, moving Toth ii's pass on to Kocsis for the inside-right to drive in his shot leaving Brazil's defence bemused. At this point the Hungarians seemed altogether too quick in thought and pace for the Brazilians. But some of the virtue now went out of them, and Brazil's abundantly gifted, if tempestuous, team came more and more into the game. Their apologists later maintained that the burly Hungarian defenders maddened them with a series of commonplace but irritating fouls. At the same time, those who proceeded from here to discern weaknesses, possible vulnerabilities, in Hungary's team, were surely out of order; for how could they be properly assessed without Puskas? What was perfectly plain was that Brazil had not assimilated the third back method of defence; which, indeed, would be abandoned by 1958.

After seventeen minutes a move between Didì and Indio was brusquely ended when Buzansky felled Indio. Djalma Santos thumped in the penalty. By half-time the Brazilians were giving quite as good as they got, Julinho was marauding on the right wing; and Toth i, his Hungarian equivalent, was a limping passenger.

The second half was soon besmirched with sly fouls, deliberate obstructions which in turn bore fruit in another penalty. Pinheiro handled Czibor's pass to Kocsis, and this time it was the turn of Lantos to score from the spot with tremendous power.

Just as powerful, however, was the ferocious, right-footed shot with which the brilliant Julinho beat Grosics, after an amazing undulating dribble, to make it 2–3. Twenty-four minutes were left, the game was open, the moral climate abysmal. Six minutes more, and two great players, Bozsik and Nilton Santos, came squalidly to blows and were both sent off, Bozsik having reacted to Santos' harsh tackle. Twice Julinho got away again, once to shoot wide and then to give Didì a ball which he struck against the bar.

The Brazilians were now on top, but their very insistence left them open, Hungary breaking in the forty-fourth minute of the half for Czibor to dash down the right and cross, and Kocsis to head past Castilho. It must have been especially gratifying to Czibor, who at one point had been chased about the field by an incensed and threatening Djalma Santos.

There was still time for Humberto Tozzi, the young Brazilian inside-left, to kick Lorant and be expelled in his turn, though he fell weeping on his knees to plead with Arthur Ellis. Then the violent match was over, giving way to worse violence still in the dressing-rooms, where bottles and football boots were swung and Gustav Sebes had his cheek cut open. Perhaps it should be recorded that Castilho had tried to calm his colleagues, that Kocsis and Hidegkuti stayed steadfastly aloof—but these were small comforts. To the Battle of Bordeaux now had to be added the Battle of Berne.

## Uruguay v. England

The game between Uruguay and England produced the same score but none of the same brutality. Though there were several injuries, mostly to Uruguayans, the match was a clean and memorable one, in which Matthews, for England, and Schiaffino, for Uruguay, were superb.

Though the cupholders were unquestionably the better, more gifted team, and won despite the fact that Varela, Abbadie and Andrade pulled muscles, they were much helped by Merrick's feeble goal-keeping. He should certainly have saved two of the goals; he might well have saved three, a fact particularly galling to an English defence inspired by Billy Wright to resist splendidly. In attack, Matthews was the driving force, again playing not merely on the wing but often in the middle, at inside-right or left.

Uruguay opened the score with a lovely goal, after only five minutes. The masterly Schiaffino sold the dummy to McGarry, who never dominated him, and unleashed Borges. The outside-left raced away, crossed a long diagonal ball to Abbadie and, with England's defence entranced, raced in to convert the return pass.

England rode the punch well and equalised eleven minutes later, when Matthews turned the defence with a clever ball behind Varela, Wilshaw ran on to it and gave Lofthouse a reverse pass to score. For twenty bright minutes England called the tune, but now one saw the flexibility of the Uruguayan methods; saw that the allegedly 'open' defence could be manned, when necessary, by seven or eight players. Lofthouse had a fine shot beaten out by Maspoli; Wilshaw shot just wide when a goal seemed sure. A sly shove was largely responsible.

Two minutes from the interval, Uruguay delivered a counter-punch —to the solar plexus. Varela shot from near the edge of the area, and Merrick allowed the ball to pass across him—and home. It was bad enough that England should go in at half-time a goal down when they could have been a goal up. It was still worse to fall a second goal behind almost immediately afterwards; and a dubious goal, at that. Varela picked the ball up for a free kick and was allowed, inexcusably, to drop kick it. Schiaffino ran through a bewildered English defence to score.

With three players limping, it was inevitable that Uruguay should find the second half difficult, but with Schiaffino now playing splendidly in Varela's position they kept the lead. After sixty-seven minutes Maspoli got his hand to a shot by Tom Finney, and the ball bounced into the net to make it 2–3. Matthews hit the post and had one shot punched by Maspoli for a corner, but the last word was Uruguay's.

With thirteen minutes left, Miguez found Ambrois, who scored with a shot which Merrick should have saved, just as he should have saved Schiaffino's. England were out; but at least, by comparison with the Scots, they had gone out with honour.

### Austria v. Switzerland

At Lausanne that same Saturday, Austria and Switzerland produced one of the highest-scoring World Cup matches there has ever been; twelve goals, seven of them to Austria.

It was an astounding match in which the Swiss, roared on by their crowd, scored three in the first twenty minutes; only for the defiant Austrians to reply with three in three minutes, five in seven minutes, building a 5–4 lead by half-time—and missing a penalty into the bargain!

The strange score was partly to be accounted for by an uncharacteristically poor display by Roger Bocquet, the Swiss captain; behind which lurked a sad tale.

Bocquet, in fact, had been suffering for some time from a tumour. His doctor had earnestly advised him not to play, but Bocquet, perhaps his country's most celebrated player of the era, replied, 'Afterwards, I shall be going into hospital for an operation, and I don't know whether I shall survive.'

Play, therefore, he did, and the intense heat provided the worst possible conditions for his tumour. Several times Karl Rappan, the Swiss team manager, tried to persuade him to move from his vital position at centre-half, but on each occasion Bocquet told him, 'It's all right, it's all right!'

'We all felt,' said a Swiss Federation official years afterwards, 'that he was playing in a sort of trance, and didn't know what happened on the field.'

In due course, Bocquet had his operation, which was happily successful; though it left him with a fearful scar, and the need to wear dark glasses, in consequence.

Austria, who so comprehensively overturned the Swiss *catenaccio* which had mastered Italy, did it in a most un-Viennese manner: with sizzling long shots after runs by the Koerners down the wings. At 5–3 to Austria, Ballaman replied for the Swiss. 'All goals scored against Switzerland owing to the sun,' announced the official, unblushing Press *communiqué* at half-time, though it was true that Parlier, the Swiss 'keeper, had a touch of sunstroke. But even with the sun at their backs the Swiss could not recover. In the second half the forceful Theo Wagner ran through for his third goal and Austria's sixth. Though Hanappi put the dynamic Hugi's shot past his goalkeeper for Switzerland's fifth, Probst dribbled through for the most spectacular goal of all. 7–5. It had been a magnificent game for Ernst Ocwirk, and for two forwards who did not score: Stojaspal of Austria and the dark Roger Vonlanthen of Switzerland.

### West Germany v. Yugoslavia

In Geneva the following day the West Germans sprang their first great surprise of the tournament. They beat Yugoslavia. The match proved that the Yugoslavs had the finesse, but not the finish, whereas the Germans had muscle, stamina, and immense determination. Moreover, after ten minutes they were presented with a goal.

Ivan Horvat, the tall Yugoslav centre-half, was possibly the best in the tournament; a Titan in this match, too. But running back with Schaefer towards a ball headed on by Morlock, he headed it in his turn, without observing that Beara had come off his line. 1–0 to Germany. Their second goal came four minutes from the end when Schaefer put through Rahn—offside, in the opinion of some critics— who ran on, on, on before beating an injured Vladimir Beara unable now to move. It was absurd, wrote an Italian critic, that a team like Germany should be in the semi-final when a team like Brazil was out, but this was irremediably what could happen in Cup competitions.

Germany would now play Austria, their victims in the third-place match of 1934, their companions in the World Cup of 1938. The Uruguayans, who had enraged their fellow hotel guests by perpetually and loudly playing a record which proclaimed their virtues, would meet Hungary. They promised there would be no violence; the Brazilians, they said, had lost their heads.

### The Semi-Finals  Hungary v. Uruguay

Uruguay kept their word at Lausanne in one of the classic matches of World Cup history. Either team might have won, for the game went into extra time. Moreover, it lacked a key player in each side, for if Puskas did not play for Hungary, Varela could not play for Uruguay. Each side, moreover, had to change its outside-right—Abbadie being forced to give way to Souto, while Budai replaced the injured Toth 1, whose brother was succeeded by Palotas. This enabled Czibor, in turn, to go back to the left wing. Miguez, another absentee, was succeeded as Uruguay's centre-forward by Hohberg, though Schiaffino nominally played there. Hungary were favoured, but Uruguay had never yet been beaten in a World Cup.

The Uruguayans were slightly faster and more energetic than they had previously been; but after a quarter of an hour Hungary went ahead. Kocsis headed a pass by Hidegkuti to Czibor, and the left-winger volleyed the ball past Maspoli. Just after half-time, Hungary doubled their lead when Buzansky intercepted a poor clearance by Carballo, Varela's deputy. He sent Budai and Bozsik flying away, and when Budai crossed Hidegkuti flung himself at the ball to head it in.

Uruguay seemed beaten beyond hope, but their marvellous morale, not to mention their skill, brought them back into the game. Schiaffino began to work his spells, nicely supported by Juan Hohberg, a naturalised Argentinian who would manage their World Cup team of 1970. Lorant had to clear on the line, Schiaffino had a couple of near misses, and then at last, fifteen minutes from the end, Schiaffino gave Hohberg the chance to beat Grosics. Three minutes from the end Schiaffino and Hohberg did it again, Hohberg being so violently felicitated by his team mates that they knocked him out.

His goal necessitated extra time, and soon after it had started Schiaffino put him through yet again, this time for a shot which smacked the post.

Poor Uruguay; it was not to be their night. In the second extra period, the peerless Andrade was hurt in a tackle and, desperate to get back into the game, was still having treatment behind the goal when right in front of him Budai centred for Kocsis to soar and head past Maspoli.

Seven minutes from the end Kocsis headed another memorable goal, and Hungary had won 4–2. 'We beat the best team we have ever met,' said their manager, Gyula Mandi.

### West Germany v. Austria

At Basel a crowd of 58,000 saw the Austrians fall to pieces like a burning house. They had been expected to win quite easily; their technique was far ahead of the Germans', and they had scored a cascade of goals against the Swiss. In the meantime, Sepp Herberger had worked hard at training Toni Turek, whom he felt should have made Kohlmeyer's saves on the line superfluous. Austria, for their part, made the cardinal mistake of dropping Schmied and restoring the famous Walter Zeman—a goalkeeper previously omitted precisely because he had lost form.

It proved a disastrous error, for Zeman, once so polished and authoritative, played like a man who had lost his nerve, running about his area like a chicken with its head cut off, utterly confused by crosses. Two of the goals, indeed, came from centres, two more from corners; a damning commentary on Austria's defence in the air. The other two were from penalty kicks.

The Germans now showed that they were a great deal more than mere destroyers, a mincing machine for other people's talent. Their football was sweepingly effective, splendidly incisive, with Fritz Walter the supreme strategist, scorer of two penalties to boot, and Helmut Rahn as powerfully effective a right-winger, in his muscular way, as the exotic Julinho.

During the first half there was little sign of what awaited poor Austria in the second. For twenty minutes their team did pretty things, relaxed and elegant, but on the half-hour Max Morlock sent Fritz Walter away, and Hans Schaefer flicked in his well-judged centre. At half-time it was still 1–0.

In the third minute of the second half an equally exact corner kick by Fritz Walter was headed in by Morlock, and though four minutes later Germany gave Austria a chance, Turek dropping the ball for Probst to score, the die was cast. The German attack, with only Rahn keeping his position firmly, the others switching at speed, overran the Austrians. Fritz Walter scored the third and fifth goals from the spot, each time sending the unfortunate Zeman the wrong way, while his brother Otmar headed the other two—one from Fritz's corner, one from Schaefer's cross—after Fritz had sent him down the right. In turning from the old *metodo* to the third back game, Austria seemed to have gained no more defensive solidity than Brazil.

They consoled themselves a little by beating Uruguay 3–1 in the third-place match at Zurich, Ocwirk dominating the game, but it was scarcely one in which the Uruguayans gave their all.

### The Final          West Germany v. Hungary

The great question before the Final was whether Puskas would play. He would, said the reports. He wouldn't. He was hoping to. There was no chance. There was a fifty-fifty chance; a specialist had said so. The ankle was better. It would never recover in time. The Germans had offered him special treatment; and been rejected.

In the event, however, Puskas *did* play; and it would prove a manifest mistake, a testimony to the captain's own powers of persuasion rather than the good sense of Sebes and Mandi.

Ciro Veratti, the Italian journalist, spoke to Sepp Herberger, the little German manager, and wrote of his 'formidable ascendancy' over his players, his power to make them give almost more than they possessed. There had been 30,000 Germans in Basel when they beat Austria. There would be about the same number in Berne for the Final, so they would virtually be playing at home. Living now 'in a climate of exaltation', the Germans hoped to give the lie to everybody. If it happened, 'it would be the greatest upset of the World Championship. But we don't believe it, and we are making ready to hail as champions tomorrow that marvellous goal-scoring machine which is the great Hungarian team.'

Sunday was a rainy day; rain, indeed, drenched the players and most of the 60,000 crowd at the Wankdorf Stadium throughout the match. If Hungary were the favourites, Gustav Sebes had still warned that their 'greatest enemy is not so much physical fatigue as nervous tension. I had never suspected that the World Cup would be such a test of nerves.'

Restoring Puskas, they also dropped Budai, who had played so well against the Uruguayans but had never been *persona grata* with Puskas. Germany's team was that which beat Austria, with Posipal, centre-half of the Rest of Europe team, still at right-back, Liebrich as stopper.

Once again, Hungary made a devastating, potentially a demoralising, start. Within eight minutes they were two goals up, and there seemed every prospect of another Basel. In the sixth minute, after Germany had three times menaced the Hungarian goal, Hungary counter-attacked. Bozsik sent Kocsis through, his shot hit a German defender in the back, the ball ran to Puskas, and that formidable left foot drove it past Turek.

Within a couple of minutes Kohlmeyer, Germany's saviour against the Yugoslavs, had given Hungary their second goal with the complicity of Turek. His misjudged back pass, suddenly bewitched, sprang out of Turek's grasp and Czibor drove the ball in.

It was enough to unhinge most teams; but not Germany. Within three minutes, shaking off the effects of so depressing a goal, they had struck back. Hans Schaefer crossed, Rahn returned the ball to the centre and this time Bozsik erred, fractionally deflecting it into the path of Morlock. The inside-forward stretched out a telescopic leg, and jabbed it past Grosics.

It was becoming plain that for all the fury of their beginning, Hungary were not running smoothly. Puskas, clearly hampered by his ankle, was unwontedly heavy and slow, and now threw away a chance when he insisted on carrying on alone, losing the ball, when Czibor was free and better placed. Czibor, meanwhile, switched to the right, was obviously not at ease there, and things would go better when he moved to the left after half-time.

So, after sixteen minutes the Germans equalised. Taking the third of three successive corners, Fritz Walter curved an insidious ball which was missed both by his brother's head and by Grosics' hands. It thus reached Helmut Rahn, who drove it thunderously back into goal.

To this the Hungarians responded vigorously, Turek making the first of his many gallant saves from a header by Kocsis, then being saved by a post when beaten by Hidegkuti. Thus reprieved, the Germans attacked in their turn, and banged away at the Hungarian goal for a full three minutes. At half-time, the game was pulsatingly open.

The Hungarians began the second half with a new and furious assault on the German goal, and only Turek denied them. Twice he saved gloriously from Puskas—who on one occasion was alone in front of goal—once Kohlmeyer kicked Toth's shot off the line; once Kocsis' header from Toth's cross skidded off the bar.

The storm weathered, Germany returned to the attack; the Hungarians were now beginning to look weary. Yet twelve minutes from the end of a game so well refereed by Bill Ling, the fast, dark Czibor broke brilliantly away, Turek saved his shot, the ball reached Hidegkuti; and Hidegkuti missed. Five minutes later came the *coup de grâce*.

Leaving Bozsik behind, Hans Schaefer got away down the left wing and crossed. The ball flashed over a crowded, pullulating goalmouth, touched, perhaps, by Otmar Walter's head. For a moment Lantos seemed to have it, then it escaped him, reaching Rahn. The big outside-right controlled it, advanced with it, and seemed, for a moment of pregnant hiatus, to stop and deliberate. Then he drove it past Grosics with his left foot.

Frantically the Hungarians sought to equalise, and two minutes later it seemed they had. Toth, from the right, took Posipal out of the game with an exquisite through pass and Puskas, seeming to judge the moment perfectly, darted through the gap to beat Turek in his old, irresistible style. The Hungarians embraced; but the flag of Mervyn Griffiths, the Welsh linesman, was up. Puskas had been given offside, and to this day the decision is argued.

Hungary had one shot left in their locker. Suddenly Zoltan Czibor was away once more, to let fly a strong, precise shot which Turek elastically reached again to punch clear, while Czibor rolled on the ground in despair.

So, in the drenching rain, it was over, and Jules Rimet, the retiring President of FIFA, gave to Fritz Walter the Cup which had seemed destined for Puskas. In the dressing-rooms, Gustav Sebes spoke of bad luck, and slumped on a bench; Herberger spoke of seriousness and enthusiasm. His team, physically exceptional, morally resilient, tactically straightforward, had won a remarkable triumph.

# RESULTS: Switzerland 1954

## Pool I

Yugoslavia 1, France 0 (HT 1/0)
Brazil 5, Mexico 0 (HT 4/0)
France 3, Mexico 2 (HT 1/0)
Brazil 1, Yugoslavia 1 (HT 0/1) after extra time

|  | P | W | D | L | GOALS F | A | Pts |
|---|---|---|---|---|---|---|---|
| Brazil | 2 | 1 | 1 | 0 | **6** | **1** | 3 |
| Yugoslavia | 2 | 1 | 1 | 0 | **2** | **1** | 3 |
| France | 2 | 1 | 0 | 1 | **3** | **3** | 2 |
| Mexico | 2 | 0 | 0 | 2 | **2** | **8** | 0 |

## Pool II

Hungary 9, Korea 0 (HT 4/0)
Germany 4, Turkey 1 (HT 1/1)
Hungary 8, Germany 3 (HT 3/1)
Turkey 7, Korea 0 (HT 4/0)

|  | P | W | D | L | GOALS F | A | Pts |
|---|---|---|---|---|---|---|---|
| Hungary | 2 | 2 | 0 | 0 | **17** | **3** | 4 |
| Germany | 2 | 1 | 0 | 1 | **7** | **9** | 2 |
| Turkey | 2 | 1 | 0 | 1 | **8** | **4** | 2 |
| Korea | 2 | 0 | 0 | 2 | **0** | **16** | 0 |

Play off Germany 7, Turkey 2 (HT 3/1)

## Pool III

Austria 1, Scotland 0 (HT 1/0)
Uruguay 2, Czechoslovakia 0 (HT 0/0)
Austria 5, Czechoslovakia 0 (HT 4/0)
Uruguay 7, Scotland 0 (HT 2/0)

|  | P | W | D | L | GOALS F | A | Pts |
|---|---|---|---|---|---|---|---|
| Uruguay | 2 | 2 | 0 | 0 | **9** | **0** | 4 |
| Austria | 2 | 2 | 0 | 0 | **6** | **0** | 4 |
| Czechoslovakia | 2 | 0 | 0 | 2 | **0** | **7** | 0 |
| Scotland | 2 | 0 | 0 | 2 | **0** | **8** | 0 |

## Pool IV

England 4, Belgium 4 (HT 2/1)
England 2, Switzerland 0 (HT 1/0)
Switzerland 2, Italy 1 (HT 1/1)
Italy 4, Belgium 1 (HT 1/0)

|  | P | W | D | L | GOALS F | A | Pts |
|---|---|---|---|---|---|---|---|
| England | 2 | 1 | 1 | 0 | **6** | **4** | 3 |
| Italy | 2 | 1 | 0 | 1 | **5** | **3** | 2 |
| Switzerland | 2 | 1 | 0 | 1 | **2** | **3** | 2 |
| Belgium | 2 | 0 | 1 | 1 | **5** | **8** | 1 |

Play off Switzerland 4, Italy 1 (HT 1/0)

## Quarter-finals

*Geneva*

**Germany 2** — **Yugoslavia 0**

Turek; Laband, Kohlmeyer; Eckel, Liebrich, Mai; Rahn, Morlock, Walter, O., Walter, F. (capt.), Schaefer.

Beara; Stankovic, Crnkovic; Cjaicowski, Horvat, Boskov; Milutinovic, Mitic (capt.), Vukas, Bobek, Zebec.

SCORERS
Horvat (own goal), Rahn for Germany
HT 1/0

*Berne*

**Hungary 4** — **Brazil 2**

Grosics; Buzansky, Lantos; Bozsik (capt.), Lorant, Zakarias; Toth, M., Kocsis, Hidegkuti, Czibor, Toth, J.

Castilho; Santos, D., Santos, N.; Brandaozinho, Pinheiro (capt.), Bauer; Julinho, Didì, Indio, Tozzi, Maurinho.

SCORERS
Hidegkuti (2), Kocsis, Lantos (penalty) for Hungary
Santos, D. (penalty), Julinho for Brazil
HT 2/1

*Lausanne*

**Austria 7** — **Switzerland 5**

Schmied; Hanappi, Barschandt; Ocwirk (capt.), Happel, Koller; Koerner, R., Wagner, Stojaspal, Probst, Koerner, A.

Parlier; Neury, Kerner, Eggimann, Bocquet (capt.), Casali; Antenen, Vonlanthen, Hugi, Ballaman, Fatton.

SCORERS
Koerner, A. (2), Ocwirk, Wagner (3), Probst for Austria
Ballaman (2), Hugi (2), Hanappi (own goal) for Switzerland
HT 2/4

*Basel*

**Uruguay 4** — **England 2**

Maspoli; Santamaria, Martinez; Andrade, Varela (capt.), Cruz; Abbadie, Ambrois, Miguez, Schiaffino, Borges.

Merrick; Staniforth, Byrne; McGarry, Wright (capt.), Dickinson; Matthews, Broadis, Lofthouse, Wilshaw, Finney.

SCORERS
Borges, Varela, Schiaffino, Ambrois for Uruguay
Lofthouse, Finney for England
HT 2/1

## Semi-finals
*Basel*

---

**Germany 6**    **Austria 1**

Turek; Posipal, Zeman; Hanappi,
Kohlmeyer; Eckel, Schleger; Ocwirk
Liebrich, Mai; Rahn, (capt.), Happel, Koller;
Morlock, Walter, O., Koerner, R., Wagner,
Walter, F. (capt.), Stojaspal, Probst,
Schaefer. Koerner, A.

SCORERS
Schaefer, Morlock, Walter, F. (2 penalties),
Walter, O. (2) for Germany
Probst for Austria
HT 1/0

*Lausanne*

---

**Hungary 4**    **Uruguay 2**

(after extra time)
Grosics; Buzansky, Maspoli; Santamaria,
Lantos; Boszik (capt.), Martinez, Andrade
Lorant, Zakarias; (capt.), Carballo, Cruz;
Budai, Kocsis, Palotas, Souto, Ambrois,
Hidegkuti, Czibor. Schiaffino, Hohberg,
Borges.

SCORERS
Czibor, Hidegkuti, Kocsis (2) for Hungary
Hohberg (2) for Uruguay
HT 1/0

## Third place match
*Zurich*

---

**Austria 3**    **Uruguay 1**

Schmied; Hanappi, Maspoli; Santamaria,
Barschandt; Ocwirk Martinez; Andrade
(capt.), Kollmann, (capt.), Carballo, Cruz;
Koller; Koerner, R., Abbadie, Hohberg,
Wagner, Dienst, Mendez, Schiaffino,
Stojaspal, Probst. Borges.

SCORERS
Stojaspal (penalty), Cruz (own goal), Ocwirk for
Austria
Hohberg for Uruguay
HT 1/1

## Final
*Berne*

---

**Germany 3**    **Hungary 2**

Turek; Posipal, Grosics; Buzansky,
Kohlmeyer; Eckel, Lantos; Bozsik, Lorant,
Liebrich, Mai; Rahn, Zakarias; Czibor,
Morlock, Walter, O., Kocsis, Hidegkuti,
Walter, F., Schaefer. Puskas, Toth, J.

SCORERS
Morlock, Rahn (2) for Germany
Puskas, Czibor for Hungary
HT 2/2

# Sweden

## 1958

Played in Sweden, the 1958 World Cup was notable for the emergence of 4-2-4, the explosion of Pelé, the first victory by Brazil, the surprise of France and Fontaine. Though it was won by an immensely distinguished team it was not, overall, a distinguished competition.

## The Contenders  Sweden

For the Swedish team, which ultimately and admirably became runners-up, it was a World Cup of nostalgia. At last the Swedish Federation had decided to allow overtly professional football and overtly professional footballers, a corollary of which was not only that such great players as Gunnar Gren returned to Sweden but also that others were recalled that summer from Italy. George Raynor, meanwhile, came back as team manager after the heartaches and the thousand natural shocks of management in Italy and to make his team happy.

One of the most beguiling features of the side was that it harked back not merely to 1950 and Sweden's last World Cup in Brazil, but even earlier—to the 1948 Olympic Games. From these, Gren and Liedholm were mighty survivors. Like the powerful and prolific centre-forward Gunnar Nordahl, they had left Sweden for Milan, making up the so-called Grenoli trio, with Nordahl in the middle, 'The Professor' Gren at inside-right, Nils Liedholm at inside-left. Liedholm, indeed, after a long and impressive spell at right-half, had just played splendidly at inside-left for the Milan team which had lost 3–2 to Real Madrid in the European Cup Final in Brussels.

The little, tow-haired Nacka Skoglund was back, too, after eight splendid years with Internazionale of Milan. On the right wing, a more recent Italian 'export' was Kurt (Kurre) Hamrin, a sturdy little man, coolly insulated and taciturn, with superb powers of dribbling and acceleration and the ability and courage to strike through the middle as well as from the wing.

At centre-half was another Italo-Swede, Julli Gustavsson, a former policeman playing for Atalanta who had been at right-back for the Rest of Europe team which beat Great Britain in Belfast in 1955. Atalanta, indicted by the Italian Federation for alleged corruption, had a vital play-off game against Bari coming up, and at first were reluctant to let Gustavsson go. Eventually they compromised grudgingly, after a tense time when it seemed that he would be unable to play for Sweden in the semi-final, allowing him to go on provided that if he wished to take part in the Final he would pay the massive indemnity of 25,000 crowns! Gustavsson, who had a superbly dominating match against Russia in the quarter-finals, did play the Final.

Ironically, however, the Swedish Press and public had no initial confidence in their team's chances, despite home advantage and the return of the Italian brigade. But as the Swedish team made more and more progress, won one match after another, the patriotic euphoria of this traditionally neutral, peaceable, unchauvinist nation rose to an orgy of patriotism in the semi-final match against West Germany. It was a riveting and somewhat alarming study in national behaviour.

### Russia

The Russians were competing for the first time in a World Cup, under the managership of the blond, Cagneyesque figure of Gabriel Katchaline assisted by the huge Mikhail Yakushin, who resembled some craggy hero of the revolutionary war and had taken Moscow Dynamo on its famous tour of Britain and Sweden in 1945. Thereafter the Russians, whose elegant, enterprising football had been excitingly successful, withdrew into splendid isolation till the Olympic tournament of 1952 in Helsinki, where they were put out 3–1 by Yugoslavia after an astonishing, oscillating 5–5 draw. They had just drawn a lively game against England in Moscow, and would now contest the same group in Gothenburg, together with Brazil and Austria.

They had gifted players in Simonian, the mobile little Armenian centre-forward; Lev Yachine, the superb goalkeeper who had succeeded and surpassed 'Tiger' Khomich in the Moscow Dynamo goal; Salnikov, a thoughtful inside-left; and Igor Netto. This blond left-half, captain of the side, who had helped it to win the Olympic title of 1956 in Melbourne, had hurt his left knee and was an uncertain starter; a blow to a Russian team which greatly depended on his lively, attacking play.

### Northern Ireland, Wales and Scotland

Of the British teams, England were the most fancied, Northern Ireland the most intriguing. It was the first occasion on which all four had qualified for the Finals.

England's chances were severely affected by the disastrous Munich air crash the previous February, when the Manchester United team's Elizabethan, twin-engined aircraft failed to gain sufficient height on a snowy day and hit a building at the end of the runway. The team, which had just drawn a European Cup tie 3–3 in Belgrade, was cruelly afflicted. Among those who died instantly were the captain, England's resourceful left-back Roger Byrne, and Tommy Taylor, their excellent centre-forward, a fine player in the air and a vigorous one on the ground. Duncan Edwards, still only twenty-one years old, a superbly powerful player thought by many to be the finest left-half to have played for his country since the war, died pitifully in hospital after fighting for life with the help of a kidney machine. The experience profoundly disturbed the twenty-year-old Bobby Charlton, whose natural shyness became a persistent melancholy which would remain with him for the next decade. He had played for England on their pre-World Cup tour, done badly in Belgrade, when they lost 5–0 in intense heat to Yugoslavia, and would not play a single World Cup match. This represented a perverse decision by team manager and selectors but, as we shall see, it may have been better for Charlton, in the circumstances, that he did not play.

Northern Ireland had won their way to the finals against all expectation by eliminating Italy—and their cohorts of South Americans. Unlucky to lose 1–0 in Rome, when the tough but tiny Wilbur Cush played successfully at centre-half and Sergio Cervato slyly moved the ball to the right to make a gap through which he could score from a free kick, they finished the job in Belfast. The decisive game should have taken place in January, but Istvan Zsolt, the Hungarian referee and theatre director, was held up in the fog, the Italians refused to accept an Irish referee and what followed was the unfriendliest friendly which can ever have been seen in Belfast.

Juan Schiaffino, star of the previous two World Cups with Uruguay, now playing for Milan and—on tenuous qualification—for Italy, broke Wilbur Cush's shinpad with a kick; Chiapella, the Fiorentina right-half, jumped with both knees into McAdams' back after a challenge on the goalkeeper, and when the final whistle blew on a 2–2 draw the crowd invaded the field. Danny Blanchflower, the Irish captain, allocated each Italian player to an Irish one. Ferrario, the huge centre-half who had jumped feet first at two Irish forwards at a corner, knocked down a couple of invaders, then panicked and cowered on the ground, and the police badly beat up a fan who had come on merely in quest of an autograph. It was a brutal, sombre affair, but Ireland eventually won the real match 2–1 on their merits, with goals by McIlroy and the ill-used Cush. Alcide Ghiggia, another Uruguayan hero of the 1950 World Cup called up by Italy, was sent off, ironically for a trivial offence.

Having fought their way through so bravely to the finals, the Northern Ireland team then had to fight again—against pressure in Ulster to prevent their playing on Sundays, an unavoidable necessity in the World Cup. The Irish Football Association was torn, but eventually sanity prevailed over bigotry.

Northern Ireland's extraordinary improvement and success was the result of the inspired managership of Peter Doherty and the emergence of a nucleus of greatly talented players—notably Gregg, the Blanchflowers, Peacock, McParland, Cush, McIlroy and Bingham.

Doherty was fortunate in having two splendid lieutenants to implement his policies on the field. Danny Blanchflower, the right-half, and Jimmy McIlroy, the Burnley inside-forward, were two drily witty, technically gifted, tactically sophisticated footballers whose good influence permeated the rest of the team. Before the World Cup, in which Ireland were drawn in a group with the West German holders, the Czechs and the Argentinians, Blanchflower whimsically observed that their plan would be to equalise before the other side had scored.

Billy Bingham, the well-sprung little Sunderland and Luton outside-right, who would form such a fine right wing with Cush in the World Cup and later become team manager himself, attributed the team's success to Doherty's 'pep talks', his double centre-forward plan which largely made up for the lack of a sufficient centre-forward, the devoted rehearsal of free kicks, corners and throws-in, and the fact that the minimal changes Doherty made ensured that the team became 'more like a club side'.

This was true of the equally impressive Welsh. Initially Wales were lucky to be going to Sweden at all, for they had been eliminated by the Czechs. When the withdrawal of all Israel's opponents—on political grounds—left them with a free passage to Sweden, FIFA decreed that those countries which had taken second place in their group should be put in a hat, the team drawn out to meet Israel, home and away. Uruguay proudly refused, Wales came out of the hat, won 2–0 home and away, and went to Sweden, their chances improved by Juventus's release of the massive, formidable John Charles to play centre-forward. Charles, who had made his international debut as a seventeen-year-old centre-half, had just finished a wonderfully successful first season in Italy. The Welsh team manager was the lively Jimmy Murphy, who had efficiently taken over Manchester United when Matt Busby was badly hurt in the Munich crash, and there were other famous players in Jack Kelsey, a strong, calm, agile goalkeeper, and the classical inside-left, Ivor Allchurch.

Scotland had done well to eliminate Spain, but they had just been thrashed 4–0 by England at Hampden and would predictably finish bottom of a group which included Paraguay—Uruguay's unexpected conquerors—Yugoslavia and France.

## Hungary

The Hungarians, moral victors and actual losers in 1954, were a parody of their great team of the early 1950s. Comes the Revolution;

in this case, the Hungarian Revolution of 1956. Honved, the army team into which, willy nilly, the authorities had stuffed almost all their best footballers, was touring abroad; and the authorities were properly hoist with their own petard. The incomparable, irreplaceable inside-forwards, Kocsis and Puskas, exiled themselves and eventually, like Kubala before them, found gainful employment in Spanish football. The excellent winger, Zoltan Czibor, expatriated himself, too, and though Josef Bozsik and Nandor Hidegkuti duly went dutifully home, they were fading veterans by now.

Moreover, it was alleged that there had been a descent by police on the Hungarian players at Budapest airport to confiscate money which they were taking out of the country to buy goods. It may well have been true, for the players seemed very much down in the mouth. Gustav Sebes, who led them in the 1954 World Cup, remarked, 'I have never seen a Hungarian team in such a deplorable physical condition and nervous state.' The myth of Hungarian superiority, their supremacy in tactics, men and training, went to the winds, though the comfortable journalese soubriquet of Magic Magyars would be with us for a few wistful years to come.

## France

The French arrived nineteen days before the competition started at Kopparberg under the inspiring and benevolent guidance of Monsieur Paul Nicolas, once an international himself, with their former splendid goalkeeper Alex Thépot among the selectors and Albert Batteux an excellent manager assisted by Jean Snella. No one thought France a serious candidate, which if anything helped them by removing pressure. They had not won a game that year, though the release of little Raymond Kopa by Real Madrid was sure to improve them. Banished to the wing at Real by the dominating Alfredo Di Stefano—who could not, even with Kubala's help, enable Spain to eliminate Scotland—Kopa flourished anew when back in the middle and on the conductor's podium. A superbly balanced player with exquisite control and a splendid eye for the through pass, his partnership with Just Fontaine would be one of the features of the tournament, bringing Fontaine a record thirteen goals.

Fontaine, born in Morocco, had come to Sweden quite reconciled to being a reserve, and even said, 'I'm centre-forward only till Kopa comes'. When René Bliard kicked the ground in training, hurt his ankle and went home—singing Fontaine's praises—his choice was assured. Dark, sturdily built, a fast and determined runner with excellent acceleration and a fine shot, Fontaine was also extremely intelligent in his responses to Kopa's splendid prompting.

### West Germany

Since their victory in Berne little had gone right for the West Germans. Almost at once their team had been smitten with an epidemic of jaundice, which led to wide but unsubstantiated charges that they had been on drugs. No fewer than seven of the 1954 team had fallen by the wayside: Turek, Kohlmeyer, Liebrich, Mai, Otmar Walter and Morloch. But Fritz Walter was still there to be the chief strategist at the age of thirty-seven, and Hans Schaefer would resume his dialogue with Rahn on the wings. Rahn, the enormous right-winger, bombardier of the last World Cup Final, had been drinking heavily since then, but he was rehabilitated, morally and physically, in time to play admirably in Sweden. Moreover, there were two exciting additions to the team in the strong young left-half, Horst Szymaniak, and Uwe Seeler, a stalwart, highly mobile and combative centre-forward from Hamburg, who had been capped initially in 1954 at the age of eighteen and would become the very symbol of German football for years to follow.

### Argentina

Argentina played in West Germany's group, but their team had been sadly plundered by the Italians. Only a year before, its young 'Angels with Dirty Faces', its *Trio de la Muerte* of Maschio, Angelillo and Sivori, had won it a spectacular South American title in Lima. In swooped the marauding Italian clubs to sign all of them, and the accomplished inside-left Ernesto Grillo for good measure.

It was only by rehabilitating the famous forty-year-old inside-left Angel Labruna of River Plate, that Argentina had managed to scrape through the qualifying rounds, in which they had the shame of losing to obscure Bolivia. Another celebrated veteran in the giant, perambulating centre-half, Nestor Rossi, was in the side, but the omens were poor.

### Brazil

Not that Brazil had had an easy passage to Sweden, even if they were the favourites by the time they got there. Their last, all-important qualifying match—against Peru in Rio—had been won only by 1–0, thanks to one of Didì's celebrated *foglia secca* (falling leaf) free kicks; which by 1970's World Cup would be known as banana shots. Yet Didì was very nearly not brought to Sweden, and his place was in doubt until the opening game. First, he was criticised for being, at the age of thirty, too old! Second, he had married a white woman; third, he was supposedly not trying hard enough. 'It would be funny if they left me out,' he remarked with irony, 'after I had paid for their ticket.' He had the remote, brooding aspect of a great negro jazz musician.

Vicente Feola, a São Paulo man of Salernitan descent, brought to Sweden the best, most thoroughly organised Brazilian side ever to visit Europe. His right-hand man was the large and imperturbable doctor Hilton Gosling, who had covered hundreds of miles in Sweden before he found the ideal place for a training camp among the trees of Hindas outside Gothenburg. The Russians too, had taken up residence there, and sometimes, when they were not fishing, would come lumbering out of the woods like bears to watch the Brazilians joyfully train, with the cacophony of a male voice choir gone berserk.

The Brazilians not only had Gosling, whom the players treated as father or father-confessor, they also had, with memories of Berne in mind, their own psychologist, an amiable eclectic from São Paulo, grey-sweatered, often unshaven, whose precise methods were a little hard to comprehend. He did not, he said, believe in haranguing the players in groups, yet neither did he believe in talking to them individually, since this made their problem bigger. He believed in getting them to draw pictures of a man. The more cerebral players drew sophisticated pictures, the instinctive players drew virtual matchstick-men. The two made good wing partnerships. Forwards must project their aggression, defenders must contain it; a theory which must have taken heavy punishment if he chanced to see such defenders as the terrible Erhardt of West Germany.

Feola, meanwhile, shook his heavy head and said, 'How can he know the ambience?' He was also critical of his nineteen-year-old, blond centre-forward José Altafini, known then by the nickname of Mazzola for his resemblance to the old captain of Italy and father of Sandrino. Altafini had just been transferred for a large fee to Milan— the team, indeed, had played two impressive matches in Italy en route to Sweden. 'He's nineteen,' complained Feola. 'All the publicity about his transfer to Milan; how can it help but go to his head? He doesn't fit in with the team.'

Feola's preference and ultimate choice went to the Vasco da Gama centre-forward, Vavà, a sturdy, Aztec figure, while there were two other imponderables. The seventeen-year-old Pelé, already described as the finest player ever produced by Brazil, was injured, while Feola was reluctant to choose the forward the psychologist regarded as the most unsophisticated of all, the outside-right Garrincha.

Garrincha, 'the Little Bird', was all the more dangerous and un-predictable because he had been crippled since childhood; he was a footballer of superb natural gifts, astonishing speed and swerve, but utterly inconsistent. The safe and early choice was Flamengo's Joel—

with another Flamengo winger in Zagalo on the left, and their club mate Dida at inside-right, beside Vavà.

The 4-2-4 system, adopted instead of the third back game which was foreign to them, solved the old Brazilian problem of pivotal covering in defence by simply putting the left-half alongside the centre-half; just as Hungary had done with Zakarias. Two players foraged and passed in midfield, while two wingers and two central strikers stayed in attack. If you had the extraordinary talent at your command that the Brazilians had, it was a marvellous system. If not, it would present as many difficulties as it solved, especially in midfield.

### England

England, who were expected to qualify from Gothenburg with Brazil, had compounded the problems created by Munich with their odd choice. They brought only twenty players, though entitled to twenty-two (the Czechs brought only eighteen) and these twenty included neither Stanley Matthews nor Nat Lofthouse, both successes of the 1954 World Cup and both still in imposing form. Matthews, indeed, had run ragged the usually impeccable Brazilian left-back Nilton Santos at Wembley in 1956—at the age of forty-one—while Lofthouse had just scored both Bolton's goals in the Cup Final.

The loss of Edwards, Byrne and Taylor was thus exacerbated. Any hope of overcoming it was severely compromised by the fact that Fulham and Blackburn Rovers had just been engaged in a fierce, exhausting struggle to emerge from the Second Division which had left its mark on Johnny Haynes, the young Londoner whose superb crossfield and through passing made him the key man in attack, on Bobby Robson, his inside-forward partner at Fulham, and the talented little right-winger, Blackburn's Bryan Douglas. Ronnie Clayton, Blackburn's captain and right-half, gained a place only in the group's play-off.

### Group Matches

Worse still was to come, for in the opening game in Gothenburg's new Ullevi Stadium where the roof, with its wire suspensions, suggested a monster puppeteer, Tom Finney was hurt. It did not prevent his inspiring the English revival in the last half hour or equalising from a penalty six minutes from time when Douglas was tripped, but his loss was a dreadful blow. Beyond question he was the one forward of world class England possessed, and there was no one now to compensate for the staleness of Haynes, Douglas and Robson, the banal crudities of the huge centre-forward Derek Kevan, the patent inadequacy of his

successor Alan A'Court—and Walter Winterbottom's astonishing
reluctance to make changes.

It was Salnikov, not Haynes, who was the arch strategist of this
interesting match, one in which Russia played much clever football,
even without Netto. Voinov and Tsarev, the robust wing-halves, made
up for his absence, Krishevski dominated the centre, and it was as well
that England's cool new goalkeeper, Colin McDonald of Burnley, was
the equal even of Yachine.

After thirteen minutes, however, he could only block a shot by the
vivacious left-winger Ilyin, and Simonian, who usually lay deep, was
there to score. England's short, square, unimaginative passing was
making no progress against a Russian defence whose methods often
transgressed the rules.

Ten minutes into the second half the second Russian goal arrived.
The English defence, in these pre-overlapping days, stood bemused as
Kessarev, the right-back, advanced, crossed beautifully; and Ivanov
scored. It was Finney's mastery of Kessarev, however, which began to
turn the tide. After sixty-five minutes Billy Wright, an indomitable
centre-half and a fine captain, booted a free kick high into the goalmouth. Kevan's fair head rose above the defence, even above Yachine,
and headed down into goal.

Brazil, meanwhile, had had no trouble with ponderous Austria at
Boras' little ground, Mazzola scoring twice, and Nilton Santos strolling
through from left-back to get the third. Their critics, however, were
dissatisfied, in particularly accusing Dida, who had done some good
running off the ball, of lack of courage. Dida promptly disappeared
from the side.

Elsewhere there were various alarms and excursions, though Sweden
had opened the ball, unscathed, on the afternoon of June 8 with a 3–0
win in Stockholm over indifferent Mexico. Two of their goals were
scored by a tall, talented young centre-forward, Agne Simonsson,
while thirty-six-year-old Liedholm, at right-half for the moment, got
the other from a penalty.

In Group 1, the astonishing Northern Irish beat Czechoslovakia by
Cush's solitary goal at Halmstad, while the holders, West Germany,
showed up Argentina's deficiencies at Malmö, defeating them 3–1.
Poor Fritz Walter, who would end the tournament in bed nursing his
injuries, was horribly fouled by Rossi towards the end; a foul which
many thought deserved to be punished with expulsion.

Not even a goal scored by Argentina's slim and dangerous little
outside-right Corbatta in two minutes, cutting past the muscular
Juskowiak, could give them the impetus they needed. The Germans
were superior in teamwork and stamina, the Argentinians too much
inclined to play off the cuff. So Rahn, half an hour after the goal,

equalised with a sudden ferocious left-footer from the inside-left position when served by Walter, and five minutes from half-time Seeler,
giving and receiving from Schaefer, lunged forward to make it 2–1.
Even an injury to Eckel which had him limping on the left wing for
most of the second half could not tip the balance, and ten minutes
from the end Rahn bent his shot past the veteran Carrizo with the
outside of the foot. 3–1.

The Irish used the young Derek Dougan at centre-forward. The
first choice, Billy Simpson of Rangers, had pulled a muscle after a
mere five minutes' training in Sweden. Dougan had an awkward first
half, but when Billy Bingham was pushed into the middle in the second
he made good use of his fine acceleration. Harry Gregg allayed all fears
with his performance in goal, Bertie Peacock had an exceptional game
at left-half and Wilbur Cush headed the only goal from the rugged
Peter McParland's centre. The lack of Jackie Blanchflower had a
seriously negative effect on the team, obliging his brother to play a far
more defensive game alongside their makeshift centre-half, the full-back
Willie Cunningham, but the defence held out well under vigorous
pressure in the closing phases.

France got away to a spectacular beginning, annihilating the Paraguayans 7–3 at Nörrkoping, five of their goals coming in the second
half; a rampant Fontaine got three. Paraguay actually scored first
through Amarilla, and were level, 2–2, at half-time. Thereafter the
superb combination of the French inside-forwards, Kopa, Fontaine
and the incisive Roger Piantoni, was simply too much for them.

Scotland, at Vasteras, did a great deal better against Yugoslavia
than had feeble England in Belgrade, holding them to a 1–1 draw in a
strangely schizophrenic match.

Yugoslavia, far superior in technique, began the game as if they
were going to treat Scotland as they had England. With the blond,
elegant Milos Milutinovic in splendid form at centre-forward and
abetted by a new star, the dark little gipsy inside-left Dragoslav
Sekularac, and the admirable Boskov at wing-half, they assailed the
Scottish goal. At first, wrote one commentator, the Scots seemed like
juniors getting a lesson. The right-winger Petakovic gave Tommy
Younger, the big, blond Scots goalkeeper, no hope; from Milutinovic's
pass Eric Caldow kicked off the line; Younger made a fine save, and
somehow no more goals resulted.

In the second half Scotland's immense determination and robust
challenge ground down the more fragile Slavs. Petakovic had scarcely
hit a post when Turnbull crossed, Beara—in goal—and Krstic confused one another, and Murray headed the equaliser. Though
Veselinovic also hit the post, Yugoslavia had lost their command.

In Group I Wales held Hungary to a draw at Sandviken. In Gothen-

1. Italy's goalkeeper Combi beaten by Puc: the Czechs lead 1–0 in the 1934 Final

2. Italy's team manager Vittorio Pozzo instructs his players before the start of extra time in the 1934 Final

3. World Cup 1938: Sweden v. Hungary. Sweden's keeper clears from Hungary's Dr Sarosi

4. 1938. Brazil 6, Poland 5. Brazil attack the Polish goal

5. World Cup Final 1938. Italy's right-back Alfredo Foni clears with an overhead kick

6. 1954. The Battle of Berne. Brazil's keeper Castilho plunges for the ball, watched by Hungary's J. Toth

7. 1954. Uruguay v. England. Nat Lofthouse beats Maspoli to score for England

8. 1954. Uruguay v. England. England attack, Maspoli to the rescue

9. World Cup 1954: Hungary's Gyula Grosics, beaten from the penalty spot by Brazil's Djalma Santos

10. World Cup 1958. Northern Ireland's airborne keeper Harry Gregg fails to stop Uwe Seeler equalising for West Germany

11. World Cup Final 1958. Svensson, Sweden's keeper, challenged by seventeen-year-old **Pele**

12.   World Cup 1962. Italy's Omar Sivori leaps over Swiss keeper Elsener

13.   World Cup 1966. Portugal's Eusebio gets in his shot against Bulgaria

14. World Cup 1966. England v. Argentina. Argentine captain Antonio Rattin **argues at** Wembley with the German referee Herr Kreitlein before his expulsion

15. World Cup Final 1966. Wolfgang Weber's last-ditch equaliser for West Germany against England. Ray Wilson and Gordon Banks stretch in vain

16. World Cup Final 1966. Was it a goal? Roger Hunt exults as Geoff Hurst's shot beats Tilkowski to come down from the underside of the bar

17. World Cup 1970. Italy v. Sweden. One way of stopping Italy's Gigi Riva

18. World Cup 1970. England manager Alf Ramsey rashly takes Bobby Charlton off the field in Leon, against West Germany

19. World Cup 1970 semi-final. Italian joy, German despair, as Italy score in extra time

20. World Cup 1970 semi-final, Rivelino on the ball against Uruguay

21. World Cup Final 1970. Brazil's Jairzinho is too quick for Italy's Facchetti and Burgnich. Pelé looks on

22. World Cup 1974. Yugoslavia cannot stop West Germany's Gerd Muller, even when he's grounded

23.   World Cup 1974. Franz Beckenbauer, West German star in three World Cups

24. World Cup 1974. Johan Cruyff scores a splendid second goal for Holland against Brazil, at Dortmund

25. World Cup 1974. Scottish captain Billy Bremner in action against Zaire

26. World Cup 1978. Peru's Teofilo Cubillas tries to negotiate Poland's Boniek

27. World Cup Final 1978. Mario Kempes leaps between Dutch defenders Willy Van de Kerkhof and Erny Brandts

28.  World Cup Final 1978. Argentinian joy: Luque, Kempes and Bertoni

burg, England would now play Brazil for the first time in a World Cup. Bill Nicholson, Tottenham Hotspur coach, having watched the Brazilians, evolved a defensive scheme whereby Don Howe, the tall, cool West Bromwich right-back, would play as a second centre-half beside Billy Wright; Eddie Clamp, the big, dark Wolves half-back, as an attacking full-back; while another Wolves man, the studious Bill Slater, would play 'tight' on Didì.

With Pelé and Garrincha still missing from Brazil's attack, though Vavà now lined up beside Mazzola, the scheme worked remarkably well, Brazil dominated the first half, Didì and the attacking right-half, the bald Dino, dominating midfield, but Vavà hit the bar, Clamp kicked off the line, and Colin McDonald made two spectacular saves from headers by Mazzola.

In the second half, the pattern changed and England might even have won. If some had cast doubt on the English penalty against Russia, claiming that the foul took place outside the box, then England were most unfortunate not to get one when Bellini hauled Kevan down as he thundered after one of Haynes's rare through passes. But by and large, however, the England attack was as grey as it had been against Russia.

In Boras, goals by Ilyin and Valentin Ivanov gave Russia a 2-0 win over Austria and put England's qualification in doubt.

The Irish, paying for bad intelligence on the Argentinian team, lost 3-1 to it at Halmstad. The sheer skill of the Argentinians overcame an Irish team which lacked bite in the middle, Coyle's unexpected replacement of Dougan bringing no improvement. This above all was a game in which Danny Blanchflower's subtle talents, his always imaginative use of the ball, were needed not in defence but in midfield, where Rossi and the splendid veteran Labruna dominated.

West Germany at Hälsingborg brought Hans Schaefer in from the wing to inside-left, and it was his controversial goal, scored on the hour, which turned a game they seemed to be losing to the lively Czechs. Two goals down, they made it 1-2 when Schaefer charged the Czech goalkeeper Dolejsi over his line with the ball, and the goal was surprisingly allowed to stand. Helmut Rahn—again—equalised.

An unexpected result was the defeat of France 3-2 by Yugoslavia at Vasteras, despite two more goals for the prolific Just Fontaine. A lack of authority in defence, despite the composed presence at centre-half of the accomplished Bob Jonquet, an inability to get the best out of two excellent wingers in Wisnieski and Jean Vincent, a penalty refused when Fontaine was fouled; all these played a part in France's defeat. So did the opportunism of Veselinovic, who got two of the Yugoslav goals. The winner came three minutes from time when France were besieging Beara's goal. Then Yugoslavia broke away, Roger Marche—

France's bald, experienced left-back—erred, and Veselinovic scored his second.

Scotland, seemingly weary after their display against the Yugoslavs, went down 3–2 to Paraguay at Norrkoping where Silvio Parodi, an inside-forward with experience of Italian football, was the dominant player and Bobby Evans an excellent centre-half. Indeed, not one of the British teams won their match in this round, for Wales played very poorly in Stockholm, to be held 1–1 by Mexico. 'Every time you knocked one of them down, he cried,' complained the Manchester United forward Colin Webster, never the most gentle of players, but Kelsey was impressed by their ball control and fitness.

Sweden made heavy weather of winning their evening game in the same stadium against Hungary, a match notable for the tremendous right-footed shooting of Hungary's Lajos Tichy and the deadly finishing of Sweden's Kurre Hamrin.

The concluding round of matches brought, above all, the annihilation of Argentina by Czechoslovakia at Hälsingborg, a humiliation which may now be seen as the bleak turning point in Argentinian football. What was especially strange was that the Argentinians should be made to look so slow and obsolete by the Czechs, so often criticised— as they would be even in the 1962 World Cup—for one-pace football.

The Czechs, who confirmed the burly Popluhar at centre-half in his second World Cup match, simply overwhelmed the Argentinians. Borovicka, who had missed the German game—there were tales of a bitter quarrel in the dressing-room during the Irish match—returned to blend perfectly with the powerful Molnar, while Hovorka was a strong and effective outside-right, making two goals and scoring the last two. Another two went to Zikan, the outside-left, and Argentina's only reply came from a penalty by the inevitable Corbatta. With the exception of him, Menendez and Varacka—who, commentators were quick to point out, was of Czech origin—the team looked slow and unfit.

When the Argentinians arrived at Buenos Aires airport initial disbelief had turned to fury and they were pelted with rubbish. The wound went deep. In future, Argentinian football would shed its old traditions of spectacle and artistry and become more destructive than the most negative.

In Malmö, with thousands of their supporters in attendance, West Germany were held to an exciting 2–2 draw by Northern Ireland, for whom Harry Gregg, superb in goal, and Peter McParland, a deadly opportunist, surpassed themselves.

In Gothenburg, Brazil at last let slip the astonishing Pelé and the inimitable Garrincha, routing the Soviets in the process. Though the score was 2–0 it might easily have been doubled or even trebled.

Pelé had been an international for almost a year, a striking inside-forward who came from a poor black family at Tres Coracoes in the heart of the great state of Minas Gerais. As a boy he had been coached by the old Brazilian international forward, de Brito, who brought him to the Santos club where his progress had been phenomenal. Five feet eight inches tall, weighing some ten and a half stone, superbly muscled, he was at this stage a goal-scorer *par excellence*, gymnastically agile and resilient, a tantalising juggler of the ball, a fine right-footed shot with the ability to climb and head like a Lawton. Above all, his temperament was extraordinary, his coolness in the thick of the battle, the most tense and dramatic situations, uncanny.

His face, which would become so familiar throughout the world over the next decade, never lost its innocence, its boyish appeal. He was no saint; in years to come his policy under provocation was much more the Old Testament one of an eye for an eye than the New Testament's turning the other cheek, but somehow the image remained untarnished, the pristine appeal untouched.

Garrincha came into the team by popular request of the players themselves. A deputation led by Nilton Santos went to Feola and asked for his inclusion. Feola gave way. From the opening minutes, Garrincha's incomparable swerve and acceleration left his opponent Kuznetsov helpless. First he beat him to the wide, shot, and hit the left-hand post. Next, Pele hit the right-hand post. Finally, after three minutes, Didì emerged calmly and magisterially from a group of Russian opponents, and with an exquisite pass found Vavà who dashed through to score.

Didì had now found his ideal complement in the Santos right-half Zito, who had replaced Dino. Stronger in defence, much less inclined to carry the ball, an adroit passer who could strike for goal when necessary, Zito would emerge as the best half-back in the tournament.

It was extraordinary that Russia's bemused defence should hold out till thirteen minutes from time when Vavà, after an exchange of passes with Pelé, got the second. At one late, memorable instant, Garrincha had and held the ball against five encircling Russians. Genius had overwhelmed mere effort.

At Boras, in a match played on a lower plane, England laboured to a draw with the ponderous Austrians, who were twice ahead. The British sailor who ironically blew the Last Post when a histrionic Austrian went down might well have been blowing it for England. Haynes, at his best, must have made more of Kevan's dominance of the ageing Happel, Austria's stopper. He himself scored England's first goal after fifty-six minutes and made the second for Kevan. Austria's goals both came from impressive, uncharacteristic long shots, by Koller and Koerner.

In Group II France duly beat Scotland, but they found it hard. Each team changed its goalkeeper. Bill Brown, of Dundee and later of Spurs, won the admiration of Kopa and Fontaine with his agility; Abbes replaced Remetter for France. Kopa volleyed home Fontaine's cross—a brief reciprocation—but Scotland struck back forcefully. Abbes had to make a fine save from Murray; then, when the Hearts forward was fouled—by Jonquet and the talented right-half Armand Penverne—John Hewie, Charlton Athletic's South African, wastefully hit the penalty against a post.

It was as well for France that in the very last seconds of the half Fontaine, served by Jonquet, should sprint away to make it 2–0. In the second half, when they were much less good, Baird emulated him and the final score was a narrow 2–1.

At Eskilstuna a hero tottered, Vladimir Beara having one of his worst games in goal for Yugoslavia against Paraguay. The score was 3–3, and all three Paraguayan goals could be blamed on the unhappy Beara. Three times the Paraguayans, inspired again by Parodi, equalised against a Yugoslav team which had dropped the graceful Milutinovic; but the Slaves went through.

## Play-Offs for Quarter-Finals

Goal average counting for nothing, three of the British teams now entered play-offs—and two got through. It was, most unforeseeably, England who failed, losing 1–0 to Russia in Gothenburg. Almost perversely, having stubbornly refused to make changes, they now, still disdaining Charlton, capped two new forwards: Peter Brabook, the Chelsea right-winger, and Peter Broadbent, the industrious young Wolves inside-right.

In the tepid Ullevi—tepid till Sweden arrived there—England did not deserve to lose, though Haynes, apparently untouchable, had another grim game. Brabook twice hit a post; Ilyin hit one after sixty-eight minutes, and scored. Sadly for the otherwise faultless McDonald, it was his careless throw which put Russia away.

Decimated Ireland, faced by a Czech team which had swamped Argentina, patched up their team at Malmö and won, as Peter Doherty promised they would.

Norman Uprichard replaced Gregg in goal, and Jackie Scott was capped for the first time in place of the injured Tommy Casey. Uprichard was hurt, Peacock was hurt, Czechoslovakia took the lead, the game went into extra time; and still Ireland won.

Zikan gave the Czechs the lead after nineteen minutes, but on the stroke of half-time the irresistible McParland equalised after Cush had had two shots blocked. Nine minutes into extra time he volleyed home

Danny Blanchflower's free kick. Bubernik of Czechoslovakia was sent off. Ireland qualified.

So did Wales, eliminating Hungary at Stockholm; a match in which an opponent was also sent off—Sipos, for brutally kicking Hewitt; also in extra time.

Neither British team survived the quarter-final, though Wales, even without the mighty John Charles, gave Brazil immense trouble in Gothenburg. Perhaps Charles would have exploited the early centre with which Webster, his deputy, did nothing.

Thereafter, it was the iron Welsh defence against the Brazilian attack which found the going harder and harder. Mazzola was back again for Vavà, Garrincha was most cleverly played by Mel Hopkins, Dave Bowen was an inspiring captain, Stuart Williams and Derek Sullivan a muscular right flank. Behind them, Jack Kelsey held everything. 'Chewing gum,' he modestly explained afterwards. 'Always use it. Put some on my hands. Rub it well in.'

Pelé has often said that the goal with which he cut the Gordian knot after sixty-six minutes was the most important he ever scored. It was also one of the luckiest, for Kelsey had the shot covered before it struck the foot of the impeccable Williams and was deflected past him. There was a pile-up, a very pyramid of yellow-shirted Brazilian bodies in the goalmouth.

The weary and depleted Irish team, all the wearier for an ill-planned coach journey, did their best against France but blew up. The two hundred and ten-mile drive to Nörrkoping the previous day was bad enough preparation; the absence of Gregg and Peacock (with torn ligaments) and the need to play the damaged Casey still a greater handicap. There was just one early moment in which the team might have scored and thus found the morale, the magic energy, they had before. In one of their set-piece throw-ins, Blanchflower threw the ball to Bingham's head and the little winger flicked it on for McIlroy, but he, clear through, squared it instead of shooting. That was that. With McParland on this occasion lost in the middle, Wisnieski scored just before half-time and Ireland collapsed. In the second half Fontaine, twice more, and Piantoni added goals.

## The Quarter-Finals

Sweden found a weary Russian team stiff opponents in the first half at Stockholm, where the public's incredulity still kept the crowd down to less than 32,000. In the second half Kurt Hamrin embarked on a one-man siege of the Russian goal. Twice he almost headed in; eventually, after his own run and cross, the ball bobbled loose and head it

in he did. He made the second goal for Simonsson from the left-hand
goal line two and a half minutes from time.

Jasseron, an experienced French coach, observed of the Swedes that
they were a good enough team provided they were not outpaced.
Raynor knew it; Brazil would capitalise on it.

At Malmö Helmut Rahn yet again won the match for Germany, racing away from the vulnerable Crnkovic to score after twelve
minutes, Krivocuka, Beara's equally unhappy replacement, failing
to narrow the angle. It was a match blemished by the ruthlessness of
Juskowiak and Erhardt, who was lucky indeed not to give away a
penalty when, nine minutes from the end, he not only brought down
Milutinovic—restored and iridescent—but held his leg for good
measure.

### The Semi-Finals   Sweden v. West Germany

The semi-finals pitted Sweden against West Germany in Gothenburg
and Brazil against France in Stockholm. The Gothenburg match
provided an extraordinary study in national behaviour, as the Swedes'
unfettered chauvinism put even the Germans' in the shade, and very
nearly resulted in the game not being played at all.

In the first place, the Swedes outraged all the canons of hospitality by
bringing their own cheerleaders right on to the pitch before the match,
to incite the crowd. The German cheerleaders, meanwhile, were
confined to the running-track.

In the stand, an embittered row was going on between Dr Pecos
Bauwens, the Olympian President of the German Football Association, whose own chauvinistic pronouncements after the 1954 World
Cup had caused concern in West Germany, and Swedish officials.
The Swedes would not provide seats for some of the West German
supporters. Dr Bauwens threatened that if they were not forthcoming
he would withdraw his team from the match. They were provided.

The game itself was a fascinating one, even though blemished by
fouls and at least one major refereeing error. With the tremendous
Swedish choruses of *Heja, heja, heja!* thundering over the stadium, the
home team dictated the early play. Erhardt had chosen the wrong
studs and slipped about parlously on the greasy ground, while
Herkenrath looked an uncertain goalkeeper. Nevertheless, it was
Germany who broke away for a sensational goal.

Seeler, always busy and thoughtful, went to the left to catch a ball
rolling out of play and centred, and Hans Schaefer despatched it past
Svensson with a ferocious twenty-five-yard volley.

Sweden's equaliser, after Liedholm and Gren had gradually brought
them back into the game, should never have stood. Liedholm blatantly

brought the ball under control with his hand before running on with an approving wave from the referee, and Skoglund ultimately scored from a sharp angle. There were only five minutes between the goals.

It was Hamrin, already tormenting Juskowiak, who turned the game early in the second half, though in a somewhat unusual way. In the third minute Herkenrath had to plunge at his feet. In the twelfth he fouled Juskowiak, who was foolish enough to kick him. Hamrin made the most of it, rolling about in apparent agony, though when Juskowiak was sent off, his recovery was quick.

Parling, the large, blond Swedish left-half known as the Iron Stove, was just as worthy to be sent off for a dreadful foul on Fritz Walter sixteen minutes from the end. Walter was carried off for a couple of minutes, and spent the next day in bed. So Sweden, now virtually playing against nine men, finished the job.

Nine minutes from time, when Hamrin's shot was blocked, Gunnar Gren let fly immediately for the top left-hand corner, for one of his rare goals. Finally, Hamrin scored a goal of rare skill and impertinence, first stopping with the ball and walking it towards the right touchline like a man bemused, then coming to galvanic life, dancing past three men and beating Herkenrath. The slowest team in the tournament had reached the Final.

### Brazil v. France

So did Brazil, though the promised feast against France never materialised. It would have been fascinating to see how the deep central thrust of Fontaine and Piantoni, fed by Kopa, would have fared against Brazil's uncertain central defence. For thirty-seven minutes, indeed, the marvellous little Kopa caused all sorts of trouble. Didì, Garrincha and Pelé made Vavà a devastating goal in the second minute, but Fontaine had equalised within nine. Then Bob Jonquet was hurt and left the middle, Didì scored within two minutes, and in the second half the fabulous Pelé ran riot with three more goals, Piantoni scoring a late, meaningless second for France.

### **The Final**  Sweden v. Brazil

So Sweden would play Brazil, and the Brazilians worried about the effect an atmosphere as torrid as Gothenburg's might have on their emotional players. The World Cup Committee set their minds at rest by sternly forbidding the Swedes to bring cheerleaders on to the pitch again. Thus deprived of example and instruction, the crowd at Rasunda was astonishingly quiet.

As an *hors d'oeuvre* Kopa and Fontaine played ducks and drakes at Gothenburg with a weakened Germany—in which the young, blond Karl-Heinz Schnellinger made his second appearance of the series, at right-half. Kopa, the son of a Polish miner and a Frenchwoman, who might never have turned professional footballer were it not for a boyhood mining accident, was irresistible. Svengali to Fontaine's Trilby, he helped him to four splendid goals and got a penalty himself. France took the third-place match 6–3.

Thus to Stockholm, and a day heavy with rain. George Raynor cheerfully forecast that if the Brazilians went a goal down they would 'panic all over the show'. They did go an early goal down; and stayed serene.

Feola made a bold change in defence, suddenly withdrawing his right-back de Sordi to give the powerful black Djalma Santos, a veteran of 1954, his first game in the competition. The two Santoses snuffed out Hamrin and Skoglund with the nonchalance of men extinguishing a candle.

Yet Sweden had a goal in four minutes, a goal worked out by Gren and Liedholm with such facility that many seemed sure to follow. Gren gave Liedholm the ball, Liedholm picked his way precisely past two Brazilian defenders in the penalty box and beat the poised Gilmar with a low, strong shot into the right-hand corner. It was the first time in the tournament that Brazil had been in arrears.

Six minutes later they were level, thanks to the pantherine Garrincha. Receiving from Zito on the right wing, he took the ball up to Parling and Axbom, caught them both off balance with a miraculous swerve and acceleration down the line and cut the ball back hard and fast. In tore Vavà to score.

The game grew wonderfully vivid. Pelé crashed a shot against the post, tireless Zagalo headed out from almost beneath the Brazilian bar. After thirty-two minutes, however, Garrincha again left the Swedish left flank standing, and Vavà again drove in his pass.

Sweden were losing the battle in midfield and were impotent on the wings. Their last hopes died ten minutes after half-time, when Pelé scored a marvellously impertinent goal. Catching a high ball in the thick of the penalty box on his thigh, he hooked it over his head, whirled round and volleyed mightily past Svensson.

Now Zito and Didì were switching play at will, now Djalma Santos was racing up from full-back, now Pelé and Vavà were probing, interpassing. With thirteen minutes left Zagalo went past Boerjesson, then Bergmark, and shot the fourth, and knelt in tears of joy.

Next, with the overjoyed Brazilian fans keeping up a shout of *Samba, samba!*, Liedholm sent Agne Simonsson through the middle, possibly offside, for Sweden's second goal—only for Pelé to reply with

Brazil's fifth. Zagalo's was the centre, and Pelé rose to it with majestic elevation and power.

The World Cup was Brazil's at long last, and who could not rejoice with them as they ran, like ecstatic children, round the pitch, holding first their own flag, then the Swedes'? There was no doubt this time that the best, immeasurably the finest, team had won.

# RESULTS: Sweden 1958

## Pool I

Germany 3, Argentina 1 (HT 2/1)
Ireland 1, Czechoslovakia 0 (HT 1/0)
Germany 2, Czechoslovakia 2 (HT 1/0)
Argentina 3, Ireland 1 (HT 1/1)
Germany 2, Ireland 2 (HT 1/1)
Czechoslovakia 6, Argentina 1 (HT 3/1)

| | P | W | D | L | GOALS F | A | Pts |
|---|---|---|---|---|---|---|---|
| Germany | 3 | 1 | 2 | 0 | 7 | 5 | 4 |
| Czechoslovakia | 3 | 1 | 1 | 1 | 8 | 4 | 3 |
| Ireland | 3 | 1 | 1 | 1 | 4 | 5 | 3 |
| Argentina | 3 | 1 | 0 | 2 | 5 | 10 | 2 |

## Pool II

France 7, Paraguay 3 (HT 2/2)
Yugoslavia 1, Scotland 1 (HT 1/0)
Yugoslavia 3, France 2 (HT 1/1)
Paraguay 3, Scotland 2 (HT 2/1)
France 2, Scotland 1 (HT 2/0)
Yugoslavia 3, Paraguay 3 (HT 2/1)

| | P | W | D | L | GOALS F | A | Pts |
|---|---|---|---|---|---|---|---|
| France | 3 | 2 | 0 | 1 | 11 | 7 | 4 |
| Yugoslavia | 3 | 1 | 2 | 0 | 7 | 6 | 4 |
| Paraguay | 3 | 1 | 1 | 1 | 9 | 12 | 3 |
| Scotland | 3 | 0 | 1 | 2 | 4 | 6 | 1 |

## Pool III

Sweden 3, Mexico 0 (HT 1/0)
Hungary 1, Wales 1 (HT 1/1)
Wales 1, Mexico 1 (HT 1/1)
Sweden 2, Hungary 1 (HT 1/0)
Sweden 0, Wales 0 (HT 0/0)
Hungary 4, Mexico 0 (HT 1/0)

| | P | W | D | L | GOALS F | A | Pts |
|---|---|---|---|---|---|---|---|
| Sweden | 3 | 2 | 1 | 0 | 5 | 1 | 5 |
| Hungary | 3 | 1 | 1 | 1 | 6 | 3 | 3 |
| Wales | 3 | 0 | 3 | 0 | 2 | 2 | 3 |
| Mexico | 3 | 0 | 1 | 2 | 1 | 8 | 1 |

Play off Wales 2, Hungary 1 (HT 0/1)

## Pool IV

England 2, Russia 2 (HT 0/1)
Brazil 3, Austria 0 (HT 1/0)
England 0, Brazil 0 (HT 0/0)
Russia 2, Austria 0 (HT 1/0)
Brazil 2, Russia 0 (HT 1/0)
England 2, Austria 2 (HT 0/1)

| | P | W | D | L | GOALS F | A |
|---|---|---|---|---|---|---|
| Brazil | 3 | 2 | 1 | 0 | 5 | 0 |
| England | 3 | 0 | 3 | 0 | 4 | 4 |
| Russia | 3 | 1 | 1 | 1 | 4 | 4 |
| Austria | 3 | 0 | 1 | 2 | 2 | 7 |

Play off Russia 1, England 0 (HT 0/0)

## Quarter-finals

*Norrköping*

**France 4** | **Ireland 0**
Abbes; Kaebel, | Gregg; Keith,
Lerond; Penverne, | McMichael;
Jonquet, Marcel; | Blanchflower,
Wisnieski, Fontaine, | Cunningham, Cush;
Kopa, Piantoni, | Bingham, Casey, Scott,
Vincent. | McIlroy, McParland.

SCORERS
Wisnieski, Fontaine (2), Piantoni for France
HT 1/0

*Malmö*

**West Germany 1** | **Yugoslavia 0**
Herkenrath; | Krivocuka; Sijakovic,
Stollenwerk, | Crnkovic; Krstic,
Juskowiak; Eckel, | Zebec, Boskov;
Erhardt, Szymaniak; | Petakovic, Veselinovic,
Rahn, Walter, Seeler, | Milutinovic,
Schmidt, Schaefer. | Ognjanovic, Rajkov.

SCORER
Rahn for West Germany
HT 1/0

*Stockholm*

**Sweden 2** | **Russia 0**
Svensson; Bergmark, | Yachine; Kessarev,
Axbom; Boerjesson, | Kuznetsov; Voinov,
Gustavsson, Parling; | Krijevski, Tsarev;
Hamrin, Gren, | Ivanov, A., Ivanov, V.,
Simonsson, Liedholm, | Simonian, Salnikov,
Skoglund. | Ilyin.

SCORERS
Hamrin, Simonsson for Sweden
HT 0/0

| **Brazil 1** | **Wales 0** |
|---|---|
| Gilmar; De Sordi, | Kelsey; Williams, |
| Santos, N.; Zito, | Hopkins; Sullivan, |
| Bellini, Orlando; | Charles, M., Bowen; |
| Garrincha, Didì, | Medwin, Hewitt, |
| Mazzola, Pelé, | Webster, Allchurch, |
| Zagalo. | Jones. |

SCORER
Pelé for Brazil
HT 0/0

## Semi-finals

*Stockholm*

| **Brazil 5** | **France 2** |
|---|---|
| Gilmar; De Sordi, | Abbes; Kaelbel, |
| Santos, N.; Zito, | Lerond; Penverne, |
| Bellini, Orlando; | Jonquet, Marcel; |
| Garrincha, Didì, | Wisnieski, Fontaine, |
| Vavà, Pelé, Zagalo. | Kopa, Piantoni, |
| | Vincent. |

SCORERS
Vavà, Didì, Pelé (3) for
Brazil
Fontaine, Piantoni for France
HT 2/1

*Gothenburg*

| **Sweden 3** | **West Germany 1** |
|---|---|
| Svensson; Bergmark, | Herkenrath; |
| Axbom; Boerjesson, | Stollenwerk, Juskowiak; |
| Gustavsson, Parling; | Eckel, Erhardt, |
| Hamrin, Gren, | Szymaniak; Rahn, |
| Simonsson, Liedholm, | Walter, Seeler, |
| Skoglund. | Schaefer, Cieslarczyk. |

SCORERS
Skoglund, Gren, Hamrin for Sweden
Schaefer for Germany
HT 1/1

## Third place match

| **France 6** | **West Germany 3** |
|---|---|
| Abbes; Kaelbel, | Kwiatowski; |
| Lerond; Penverne, | Stollenwerk, Erhardt; |
| Lafont, Marcel; | Schnellinger, Wewers, |
| Wisnieski, Douis, | Szymaniak; Rahn, |
| Kopa, Fontaine, | Sturm, Kelbassa, |
| Vincent. | Schaefer, Cieslarczyk. |

SCORERS
Fontaine (4), Kopa (penalty), Douis for France
Cieslarczyk, Rahn, Schaefer for Germany
HT 3/1

*Stockholm*

| **Brazil 5** | **Sweden 2** |
|---|---|
| Gilmar; Santos, D., | Svensson; Bergmark, |
| Santos, N.; Zito, | Axbom; Boerjesson, |
| Bellini, Orlando; | Gustavsson, Parling; |
| Garrincha, Didì, | Hamrin, Gren, |
| Vavà, Pelé, Zagalo. | Simonsson, Liedholm, |
| | Skoglund. |

SCORERS
Vavà (2), Pelé (2), Zagalo for Brazil
Liedholm, Simonsson for Sweden
HT 2/1

# Chile
## 1962

## Background to Chile

Brazil retained the 1962 World Cup, held in Chile, showing in the process that they were very much more than a one-man—or one-demigod—team; or rather that if one hero succumbed, another sprang up to take his place. It was the World Cup of Garrincha, the World Cup of 4-3-3. That long, thin, impoverished Chile should put it on at all was remarkable. Earthquakes had devastated the country at the time they were pleading their case, and Carlos Dittborn, the President of the Chilean Football Federation, coined the magnificent *non sequitur*, 'We must have the World Cup *because* we have nothing.'

They got it, quickly building one superb new stadium in Santiago in the snowy lee of a still more superb mountain and another, small but exquisite, on the coast at Viña del Mar, where pelicans sat on the rocks and the sea wrack blew in over the pitch. A third group would play in seedy, broken-down Rancagua in the stadium of the Braden Copper Company, and a fourth thousands of miles to the north, at Arica, near the Peruvian border.

Criticisms of the country, of the organisation, were often unfair. If there was corruption over tickets, at least an official was hauled off to gaol. When there were similar stories, four years later, in England, the dirt was swept quickly under the carpet. If there were tales of over-charging for accommodation, then the police quickly made indict-ments. The two Italian journalists who indicted Chile as a backward country, and thereby exposed their own team to the calvary of the Battle of Santiago, were not even justified in their criticism. It was a country at once squalid and sophisticated, backward yet subtle, but for the visitor, Chile left more congenial memories than either Sweden or Mexico.

Brazil, playing on South American soil, were inevitably the favour-ites, though illness had obliged Vicente Feola, that rumbling, Buddha-figure, to stand down as manager in favour of Aymore Moreira, brother of 1954's Zeze. Aymore was a white-haired, patient, courteous man who, with Hilton Goslin beside him, had again ensured a climate in which the Brazilians could express their overflowing gifts in peace and with effect. They would play in the Viña del Mar group with the Czechs, Spaniards and Mexicans.

## The Contenders
### The Viña group: Brazil, Czechoslovakia, Spain and Mexico

In the four years since they had won the World Cup, the component pieces of the Brazilian team had sprung apart, then strangely and steadily come together again. Two players had gone to Madrid, with sharply varying fortunes; and had come back. Vavà, the centre-forward who scored twice in the Final was transferred to Atletico Madrid, did well for a few seasons, then returned to play in Brazil; in time to displace Pelé's precocious teenaged colleague at Santos, Coutinho, with whom he had worked many a spectacular one-two.

Didì, the great orchestrator in Sweden, and already a star in Switzerland, had joined Real Madrid, but had come home, in time to win back his place from the confident young Cinesinho.

Zito, his midfield colleague, challenged by Zequinha, had edged in front of him at the eleventh hour, while an injury precluded any chance of Pepe supplanting Zagalo on the left wing; history repeating itself. Garrincha, that extraordinary child of nature from Pau Grande, was there again.

There were changes, however, in the central defence. Mauro, a reserve in 1958, took over at centre-half and captain from Bellini. The little black Zozimo, who had toured Europe with Brazil in 1957, succeeded Orlando, who had been playing in Argentina.

The Santoses, though veterans now—Nilton was thirty-six—were irreplaceable at back; the grey-jerseyed Gilmar was as calmly efficient as ever in goal. And of course there was Pelé, as wonderfully gymnastic, as astonishingly inventive, as brave, strong, inimitable and explosive as ever. At twenty-one there was little doubt that he was now the best footballer in the world.

At Viña—or rather, just outside it at Quilpue, where Pelé rejoiced to play daringly in goal—Aymore Moreira confessed his fears of Czechoslovakia. 'The Czechs play a very athletic game, hard and vigorous, which will certainly give us trouble. And then I know that they are also good technicians!' They were known to be a gifted team though a slow one but, as one acute French journalist wrote, their very slowness, their very pessimism, were turned to advantage.

Slowness—when players were at the same time such fine ball-players —meant precision; a packed defence, a sparsely-manned attack, with large areas of space to play in. Pessimism meant lack of pressure, plus a desire to show everybody they had been undervalued. Teamwork was guaranteed by the fact that most of the side played for the Dukla Prague (Army) club; and there was an outstanding left-half in Josef Masopust, a calm, deft player who used the ball cunningly and could score goals, too. In the centre of the defence, Pluskal and the massive, bald Popluhar, both World Cup centre-halves in their time, were no mean barrier, while behind them played the bald, elastic goal-keeper Wilhelm Schroiff, whose contribution would, until the Final, be so great.

Spain were managed by Helenio Herrera, the Internazionale

manager, who had previously flanked Giannino Ferrari as coach to the Italian side. Controversy over the drugging of Inter players, and Herrera's public delight when Juventus were knocked out of the European Cup, had led to his resignation. Spain—where he had worked for many successful years—now appointed him.

It was a surprising development, which led predictably to a conflict of egos between Herrera and Alfredo di Stefano. Pulling a muscle just before leaving Spain, di Stefano announced he would be coming merely 'as a tourist'. His cheerful father arrived from Buenos Aires with a 'magic' liniment which he urged him to use, but the prevailing view was that no liniment would heal the breach between di Stefano and Herrera.

Still, there was Luis Suarez, a fine, creative inside-forward, once with Herrera at Barcelona and now with him again at Inter. There was the leggy Peirò of Atletico Madrid. There was Martinez from Paraguay, and Puskas from Hungary. The talent was there, if not the team.

The remaining country was Mexico, two of whose players had tried on their arrival in Viña to attack an Australian journalist who had written that they would be there only to live the gay life.

In retrospect, there are good reasons for calling this Zagalo's World Cup as much as Garrincha's. 'One could never sufficiently stress the key role played by Zagalo in the Brazilian victory,' wrote the French journalist Jean-Philippe Réthacker. 'An active and courageous footballer, very perceptive in his passing and positional play, precise and varied in his technique, Zagalo was certainly, with the Czech Masopust, the most intelligent player of the 1962 World Cup.'

Seriousness was the keynote of his game and his personality. In hot, gay Rio, he was the player who spent his evenings quietly with his fiancée, his Sunday mornings in church. Strength of lung and strength of will would transform him into an international star, capable now of labouring in midfield, now of bursting forward to deliver a short, deadly accurate cross, who had never been more important to Brazil than at this moment.

## The Rancagua group:
## England, Hungary, Bulgaria and Argentina

England had Walter Winterbottom in charge, for what would be his fourth and last World Cup. He had just been out-voted for the Football Association's Secretaryship, in which he was expected to succeed his mentor, Sir Stanley Rous, now President of FIFA. He was assisted as coach by the English Footballer of the Year, Burnley's Jimmy Adamson, a tall, lean, humorous Geordie, captain and future manager of his club, who would subsequently turn down Walter Winterbottom's job.

Yet although they had scouted the ground this time, had got the retreat that everybody wanted, there was still something vaguely amateurish and haphazard about the English preparation. What other team, for instance, would include in its practice matches a middle-aged Australian millionaire businessman?

The 1958 side had largely evaporated, with one major exception; the attack was still built round Fulham's inside-left Johnny Haynes, who was now the captain. 'Why is everything with England number 10?' a Yugoslav coach would demand rhetorically, as his team's aeroplane finally flew out of Santiago. 'Number 10 takes the corners! Number 10 takes the throw-ins! So what do we do? We put a man on number 10! Goodbye, England!'

It was exactly what the Hungarians would do in the first match at Rancagua, when Rakosi dogged Haynes' every move. And indeed, the nemesis of making one man so important was precisely that if he failed, so did the team. Haynes had failed in Gothenburg; he would fail, alas, again in Chile. But since he was captain, the failure would if anything be more costly. A most gifted player with a superb left foot, brisk control and high strategic flair, Chile saw him at his least amenable. There was a thin-skinned petulance about him which seemed to permeate the team, and led to strained relations with the Press. On the other hand, it was not Haynes' fault that the over-hierarchical atmosphere of the England team was so marked that players still tended to give less for England than they gave for their clubs; and they still travelled without a doctor, an omission which might have had fatal results for Peter Swan, the reserve centre-half, in Viña del Mar.

Bryan Douglas, the skilful little Blackburn outside-right, who had scored an important goal in the vital qualifying match against Portugal, also survived from Sweden. As for Bobby Charlton, the blameless cause of such controversy in 1958, he had developed in these years from a goal-scoring inside-forward into an outside-left of classical gifts, marvellous acceleration, a willowy swerve, a prodigious shot not only in his left foot but now in his right.

Then there was Jimmy Greaves, quintessentially Cockney, a 'boy-wonder' still more remarkable than Charlton; an East Ender who at the age of seventeen had walked straight into the Chelsea First Division team on the opening day of the season at Tottenham to embark on a dazzling series of goals. His turn of speed was extraordinary, his confidence more remarkable still, his left foot a hammer, his instinct for being in the right place near goal almost psychic. The previous year he had gone briefly and reluctantly to A.C. Milan, hated the atmosphere and the disciplines, and obliged them to transfer him home; but to Tottenham, not to Chelsea. He was one of the most exciting talents England had thrown up since the war; yet now, when the chips were truly down, he would be as disappointing as Haynes.

Another East Londoner had just won a place in the team—Bobby Moore, capped for the first time in Peru *en route* to Chile. England had played extremely well, winning 4–0 on a ground where, three years earlier, they had lost 4–1, and the twenty-one-year-old Moore, tall, blond, quite imperturbable, had had a fine game at right-half. This imperturbability was evident even when he was a West Ham United youth player, running up a record number of youth caps for England. Haste seemed anathema to him; even in the tightest goal-line situations he would remain calm and relaxed.

Encouraged by Ron Greenwood, West Ham's manager, a disciple of Winterbottom, he had worked hard at his football, developing from a centre-half of great poise but unexceptional talents into a defensive wing-half who read the game superbly, covering and tackling fault-lessly, using the long ball well. If he had weaknesses, they lay in strange, transient lapses in concentration and a vulnerability to small, quick-turning forwards who would play close up on him.

He well deserved his place, and would have an excellent World Cup, but the choice of the equally bold, equally large, straightforward Ron Flowers as the other wing-half meant that England lacked the ball-playing half-back they needed in a 4-2-4 formation. Bobby Robson, who had developed since 1958 into a thoughtful half-back, had dropped out in Lima through injury, and would otherwise have been a more sensible choice in the circumstances.

In goal was yet another Londoner, the cheerful, robust, fearless Ron Springett of Sheffield Wednesday. He was Fulham-born, resilient on the line, but vulnerable to shots from afar, as his colleagues knew. There was a worrying doubt about his vision.

At full-back there was a resilient pair in the calm, pipe-smoking Jim Armfield and the tough ebullient Ray Wilson, while at last there was a choice between two tall and powerful centre-halves, Tottenham's Maurice Norman and Sheffield Wednesday's Peter Swan. For centre-forward there was the brave, blond Shropshire miner, Gerry Hitchens, who unlike Greaves had stayed happily that season in Milan, scoring freely for Inter. He arrived in Chile, to the admiration of his colleagues, dressed to kill.

Hungary, Bulgaria and Argentina were the other teams in the Rancagua group, where England were favoured. Their own critics, however, feared they might again distil the familiar, bitter-sweet essence of mediocrity for which they were known in World Cups; and the opening game would bear out this pessimism.

Hungary, though they had just lost to Italy B, were in better plight than in 1958. They had beaten England two years before in Budapest, thanks to the prowess of Florian Albert, a fluent young centre-forward whose skills evoked the earlier Hidegkuti, and who combined beautifully with the lean Gorocs while Tichy was still there to fire his right-footed shells. Gyula Grosics alone survived from the great team of the 1950s. There was a tall, supple, blond, linking right-half in Erno Solymosi, a formidable double pillar in defence in Sipos and Meszoly, and an insidious right-winger in dark little Karoliy Sandor who played, like Kurt Hamrin, with his socks around his ankles.

The Argentinians had a new young manager in Juan Carlos Lorenzo, but were still playing with the traditional roving centre-half; this time the fair-haired Sacchi. He, with the strong, blond, attacking left-back, Silvio Marzolini, would give the team much of its propulsion. José Sanfilippo, their free-scoring inside-left, had tried to drop out after a period of poor form. Lorenzo had him medically and psychiatrically examined, got highly positive reports—and picked him.

The Bulgarians, built around the CDNA (Sofia) Army team, had beaten France in a play-off, yet seemed to have little to offer apart from the clever left wing of the experienced Ivan Kolev and the young Yakimov. Kolev, with his speed and ball skills, had now moved to the flank.


### The Santiago group:
### Italy, Chile, West Germany and Switzerland

Italy, playing in Santiago, had arrived in their customary state of chaos, warned by Herrera that it was always a bad thing to fall into the group which included the host country. At once flamboyant and dictatorial, hooded and extrovert, a coiner of slogans and of money, a ruthless manipulator and a superb preparer of players, Herrera had become the best paid, most controversial manager in the world, though the World Cup would elude him.

By now, *catenaccio* had Italian football in its clammy grip, and bright young players who began with all the traditional joy in ball play and invention soon had it bred out of them when they reached the stony reality of Serie A, the First Division.

To qualify, Italy had to negotiate the low hurdle of Israel; yet at one point in the game in Tel Aviv they found themselves two down. They recovered to win 4–2, thanks partly to the accomplished left-footed finishing of the Veronese, Mario Corso of Inter. By the time the World Cup was due, however, Corso was dropped from the chosen twenty-two. It chanced that shortly before the party flew off he played a leading part in Inter's victory at San Siro over the Czech World Cup team.

Chilean hostility to the Italians had been aroused by the old policy of *oriundi*. José Altafini, lately Italy's chief goal-scorer, had in 1958's World Cup played centre-forward for Brazil. Humberto Maschio and the immensely talented little inside-left, Omar Sivori of the rolled-down socks, limpid control and deadly left foot, would have played for Argentina in the 1958 World Cup had Italian clubs not swooped on them in 1957. No policy could be more perfectly calculated to offend the South Americans in general, and the Argentinians, playing only ninety kilometres away in Rancagua, in particular.

As though this, and the presence of Italian club scouts hanging round the South American training camps, were not enough, two Italian journalists sent home disparaging articles about Chile which raised local hostility to a crescendo. One had, at all events, to sympathise with the poor Italian (or putatively Italian) footballers, who would be obliged so painfully to bear the brunt of what had been written.

If there were *oriundi* in the team, there was also an authentic Italian star in Gianni Rivera, one of the most precocious and gifted footballers produced since Meazza. He was still only eighteen, yet already he had been capped against Belgium in their last international, won in Brussels. Already he had had two seasons as strategist of the Milan attack. He was a dark, grave, faunlike figure who, playing in the Olympic football team at the age of sixteen, had already been talking like a man of thirty. His technique was flawless; despite a fragile physique, he struck a ball beautifully, and his passing was wonderfully imaginative.

West Germany were also in this group, bringing with them such doughty warriors as Uwe Seeler, Horst Szymaniak, Hans Schaefer and Karl-Heinz Schnellinger. They had qualified without hardship against Greece and Northern Ireland and, under the cunning leadership of Sepp Herberger in his last World Cup, had the tactical expertise, the physical hardness, to worry anyone.

Switzerland, the fourth team in the group, had accounted for Sweden in a play-off in Berlin, but were little fancied.

Of the Chileans themselves not a great deal was known, though they had lately thrashed and drawn with Hungary, and lost narrowly to Russia in Santiago. They were under the sophisticated managership of Fernando Riera, a debonair, good-looking man who had played football in France, they used a 4-2-4 formation, and were bound to be galvanised by an impassioned crowd.

### The Arica group: Uruguay, Russia, Yugoslavia, Colombia

Finally, in Group I, up in remote Arica, there were three giants and a probable pygmy. The giants were Uruguay, twice Cup winners;

Russia, who had beaten them during their splendid November tour of South America; and Yugoslavia. The pygmy was Colombia, who had come down from high altitudes after unexpectedly putting out Peru. There were Yachine, Sekularac, Gonçalves.

## The Opening Games

In their opening game, Chile showed they would need to be reckoned with by beating Switzerland 3–1 in Santiago before a delighted 65,000 crowd. The *mis-en-scène* was glorious—bright sun, a soaring, snowy mountain. The President of Chile spoke, Sir Stanley Rous spoke and the President of the Chilean Federation spoke. After this came what seemed a brisk anticlimax when, in only seven minutes, a banal error by the Chilean defence allowed Wuthrich to score from over twenty-five yards. The Swiss *verrou* was working wonderfully.

Chile, with the tall, strong left-half Eladio Rojas and the energetic inside-right Toro giving them power in midfield, took half an hour to get into their stride. Their equaliser came at the most delicately telling moment—a minute before half-time, Leonel Sanchez, the rapid outside-left and son of a professional boxer—there would be reason to remember this—converting Landa's centre.

In the first ten minutes of the second half, Chile grasped their psychological advantage, overrunning the Swiss defence. Ramirez gave them the lead. Leonel Sanchez, tackling Grobety, beating man after man, then shooting home from the twenty-five yards, got the third.

In the same group the following day, Italy and West Germany walked round and round one another like two cautious boxers, under a suitably leaden sky. There were no goals. Italy played, as expected, with the tough Torino half-back Ferrini as 'false' outside-right; a decision which, in those still relatively innocent days, had roused much displeasure in their Press. Salvadore was sweeper; the inside forwards were Rivera, Altafini and Sivori. Germany, too, played *catenaccio*, with Schnellinger as sweeper. The two stoppers, Erhardt, a forbidding force in Sweden, and Willy Schulz, tackled implacably, and Seeler once struck the bar, but there was little variation of pace. Italy, matching greater power with greater skill, held their own, till the game degenerated into a kind of tank battle; a few of their movements were beautifully conceived and carried out. Their morale seemed to equal their skill, their possibilities seemed great; but for the Chilean match, they would make six silly changes, and their hopes would go out of the window.

In Rancagua, Argentina began by beating Bulgaria 1–0 through Facundo's early goal in a harsh, dull game, while Hungary beat England 2–1 the day after. The Argentinians, far from backward in

physical contact, themselves cut an impressive figure when similarly
treated. The gesture of hurt incomprehension, the slow, concertina-
crumpling to the ground, the final, corpse-like prostration, would have
touched a heart of stone.

England's prosaic attack found Hungary's packed defence an
insoluble puzzle. No English player could match the splendidly supple
Albert and Solymosi, and it was a glorious individual goal by Albert
which won the game, eighteen minutes from time. One of Tichy's
long-range cannon balls had given Hungary the lead on the quarter-
hour, and shown up Springett's costly weakness; Ron Flowers had
equalised on the hour from a penalty given away by Meszoly's handling. So England went dispiritedly up the hill to Coya. 'You *want* us to
lose,' Haynes reproached a journalist.

In Viña's little jewel of a seaside stadium, Brazil were given a
surprisingly hard time by a brave Mexican team which lost four or
five good chances to score. Brazil, aware that several of their team were
bearing the burden of the years, had already pulled Zagalo deeper, in
a 4-3-3 formation, and Zagalo it was, from the brilliant Pelé's cross,
who headed the first goal.

Pelé, in splendid form, scored the other goal against Mexico—both
came in the second half—after beating four defenders and then
Carbajal, with a prodigious shot.

The Czechs then beat Spain 1–0 with a goal scored by their right-
winger Stibranyi ten minutes from time; a brisk piece of opportunism
when the injured Reija failed either to control a ball or to reach
Santamaria (Uruguay's 1954 stopper) with his pass. That the Czechs
were by then in a position to win was thanks to the way their defence,
especially the impressive Schroiff, had withstood Spain's early pressure.
Finally the ponderous Martinez had vented his frustration by kicking
Schroiff in the stomach; which simply moved the stronger Czechs to
punish their opponents with a series of mighty tackles. Schroiff continued, undaunted, to perform small miracles, and at last Spain
exposed themselves to the counter-thrust which brought Stibranyi's
goal. Czechoslovakia, with Masopust and the tall, lean, jog-trotting
Kvasniak so skilful in midfield, had announced their candidature.

In far-off Arica, strange things were happening. Little Colombia,
opening the ball, took the lead against Uruguay from a penalty and
succumbed, 2–1, only a quarter of an hour from the finish. It took a
characteristically clever run by little, dark Cubilla, the Uruguayan
outside-right, and a thumping shot by Sasia to beat Sanchez, Colombia's fine goalkeeper, after half-time.

The next day a Russian team, including such heroes of 1958 as
Yachine, Voronin, Ivanov, Netto and two lively wingers from Torpedo
in Metreveli and Meshki, beat Yugoslavia 2–0 in a grim game. The

Yugoslavs committed themselves furiously to the conflict, Mujic going so far as to break Dubinski's leg and to be sent home by his team in consequence. For all this, it was a fine, technically pleasing match; the only one in which the celebrated Yachine would justify his immense reputation.

Ponedelnik, Russia's muscular new centre-forward, was involved in both goals. After fifty-three minutes he struck a thundering free kick against the bar, and Ivanov beat Soskic, Yugoslavia's fine goalkeeper, to the rebound. Four minutes from the end Ponedelnik himself scored the second. He would later complain that his team's atmosphere was too cold, too impersonal; that at one crucial stage he and his room-mate had lain awake, side by side in their beds, far into the night, unable to speak a word to one another.

In the second round of matches Germany, in Santiago, beat Switzerland 2–1 in a tedious game which was spoiled when Szymaniak's brutal tackle broke a leg of the Swiss forward, Norbert Eschmann, after fourteen minutes. In the circumstances, the Swiss did well to hold the score to 2–1 and to have the last word, the last goal, themselves, when Schneiter scored fifteen minutes from the end.

The game was played in the deep shadow of what had gone on the day before in Chile's ghastly game against Italy; a game which produced two expulsions, a broken nose and a welter of violence. The ground, as we have seen, had been abundantly prepared by those two inflammatory articles, while the question of the *oriundi*, the recent accusations of drug-taking among Italian clubs, had made things worse.

For the Italian players, as their own correspondents wrote, were far too easily provoked by the Chileans, who were from the first busily spitting in their faces. The referee himself, tall Ken Aston, was accused by the Italians of being 'hostile and provocative'. He in turn, limping through the rest of the World Cup, *hors de combat* with a damaged Achilles tendon, insisted that the match was 'uncontrollable'. What is beyond dispute is that from this day Aston's career in refereeing went from strength to strength; to membership of FIFA's Referees' Committee, to the surveillance of World Cup referees in 1966 and 1970.

Certainly he was ill-served by his linesmen who, when Leonel Sanchez, behind his back, broke Maschio's nose with a left hook that was televised around the world, elected to behave like the three wise monkeys. Thus Sanchez stayed on the field while Ferrini, for hacking down Landa in the seventh minute, and David, for a retaliatory kick at Sanchez's head, went off. Reduced to nine men, Italy still resisted till fifteen minutes from time, when Ramirez headed in Leonel Sanchez's free kick, Toro adding the second, in the last minute. It had been altogether a dreadful day for football.

The group concluded with a 2–0 win by a much more sophisticated, economical German team over Chile, and an easy but meaningless 3–0 victory by Italy against Switzerland. So Chile and Germany passed into the quarter finals.

In Rancagua, England found form at last, beating Argentina by a clear 3–1; their first World Cup victory since 1954 outside the qualifying competition.

Much was achieved with the replacement of the disappointing Hitchens at centre-forward by Middlesbrough's Alan Peacock, a tall, straight-backed, guardsman-like figure even to the short haircut, who won many balls in the air despite ill usage from Navarro. Though it was his first international, he showed great aplomb, provoking the first goal after seventeen minutes. When Charlton, in ebullient form, centred from the left, Peacock skilfully headed the ball on, Navarro desperately handled, and Flowers scored his second penalty of the series.

Argentina were clever but unincisive, but served by Sacchi and the adventurous Marzolini; but Moore and Flowers tackled briskly, Jimmy Armfield was impeccable, Bryan Douglas far more lively than he had been against Hungary. Charlton, with a crisp, low, right-footed shot, made it 2–0 before half-time.

Then Hungary, in remarkable form, whipped Bulgaria 6–1, with a goal by Albert in the first minute and four goals by the twelfth. Albert and the greyhound Gorocs worked their fluent one-twos, their clever changes of pace, as easily as they had done in the 1960 Olympiad. Deprived of Iliev and Diev, Bulgaria could do little but let the wave wash over them. Hungary's was an iridescent performance, Solymosi, Albert and Gorocs bestriding the field as in the good old days of Bozsik, Hidegkuti and Puskas. Albert scored three; the result was 6–1.

In the final game, Lajos Baroti, the shrewd Hungarian coach, told his team not to exert themselves; a point was sufficient, and it was what they got, drawing 0–0 with Argentina. Albert and Sandor were rested. Gorocs, alas, tore a muscle in the eighteenth minute, while Meszoly, the blond stopper, played so majestically that the watching England players clapped him off the field.

England themselves, next day, gave a wretchedly mediocre performance against Bulgaria, drawing 0–0 in their turn, and lucky indeed to survive when Kolev beat Armfield on the line, to expose their goal with a cross nobody converted. England, second in the group, now had the daunting task of playing Brazil in Viña del Mar; while Hungary were much favoured to beat the Czechs in Rancagua.

Brazil had cataclysmically lost Pelé, victim of a torn thigh muscle, in their 0–0 draw with Czechoslovakia. After twenty-five minutes, taking a pass by Garrincha, he shot powerfully from twenty-five yards against the foot of the post; then hobbled off the field and out of the 1962 World Cup.

Brazil, with Pelé useless on the wing, drew all but Vavà and Garrincha back in defence; the Czechs gladly settled for a stalemate. No longer threatened by Brazil's explosive change of pace, they went their precise, skilful, somewhat monotonous way to a draw.

Brazil now pulled out of the hat the twenty-four-year-old Amarildo, Botafogo's inside-left; no Pelé, certainly, but a lithe, quick enterprising player with a nose for a goal, a cheerful and emotional child of nature, brown-skinned, curly-haired, effervescent. Succeeding Pelé was clearly less of a burden than an adventure.

The final qualifying match, against Spain, proved a tough one. A goal by Peirò in the last minute had given Spain meagre victory against surprising Mexico, so well coached by the Argentinian, Scopelli. Carbajal, in his fourth World Cup, had kept an impeccable goal, and now Spain needed at least a draw, probably a win, to qualify. Herrera gambled by dropping his two famous forwards, del Sol and Suarez, his goalkeeper Carmelo, and his centre-half Santamaria. Now Puskas would lead an attack which had three Atletico Madrid players, and the flying Paco Gento at outside-left. This was the game, one had heard, in which Didì planned his revenge on di Stefano for the humiliations of Madrid; but di Stefano was still not playing. Greatest all-round forward of his generation, inexhaustibly versatile, he never took part in the finals of a World Cup.

The 'new' Spain played with immense commitment and no little flair. Indeed, the match was possibly the best of the whole tournament, and it took the sudden, soaring flight of Garrincha to save and win it for Brazil.

Herrera, high priest of *catenaccio* with Inter, now used it with Spain, Rodri playing sweeper, the other defenders marking man to man. For an hour these tactics, given force and bite by the team's intense commitment, had Brazil at full stretch, and in the thirty-fourth minute a short, swift dribble by Puskas, a clever pass, made a goal for the energetic Adelardo.

For thirty-eight minutes, Spain deservedly kept their lead, their drive and *brio* several times taking them close to another goal; once especially, through Peirò. Then Amarildo, rising splendidly to the occasion and the opportunity, converted Zagalo's centre to equalise. Again Spain almost scored, this time through Verges, but with four minutes left Garrincha got electrically away, crossed, and Amarildo darted in to head the winner. It was a very near thing; and a manifest injustice to Spain.

The last game of the group produced the strangest result, Mexico defeating Czechoslovakia 3–1 and giving one of the best performances in their long but mediocre history in the World Cup. It meant that in the quarter-finals Czechoslovakia would play Hungary at Rancagua, while England came to Viña to meet Brazil.

Back in Arica, and Group I, Russia, who had walloped the Uruguayans 5–0 in Moscow the previous month, now found that Uruguay in and Uruguay out of World Cups were two different teams; their 2–1 win was achieved only after eighty-nine minutes, and was extremely lucky. Reduced to ten men for an hour by an injury to Eliseo Alvarez, Uruguay pulled back their fine winger, Domingo Perez, and had the best of the argument, equalising Mamikin's goal through Sasia after fifty-four minutes, and hitting the post three times. Their 4-2-4, with Nestor Gonçalves deploying his unhurried skills in midfield, would surely have prevailed at full strength.

Not that Russia had covered themselves with glory in their second game. Colombia, astonishingly, had held them to a 4–4 draw which *L'Équipe*'s annual described as 'one of the greatest surprises of modern football'. Russia, after all, were 3–0 up after eleven minutes, and if Acero reduced it to 3–1, that was still the score at half time, while Ponedelnik brought it to 4–1, early in the second half.

It was then, after sixty-eight minutes, that something very strange happened. Lev Yachine, of all people, gave a goal away straight from a corner. Suddenly the options were open. The little black inside-forward, Klinger, began tearing holes in the strapping Russian defence, the whole team ran like furies, Rada scored a third goal, Klinger equalised. Though Yachine did make a couple of fine saves, *L'Équipe*'s annual solemnly, and prematurely, recorded that the match 'certainly marked an historic date, the end of the greatest modern goalkeeper, if not of all time: Lev Yachine.'

Yugoslavia, meanwhile, were winning their key match against Uruguay 3–1, with Sekularac in such transcendent form, working such wonders of control and construction that the very Uruguayans bore him off on their shoulders at the end! His henchmen were the powerfully made, thrusting double spearhead, Galic and Jerkovic, scorers of the second and third goals. The first came through Josip Skoblar, a young left-winger later to make a great name in Marseilles, from the penalty spot, equalising Cabrera's goal.

Beating a now exhausted Colombia 5–0 in their third match, Jerkovic scoring three, Yugoslavia finished second in the group. Their quarter-final opponents, for the third consecutive World Cup, would be . . . West Germany.

**The Quarter-Finals**　　Brazil v. England

At Viña, Brazil—and Garrincha—accounted for England. Perhaps because he was no longer rivalled and obscured by Pelé, Garrincha continued in a vein of luminous virtuosity which would persist into the semi-final. Wilson did what he could with him; but it was inevitably little. To the panther swerve and acceleration, the deadly goal-line cross, which one had seen in Sweden, Garrincha had now added a thumping shot in either foot and remarkable power in the air. The first Brazilian goal, after thirty-one minutes, came when he, at five foot seven, utterly outjumped Maurice Norman at six foot two, to head in a corner kick. That it was no fluke, no mere aberration by Norman, was shown when he did just the same against Chile.

A much worse error by Ron Flowers would have put Brazil 2–0 up, were it not for a marvellous save by Springett. Flowers, retrieving a ball on the right, bemusedly turned and pushed it straight across his own goal area. Amarildo was in like a ferret; only for Springett, still quicker, to dive and block at his feet. It was a save too easily forgotten afterwards when attempts were made to turn Springett into a scapegoat.

Within five minutes of the second half, Garrincha decided the game. After fifty-four minutes, his fulminating, swerving free kick bounced off Springett's broad chest for Vavà to score as easily as Hitchens; then his diabolical swerving long shot utterly deceived the goalkeeper and curled in by the right-hand post. Brazil had won their place in the semi-finals.

Yugoslavia v. Germany

Yugoslavia flew down to Santiago to play Germany. Milovan Ciric, the Yugoslav manager, a large, bald, consistently amiable man, deplored his lack of wingers and smilingly promised that his team would know how to cope with Germany's physical challenge.

Third time proved lucky; for at last Germany were conquered, at last their sheer, forbidding muscularity did not subdue Yugoslavia's greater finesse. The Germans played *catenaccio* again, the Yugoslavs 4-2-4. It was a spirited and splendid game, perhaps decided by its tactics. For the Germans, playing so tightly and cautiously, gave Radakovic, the little Yugoslav right-half, a scope and space that finally proved fatal.

Germany favoured the long pass, Yugoslavia the short. In an absorbing half Germany initially forced the game, Seeler hitting a post, but then until the half-hour it was the Yugoslavs who dominated, making but not taking chances. The second half, though still exciting, was less distinguished, both teams appearing tired. Schnellinger, curiously anticipating Germany's 'total football' of a decade later, often left his post as sweeper to join in attacks, a dangerously effective stratagem which several times almost brought a goal. As for the Yugoslavs, they now had Radakovic, who had collided with Seeler, playing with a bandaged head, and somewhat diminished in consequence.

Extra time seemed certain, a German win the more likely, when at last, after eighty-six vibrant minutes, Galic pulled the ball back to Radakovic whose shot, from fifteen yards, flew under the bar to beat the able Fahrian.

## Chile v. Russia

In Arica, Chile astonished and uplifted their supporters by defeating Russia, with Yachine once more betraying strange deficiencies. He should have saved both Chilean goals, each a long shot. Leonel Sanchez got the first after ten minutes from a twenty-five-yard free kick, a searing cross shot from the left. Eladio Rojas, the attacking half-back, scored the winner eighteen minutes later; two minutes after Chislenko had equalised from fully thirty-five yards. For all its formidable power, how so long a shot beat a goalkeeper as great as Yachine remains a mystery.

The Chileans, for the occasion, pulled Toro deeper, turning their 4-2-4 into a virtual 4-3-3, though at times Toro broke sharply and effectively from the back. It was not one of Chile's best days; if anything, the frenzied support of the 17,000-strong crowd, the knowledge that the whole country hung breathlessly on the result, inhibited more than it inspired them. Nevertheless, they were through.

## Czechoslovakia v. Hungary

So, in the strangest fashion, were Czechoslovakia, outplayed at Rancagua by a Hungarian team which beat a tattoo on their goalposts, but could not beat the incredible Schroiff; as brilliant that day as Yachine was fallible. Scherer, in the thirteenth minute, surprised Grosics with a cross shot in one of Czechoslovakia's pitifully rare breakaways. It was enough, however, to put his team in the semi-final, for on the one occasion when Hungary, and Tichy, seemed to have scored, Russia's Latychev, the veteran referee, gave it obscurely offside.

## The Semi-Finals    Brazil v. Chile

The Brazilians were so much superior to the Chileans that it was hardly a match. Garrincha, fiery and uncontrollable, seemed determined to win the game on his own. After only nine minutes, he pivoted on the ball in an inside-left position to beat Escutti with a killing twenty-yard left-foot shot. After thirty-two, he performed another of his trampoline jumps to head in a corner by Zagalo.

Chile, to their credit, were not supine. Ten minutes later Toro, right-footed, smashed a mighty free kick past Gilmar from the edge of the area to bring them back into the game; only for Vavà, a mere two minutes into the second half, to restore the margin, heading in Garrincha's dropping corner.

Once more the Chileans got up off the ground, inspired by the gifted Toro, the determined Rojas, the quick, slight, mobile right-back Eyzaguirre, fighting back into the game with a penalty by Leonel Sanchez for hands by Zozimo. But just as the match seemed alive again the indefatigable Zagalo moved up the left wing, spun past his man with princely ease and delivered a short centre which Vavà headed in.

The closing minutes were displeasing. Garrincha, kicked by Rojas and tired of being kicked, kicked back and was sent off. As he made his way round the field towards the dressing-rooms, to a cacophony of whistling, a bottle struck him and cut open his head. Soon afterwards Landa, the Chilean centre-forward, followed him.

### Czechoslovakia v. Yugoslavia

In Viña del Mar, a mere, miserable 5,000 supporters stood under the pines, cypresses and willows to see Czechoslovakia beat the book again, this time defeating Yugoslavia. The Slavs, as Ciric had feared, were indeed weak on the wings, and could not breach the Czechs' packed defence in the centre. Tactically, Czechoslovakia were a credit to their manager, the silver-haired, silver-toothed, Austrian-born Vytlacil; surviving the first half, they got the goals they needed in the second.

Kadraba gave them a fortuituous lead three minutes after half-time, but when Jerkovic equalised in the sixty-ninth minute, a Yugoslav win again seemed probable. Instead, Schroiff defied them as superbly as he had defied the Hungarians, Scherer scored ten minutes from time in a breakaway, and a silly handling offence by Markovic allowed the same tall player to make it 3–1 from a penalty. The Final would reunite Brazil and Czechoslovakia.

### The Final    Brazil v. Czechoslovakia

Needless to say, Brazil were favourites to beat the Czechs; but for that matter so had Hungary and Yugoslavia been in the quarter- and semi-finals. The Yugoslavs, in the third-place match, went through the irrelevant motions in Santiago and lost to a much more committed

Chile with a last-minute goal by Eladio Rojas; the commanding Soskic would have saved it had the shot not been deflected. Sekularac, however, was splendid.

Perhaps Czechoslovakia *would* have brought off their greatest surprise of all had not the one crucial constant in their previous success been missing. Something snapped—Schroiff lost his form. Like a bomber pilot who has made one raid too many, an infantryman who cracks after too many campaigns, he would fall to pieces in the Final.

The game began with a shock; the shock of a Czech goal which, with no Pelé, with Schroiff in form, might have worked wonders. After sixteen minutes a superb combination between Scherer and Masopust split Brazil's defence asunder. Scherer, deep on the right, held the ball and judged his diagonal pass as exquisitely as clever Masopust judged his run. Through the gap he went, calm and implacable, to strike the ball past Gilmar with his left foot. For the second successive World Cup Final, Brazil had conceded the first goal.

For the second time, too, they fought back, though it would take them till after half-time to get ahead. The equaliser took no time at all; and it was Amarildo's. Beating the sturdy Pluskal, he advanced on Schroiff almost along the left goal line. What would he do? Shoot for the near post or the far; or not shoot at all, pull the ball back? It was a fearful dilemma, and Schroiff's answer was wrong. Guarding the near post, he gave Amarildo enough room for an extraordinary shot, the ball flying in at the far corner, striking the side netting.

In the second half the Czechs appeared to be holding their own, at their own *adagio* pace. Kadraba had a good shot, Jelinek another; Brazil seemed to have gone into their shell. Suddenly, after sixty-nine minutes, they struck, and again Amarildo was the decisive figure, a wonderfully effective replacement for Pelé. Boxed in on the left-hand goal line, he beat his man with a sudden galvanic turn from left to right, centred across the exposed goal with his right foot—and there was Zito, to head into the empty net.

It was over and done with, and Schroiff might have been spared the small calvary of the third goal thirteen minutes from the end. Djalma Santos, reaching casually, massively backwards to a ball bouncing on his touchline, booted it with his left foot high, high up into the sun. It fell upon the dazzled Schroiff like unmerited retribution. He held up his hands to it, dropped it, and the impassive Vavà kicked it in.

Comes the hour, comes the man. In losing Pelé, Brazil had found Amarildo, and their elderly, distinguished team had kept the Cup.

# RESULTS: Chile 1962

## Group I

Uruguay 2, Colombia 1 (HT 0/1)
Russia 2, Yugoslavia 0 (HT 0/0)
Yugoslavia 3, Uruguay 1 (HT 2/1)
Russia 4, Colombia 4 (HT 3/1)
Russia 2, Uruguay 1 (HT 1/0)
Yugoslavia 5, Colombia 0 (HT 2/0)

|  | P | W | D | L | GOALS F | A | Pts |
|---|---|---|---|---|---|---|---|
| Russia | 3 | 2 | 1 | 0 | 8 | 5 | 5 |
| Yugoslavia | 3 | 2 | 0 | 1 | 8 | 3 | 4 |
| Uruguay | 3 | 1 | 0 | 2 | 4 | 6 | 2 |
| Colombia | 3 | 0 | 1 | 2 | 5 | 11 | 1 |

## Group II

Chile 3, Switzerland 1 (HT 1/1)
Germany 0, Italy 0 (HT 0/0)
Chile 2, Italy 0 (HT 0/0)
Germany 2, Switzerland 1 (HT 1/0)
Germany 2, Chile 0 (HT 1/0)
Italy 3, Switzerland 0 (HT 1/0)

|  | P | W | D | L | GOALS F | A | Pts |
|---|---|---|---|---|---|---|---|
| Germany | 3 | 2 | 1 | 0 | 4 | 1 | 5 |
| Chile | 3 | 2 | 0 | 1 | 5 | 3 | 4 |
| Italy | 3 | 1 | 1 | 1 | 3 | 2 | 3 |
| Switzerland | 3 | 0 | 0 | 3 | 2 | 8 | 0 |

## Group III

Brazil 2, Mexico 0 (HT 0/0)
Czechoslovakia 1, Spain 0 (HT 0/0)
Brazil 0, Czechoslovakia 0 (HT 0/0)
Spain 1, Mexico 0 (HT 0/0)
Brazil 2, Spain 1 (HT 0/1)
Mexico 3, Czechoslovakia 1 (HT 2/1)

|  | P | W | D | L | GOALS F | A | Pts |
|---|---|---|---|---|---|---|---|
| Brazil | 3 | 2 | 1 | 0 | 4 | 1 | 5 |
| Czechoslovakia | 3 | 1 | 1 | 1 | 2 | 3 | 3 |
| Mexico | 3 | 1 | 0 | 2 | 3 | 4 | 2 |
| Spain | 3 | 1 | 0 | 2 | 2 | 3 | 2 |

## Group IV

Argentina 1, Bulgaria 0 (HT 1/0)
Hungary 2, England 1 (HT 1/0)
England 3, Argentina 1 (HT 2/0)
Hungary 6, Bulgaria 1 (HT 4/0)
Argentina 0, Hungary 0 (HT 0/0)
England 0, Bulgaria 0 (HT 0/0)

|  | P | W | D | L | GOALS F | A |
|---|---|---|---|---|---|---|
| Hungary | 3 | 2 | 1 | 0 | 8 | 2 |
| England | 3 | 1 | 1 | 1 | 4 | 3 |
| Argentina | 3 | 1 | 1 | 1 | 2 | 3 |
| Bulgaria | 3 | 0 | 1 | 2 | 1 | 7 |

## Quarter-finals

*Santiago*

| **Yugoslavia 1** | **West Germany 0** |
|---|---|
| Soskic; Durkovic, | Fahrian; Novak, |
| Jusufi; Radakovic, | Schnellinger; Schulz |
| Markovic, Popovic; | Erhardt, Giesemann |
| Kovacevic, Sekularac, | Haller, Szymaniak, |
| Jerkovic, Galic, | Seeler, Brulls, Schae |
| Skoblar. | |

SCORER
Radakovic for Yugoslavia
HT 0/0

*Viña del Mar*

| **Brazil 3** | **England 1** |
|---|---|
| Gilmar; Santos, D., | Springett; Armfield, |
| Mauro, Zozimo, | Wilson; Moore, |
| Santos, N.; Zito, Didì, | Norman, Flowers; |
| Garrincha, Vavà | Douglàs, Greaves, |
| Amarildo, Zagalo. | Hitchens, Haynes, |
| | Charlton. |

SCORERS
Garrincha (2), Vavà for Brazil
Hitchens for England
HT 1/1

*Arico*

| **Chile 2** | **Russia 1** |
|---|---|
| Escutti; Eyzaguirre, | Yachine; Tchokelli, |
| Contreras, Sanchez, R., | Ostrovski; Voronin, |
| Navarro; Toro, Rojas; | Maslenkin, Netto; |
| Ramirez, Landa, | Chislenko, Ivanov, |
| Tobar, Sanchez, L. | Ponedelnik, Mamiki |
| | Meshki. |

SCORERS
Sanchez, L., Rojas for Chile
Chislenko for Russia
HT 2/1

| **ezechoslovakia 1** | **Hungary 0** |
|---|---|
| hroiff; Lala, Novak; | Grosios; Matrai, Sarosi; |
| uskal, Popluhar, | Solymosi, Meszoly, |
| asopust; Pospichal, | Sipos; Sandor, Rakosi, |
| herer, Kvasniak, | Albert, Tichy, Fenyvesi. |
| adraba, Jelinek. | |

ORER
herer for Czechoslovakia
r 1/0

## emi-finals

*ntiago*

| **azil 4** | **Chile 2** |
|---|---|
| lmar; Santos, D., | Escutti; Eyzaguirre, |
| auro, Zozimo, | Contreras, Sanchez, R., |
| ntos, N.; Zito, Didì, | Rodriguez; Toro, |
| arrincha, Vavà, | Rojas; Ramirez, |
| narildo, Zagalo. | Landa, Tobar, |
| | Sanchez, L. |

ORERS
arrincha (2), Vavà (2) for Brazil
oro, Sanchez, L. (penalty) for Chile
r 2/1

*ña del Mar*

| **ezechoslovakia 3** | **Yugoslavia 1** |
|---|---|
| hroiff; Lala, Novak; | Soskic; Durkovic, |
| uskal, Popluhar, | Jusufi, Radakovic, |
| asopust; Pospichal, | Markovic, Popovic; |
| herer, Kvasniak, | Sujakovic, Sekularac, |
| adraba, Jelinek. | Jerkovic, Galic, Skoblar. |

ORERS
adraba, Scherer (2) for Czechoslovakia
rkovic for Yugoslavia
r 0/0

## hird place match

*ntiago*

| **hile 1** | **Yugoslavia 0** |
|---|---|
| odoy; Eyzaguirre, | Soskic; Durkovic, |
| ruz, Sanchez, R., | Svinjarcvic; Radakovic, |
| odriguez; Toro, | Markovic, Popovic; |
| ojas; Ramirez, | Kovacevic, Sekularac, |
| ampos, Tobar, | Jerkovic, Galic, Skoblar. |
| anchez, L. | |

ORER
ojas for Chile
r 0/0

## Final

*Santiago*

| **Brazil 3** | **Czechoslovakia 1** |
|---|---|
| Gilmar; Santos, D., | Schroiff; Tichy, Novak; |
| Mauro, Zozimo, | Pluskal, Popluhar, |
| Santos, N.; Zito, Didì, | Masopust; Pospichal, |
| Garrincha, Vavà, | Scherer, Kvasniak, |
| Amarildo, Zagalo. | Kadraba, Jelinek. |

SCORERS
Amarildo, Zito, Vavà for Brazil
Masopust for Czechoslovakia
HT 1/1

# England
## 1966

## Background to 1966

The 1966 World Cup was the first for thirty-two years to be won by the home side. To this extent England's achievement was an unusual one, and indeed their form in the exciting, pleasing semi-final and Final made up for much of the tedium which had gone before.

It was a passionate and controversial World Cup; controversy persisting long after the dramatic Final was lost and won, thanks to the shot by Geoff Hurst of England which struck the underside of the bar and came down—or did not come down—behind the line. It was a World Cup distinguished by the enigmatic presence, and final triumph, of Alf Ramsey, the collapse of the Brazilians, the astonishing prowess of the North Koreans, the turbulence of the Argentinians, the absolute superiority of the Europeans over the South Americans—who cried conspiracy and threatened mass withdrawal, in consequence. It was a World Cup in which, for the second consecutive occasion, the fabled Pelé was laid low by injury, though this time in displeasing circumstances; in which Hurst scored the first hat-trick in a World Cup Final, and extra time was needed for the first time since 1934.

Whatever else may be said about the tournament's quality, the merits of England's win, there is no doubt that the Final was a glorious climax, the best there had been since 1954, and a great deal better than the one-sided Brazilian exhibition of 1970. Again, though England may not at any time have matched the technique and artistry of the Brazilian teams which won the two previous competitions, though they may have struggled all the way to the semi-final putting effort above creativity, hard work above joy in playing, the team had its undoubted stars. The commanding Bobby Moore, captain and left-half, was properly voted best player of the tournament, and this was followed by the immensely popular Bobby Charlton's election as European Footballer of the Year. Then there was Gordon Banks, whose splendid displays excelled even those of the veteran Lev Yachine —playing in his last World Cup—not to mention Geoff Hurst and the indefatigable Alan Ball, the two true heroes of the World Cup Final.

## Alf Ramsey

We have met Ramsey, in this World Cup saga, before; as England's right-back in Brazil, when the United States so saucily and painfully twisted the lion's tail. As though this were not trauma enough, he had also played in the team which was beaten 6–3 at Wembley by Hungary in November 1953.

Born to a poor family in Dagenham, the London 'overspill' town, in 1920, his early ambition was to become a successful grocer. As a footballer, he was a curiously late developer. Southampton discovered him during his Army service when he was an inside-forward, but eventually converted him to full-back where his strength, vision of play and somewhat deliberative approach put him more at his ease. By December 1948, he was good enough to play for England against Switzerland, but only as a second choice. In the summer of 1949 his career took a crucial turn when Arthur Rowe signed him for Tottenham Hotspur in a deal involving the Welsh international left-winger Ernie Jones, and which, overall, valued Ramsey at the surprisingly low figure of £21,000. It must have been the best bargain Tottenham ever made.

For Ramsey fitted instantly into the new, push-and-run, quick, wall-passing tactics devised by Rowe. Though he was not the captain of the team, his nickname at Spurs, 'The General', shows clearly enough who was in command. His moral influence over the side was immense. He may have lacked pace, but his positional sense was admirable, his tackling strong, and above all he made consistently fine use of the ball. It was long before the days of the overlapping full-back, but Ramsey was what one might call a constructive full-back, whose thoughtful, scientific play set the tone for the whole ebullient team. He was also a dab hand at penalty kicks, with one of which he would temporarily save England's unbeaten home record, in October 1953 against FIFA at Wembley. When Hungary destroyed it a few weeks later, Ramsey again, to some degree, had the last word; or at least the last goal—from the penalty spot.

His approach to the game, his unfailingly thoughtful play, made it probable he would succeed as a manager, and so he did, taking Ipswich Town, a small East Anglian club which had entered the Football League only in 1937, from the Third Division to the Championship of the First, an extraordinary feat, achieved with a team of obscure and rehabilitated players.

When, after the 1962 World Cup, it was decided to appoint a full-time team manager with no other interests—Walter Winterbottom, disappointed in his ambitions for the Football Association secretary-ship, had resigned—Ramsey was not the first choice. Indeed, he was probably no better than the third; Jimmy Adamson, the dedicated Burnley player who had coached the 1962 team, being first. He turned the job down.

Ramsey, who must have known he had got all he was ever likely to get out of his Ipswich side, poised on the verge of rapid disintegration, accepted the job, but on the specific understanding that he and he alone picked the team, that the Selection Committee which had for so many years theoretically held sway over the team manager would disappear. Ramsey never pretended to have much time for selectors and their ilk.

Ramsey built his success and his managerial reputation on the fact of being a player's man, and there is no doubt that it was his strength during the years which led to his success in 1966. Winterbottom, by contrast, had been, for all his virtues and his charm—a quality which scarcely distinguished Ramsey—an 'Establishment' man. He had been Sir Stanley Rous' choice, Sir Stanley's *protégé*, a theorist and an idealist whose chief concern, by his own admission, was the development of coaching. The players, who gave him a hard time when he first took over, came to like and accept him, but for all his own career in professional football, he did not move on their level, live in their world, talk in their terms. Ramsey did. Indeed, he seemed uncomfortable in any other world, afflicted by a feeling of social and cultural inadequacy reflected in a suspicion of the unfamiliar, a deep mistrust of the Press, a lurking xenophobia. But however tense and taut he might be with the world at large, Ramsey with his players was generally relaxed, friendly, avuncular, even humorous, cheerfully joining in their training games, never losing his authority but never wielding it in the paternalist manner of a Vittorio Pozzo.

## The Contenders   England

Ramsey's first international fixture, against France, was held in Paris in the Nations Cup early in 1963, and was a disaster; England were thrashed 5–2, though goalkeeping errors made the defeat look worse than it should have been. Having taken stock, Ramsey then quickly rebuilt the side, and by the European tour of the summer of 1963 it was a very good one; well balanced, incisive, well 'motivated'. Ramsey had also made it his business to do something which Winterbottom had not done over his sixteen years; he appointed a team doctor. As we have seen, it was only when Peter Swan, given dangerously mistaken treatment, almost died in Viña del Mar during the 1962 World Cup, that the FA woke up to the need for a regular medical adviser.

They were especially fortunate in the man they chose, a gifted Harley Street consultant called Dr Alan Bass, Arsenal's team doctor, a native of Leeds, who carried his knowledge lightly, got on splendidly with the enigmatic Ramsey and his trainer, Harold Shepherdson, and just as well with all the players.

On that 1963 tour, Ramsey's relations with the Press were for once as good as they were with the players. He conceived and patiently explained successful tactics, in which wingers were of the essence; vital in their role of getting round the back of a packed defence and pulling the ball back into the goalmouth.

Gradually, as we shall see, he abandoned this tactical conception in favour of a 4-3-3 system, modulating at times into a 4-4-2, which eschewed orthodox wingers, putting its emphasis on hard work and hard running.

That his strategic grasp was less than impeccable was shown the following summer, when he took England to play in an international tournament organised by Brazil. England lost the opening match in Rio against Brazil 5–1, and did not win either of their two subsequent games in the competition, against Argentina and Portugal. Before the Brazilian match, moreover, Ramsey had a taste of the gamesmanship he was likely to meet in major international football. The Brazilians, having fixed the kick-off time, blithely arrived over an hour late, while the English players sat and fretted in their dressing-room. Shades of Pozzo's foresight before the 1938 World Cup Final. Ramsey would see that nothing like this happened again.

The 1964 tour was also significant for his collision with Bobby Moore. The tour, ill-planned, began with a meaningless game against the United States in New York, followed by the long haul down to Rio and inadequate time to prepare. In New York, certain English players broke curfew, but more serious was the stand made by several, Moore among them, against a training session organised on the tour by Ramsey. The 'revolution' quickly petered out, but had its strange, though not uncharacteristic, sequel in Ramsey's refusal to confirm Moore as England's captain till the very eve of the subsequent match against Northern Ireland in Belfast the following October.

Ramsey has a long memory, and it was some while before he and Moore achieved a reconciliation. Indeed, before the 1966 World Cup there seemed a real possibility that Moore would be replaced by the infinitely less commanding, but considerably more aggressive, Norman Hunter of Leeds United. It was perhaps not entirely fortuitous that during the pre-World Cup tour Moore's closest companion should be another East Londoner, another player never truly *persona grata* with Ramsey, Tottenham's Jimmy Greaves.

Players like Greaves, whose immense natural talent allowed them to do in a flash what other players could not achieve with endless effort, clearly worried Ramsey. Greaves, a goal-scoring prodigy in his teens, manifestly worried him. Ramsey was not at bottom without his own particular humour, but Greaves's irreverence was not something he could easily accept or understand. Indeed, his first real fracas with the Press had come a year before, on tour in Gothenburg, when he omitted Greaves from the team, said there were no injured players, then was incensed when newspapers reported that Greaves had been dropped. It was, however, equally characteristic of the man that he should in due course cool down and have the generosity to apologise.

Greaves, on the summer tour, looked fit and sharp again after long months fighting the effects of jaundice. He scored four splendid goals in Norway but did much less well in Denmark, where on a dreadful pitch England won crudely, 2–0.

Since Ramsey's accession, and since the 1962 World Cup, the team had been greatly modified. Gordon Banks, making his debut in May 1963 at home to Brazil, and letting in, to Ramsey's displeasure, a wildly swerving free kick by Pepe, had confirmed himself as the best goalkeeper since Bert Williams; perhaps since Frank Swift.

A Sheffield man who played for Leicester City, he combined physical strength and courage with astounding agility. His high cheekbones, his narrow eyes, gave his face an almost Red Indian, rather than a Yorkshire, look. He was modest, quiet and diligent. Ramsey, he said, on the day before the World Cup Final, had convinced him that 'my mind's got not to wander'. Nor did it.

To partner the still excellent Ray Wilson at full-back Ramsey had chosen George Cohen, an immensely amiable Londoner who had played all his professional football with Fulham, a strong, fast, endlessly determined player with a penchant for overlapping and a bottomless good humour.

At right-half there was . . . Nobby Stiles, the players' player, *bête noire* of the purists, a tiny, toothless, urban, gesticulating figure, perennially in the bad books of referees and opponents, forever urging on, castigating, his own defenders, a player with no obvious physical or technical gifts, a poor passer of the ball, but a formidable marker and an extraordinary competitor. By the end of this World Cup he would be the player whom most of the footballing world loved to hate, yet his was the satisfaction of nullifying Eusebio, the tournament's leading scorer and, till then, most dangerous forward.

The attack was clearly more of a problem than the defence. Bobby Charlton had been transformed, by Ramsey and by Manchester United, from a flowing, accelerating left-winger with a terrific shot in either foot into the general of the team, the role that he preferred. 'You're active all the time, you're in the game,' he declared. He exercised this role, however, in a very different manner from Johnny Haynes. A naturally more gifted player in terms of technique—though Haynes's ball control was often undervalued—he had none of Haynes's vision of play, eye for an opening, great strategic sense. His long, powerful crossfield passes were usually cause for a delighted roar at Wembley, but often they were merely lateral and spectacular, making no real impact. Yet his sinuous ability to beat a man with a lovely swerve could set problems to a defence which then found itself obliged to commit another defender, while his glorious shooting when he did come forward was a harbinger of goals.

His brother Jack, of Leeds United, had become the regular centre-half. A veteran by now, his spectacular improvement had much to do with the new spirit at Leeds inculcated by its manager, Don Revie. Charlton, a tall, tough, laconic man from a miner's family, with a miner's robust attitudes, could scarcely have been more of a contrast to his gentler brother, whom he so admired. As children, it appeared, they had never been close. There was none of Bobby's Prince Myshkin-like quality about Jack who, immeasurably less gifted, relied on strength, experience and intelligence.

Geoff Hurst had been something of a marginal choice for the party. When a journalist in Oslo expressed surprise that the brilliant young Chelsea forward Peter Osgood had not been chosen, Hurst replied, with uncharacteristic bitterness, 'Instead of me, I suppose'. Like Bobby Moore, he owed much to the coaching and percipience of West Ham's manager, Ron Greenwood. He was superbly built, tall, with immensely muscular thighs, a fine jumper, shot and header, but he had originally been no more than a moderate wing-half, and Greenwood had countermanded a decision to sell him to a Second Division team. The son of an Oldham Athletic half-back, Hurst had moved early to Essex, for whom he had played cricket. He was marvellously philosophical about the harsh treatment he often got from opponents, superbly unselfish and intelligent in his movement 'off' the ball, especially to the left wing.

Martin Peters was a third West Ham player in the party, a quiet, almost withdrawn, Londoner whom Greenwood had described as 'ten years ahead of his time', technically exceptional, a right-half by preference and position, who had just 'made' the England team in time the previous May. Ramsey had chosen him against Yugoslavia at Wembley and he had done well; many had felt his choice long overdue. Now he would blossom in a new role as a midfield player exploiting his flair for the unexpected, Panglossian appearance in the penalty area.

The little, red-haired, twenty-one-year-old Alan Ball, Blackpool's inside-forward, was quintessentially the kind of player Alf Ramsey wanted. He had first capped him on his twentieth birthday the previous year against Yugoslavia in Belgrade. The son of a former professional inside-forward, whom physically he closely resembled and who had been the Svengali of his career, Ball was a passionate enthusiast. Some felt he was neither fish nor fowl, that he lacked the subtlety of a great midfield player, the power and acceleration of a great goal-scorer; but in the Final none would play better or contribute more than he.

Roger Hunt, the Liverpool inside-forward, was another Ramsey player *par excellence*, fair-haired, sturdily built, as quiet as Martin Peters but much less talented, a doer of good by stealth, but essentially a workhorse.

England were drawn in Group I, which would play all its matches but one at Wembley; Uruguay and France were scheduled to play at the White City, a gesture towards the owners, who had allowed it to be used as World Cup headquarters. The fourth team in the group was Mexico, and England's passage to the quarter-finals seemed pretty secure. It was unfortunate that a Football Association booklet on the competition should give the impression that should England win the group they would play the quarter-final at Wembley but the semi-final at Everton. In fact, no such decision had been taken, as FIFA's own rules made clear. Nor, as some supposed, had it been decided that the winners of Group I would, if they cleared the quarter-finals, automatically play the semi-finals at Wembley. Instead, it was left to the World Cup committee to choose the respective venues, and it was not without considerable discussion and disagreement that it did so.

Indeed, given the nature of the discussion, it is especially ironical that certain European and South American journalists, pursuing what one might perhaps call the Conspiracy Theory of football, should darkly have blamed Sir Stanley Rous for loading the dice in favour of England.

Nothing could have been farther from the truth. What in fact happened was that a strong group urged that England play their semi-final at Wembley, on purely—or pragmatically—economic grounds. This group argued that if England played at Wembley, it would be in front of a 90,000 crowd, whereas if Russia and West Germany played there, probably the crowd would be no bigger than 50,000. At Liverpool, the crowd would probably be a 'capacity' one, whoever played there. Rous argued strongly against this, but was finally persuaded to accept the majority's view.

### Brazil

Brazil were in the Liverpool-Manchester Group III, though all their matches would be on Everton's ground. Once again the 'draw' had been a somewhat premeditated affair, the admirable Dr Hilton Gosling having long since picked out the pleasant Lymm for his team's headquarters. Vicente Feola was back again as team manager. In the event the selection would display a reverence for the past bordering on gerontophilia, but in prospect Brazil seemed well equipped to defend their title and even to win it a third consecutive time. Amazingly, they had not only stayed faithful to most of the old guard of 1962, they had even recalled Bellini and Orlando, their two centre-backs of 1958.

Of Garrincha Dr Gosling said, 'He has recovered (from injuries in a motor accident) but not completely. The problem with Garrincha is this; he can't play as often as he used to play, his recovery is quite slow now.' It was a point Brazil's selectors would wantonly ignore.

An ageing Djalma Santos and a fading Zito were also among the elect, while a third survivor of 1958, the thirty-four-year-old Dino, who had gone home from Italy to São Paulo promising to retire, was now in such splendid form with Corinthians that he seemed likely to win a place. In fact he did not even get into the final party. Lima, a powerful but straightforward half-back, did, while the gifted but inconsistent Gerson, a member of the 1960 Olympic team, was the designated successor to Didì.

But when all was said and done there was always Pelé, the sublime *deus ex machina*, throbbing with power and energy, capable of resolving and transforming any game in a flash. He, too, had had his problems with injuries, but at twenty-five he was at the peak of his career.

## Hungary

Portugal and Hungary were in the same strong group. The Hungarian team manager had promised that his side would abandon 4-2-4 and play with Matrai as a sweeper, because otherwise 'we'd have no chance against Brazil and Portugal'. The Hungarians had won their qualifying group well, without losing a match. They still had the immaculate, Hidegkuti-like Florian Albert for centre-forward, and could afford the indulgence of playing Ferenc Bene, a huge success in the 1964 Olympic tournament, small and clever and fleet, on the right wing. As we shall see, however, their tactics were rather more than mere *catenaccio*.

## Portugal

Portugal had staggered through the last phases of *their* group, losing in Romania, but in Eusebio they had one of the game's few authentic stars, a very great striking inside-forward with a staggering right foot, flowing control, wonderful acceleration. Born in Lourenço Marques, Mozambique, he had at the age of nineteen established himself in the Benfica team in 1961 in a world club championship match in Montevideo, having previously electrified Paris in a friendly tournament. His face had a pristine innocence and beauty in respose, his movements were graceful yet enormously powerful. If Europe had found a rival to Pelé in spectacle and efficiency, then this was unquestionably he.

There were several other stars from a Benfica team which had played superbly in the European Cup over the past five years, winning it twice and twice losing narrowly in the Final. Eusebio himself, after his thunderous shooting had resolved the 1962 Final against Real

Madrid in Amsterdam, had been symbolically presented by Ferenc Puskas—scorer of three that night—with his jersey. José Augusto, formerly the team's fast and clever outside-right, would now play in midfield as a subtly creative inside-left, little Simoes would appear with great effect both on the left flank and on the right, while the immensely tall Torres would be a menace in the air.

Alas, two superb defenders had dropped out; and this would finally prove decisive. Costa Pereira, a tall, calm goalkeeper, and Germano, a mighty, resilient centre-half, had been the very props of the Benfica defence and there was no replacing them.

## The Groups

In England's group, Uruguay, who would be met in the curtain-raiser, were clearly the toughest nut to crack. They were managed by the elderly, dedicated, courteous Ondino Viera, a man rich in experience of South American football. They brought such stars of the 1962 team as the dazzling inside-forward Pedro Rocha in midfield, and Ladislao Mazurkiewiecz in goal, but to Viera's chagrin he could get hold of none of the Uruguayans playing in Argentina—Silveira, Pavoni, Matosas, Sasia, Cubilla.

In the Birmingham-Sheffield group there were Argentina, Spain, Switzerland and West Germany. Luis Suarez, the Internazionale (Milan) inside-forward, the first £200,000 transfer of all and a World Cup player of 1962, had given England to win. His own country had qualified most laboriously with a play-off in Paris against little Eire, won only 1–0 by a goal from Ufarte, the Atletico Madrid right-winger, who had played almost all his football in Brazil with Flamengo of Rio.

Argentina, who had progressively hardened their hearts since 1958 and had won Brazil's International Tournament of 1964, which included England and Portugal, with ruthless defensive methods, had had a palace revolution, Juan Carlos Lorenzo, their 1962 manager, replacing Zubeldia. They had unexpectedly recalled Luis Artime, centre-forward, and Ermindo Onega, inside-left, two players who had till quite recently been playing in the River Plate reserves, for all their celebrated understanding. Artime, known as *El Hermoso*, 'The Handsome', would go on scoring goals all over South America for the next six years. As the perambulating half-back in a team hanging somewhere between *catenaccio* and *metodo* there was the tall, strong, unhurried Antonio Rattin; a proper successor to Luisito Monti in more senses than one.

The Swiss had been fortunate to edge ahead of Northern Ireland, baulked by a frustrating draw in Albania, while the West Germans had come in at the expense of Sweden. The return of the ever-resilient Uwe

Seeler, amazingly recovered from an operation to fit an artificial
Achilles tendon, had enabled them to win the vital match in Stockholm.

In midfield there was abundant young talent: Helmut Haller, now
with Bologna in Italy, Wolfgang Overath and his splendid left foot,
and a tall, dark, immensely elegant young attacking right-half called
Franz Beckenbauer from Bayern Munich, who was said to be better
than either.

The Italians, who played in the north-eastern Group IV with Russia,
Chile and . . . North Korea, came with a bevy of impressive recent
victories behind them. In charge of them was the tiny, spectacled
Edmondo Fabbri, who had vacillated between the kind of large-
souled, attacking tactics which thrashed Poland 6–1 in Rome and the
wretched *catenaccio*-ridden negativity which brought about a 1–0
defeat in Scotland. The return, in Naples, was won against a much
depleted Scottish side, several of whose stars were kept at home by
their English clubs for reasons more or less convincing. Jock Stein, the
forceful and able Celtic manager who had been in charge, resigned in
disgust.

When the draw was announced, after Italy's 3–0 win over Scotland,
qualification for the quarter-finals seemed inevitable; even if, by a
malign concatenation, Chile had to be met again. Then things began
to go wrong. There was a disappointing 0–0 draw with France, in
which Inter's turbulent midfield player Mario Corso not only played
badly but previously insulted the assistant manager, Ferruccio
Valcareggi, who elected not to hear the worst of his epithets. Poor
Mora, meanwhile, after scoring a fine goal against the Scots and confirming himself as one of Italy's few natural wingers, had broken his leg.

Inter were angry enough when Corso was dropped from the team
leaving Gianni Rivera unchallenged in midfield. They were incensed
when Fabbri also left out their captain and sweeper, the superbly
combative and resilient Armando Picchi, whose presence would be so
badly missed. Fabbri also surprised the critics by omitting Giuliano
Sarti, his most experienced goalkeeper, and the heavy-scoring Luigi
Riva of Cagliari.

The Russians had made their customary pre-World Cup tour of
South America. They still had the incomparable Lev Yachine, not to
mention a fine winger in Chislenko and a forceful midfield half-back
in Voinov. The charge against them, however, was the old one of lack
of flair.

Chile no longer had their midfield pair of Toro and Rojas, both of
whom had gone abroad, and failed, while North Korea—what could
be expected of *them*? They had had to beat only Australia to qualify,
since the rest of the Afro-Asian block had walked out in a huff because
they were allowed only one representative. The two necessary games

had taken place on neutral territory, at Pnom-Penh in Cambodia. Australia, who seemed to have enough experience to win comfortably, were thrashed 6–1, then beaten 3–1, by a team of little men who moved sweetly and finished splendidly. Sir Stanley Rous, who was present, warned everyone prepared to listen that this was not a team to be taken lightly, but scepticism remained.

Little, after all, was known about the North Koreans. Their contacts with football beyond their own remote confines were small, and beyond the range of Communist countries sympathetic to Russia—rather than China—nil. A couple of games in eastern Europe on the way to the World Cup was simply not enough. Had they deserted their sombre, rather than splendid, isolation as soon as they had beaten Australia, who knows how much more they might have done; though they would, it is true, have lost their aura of inscrutability, the charisma of the unknown.

### The Opening Matches    The First Round

The opening match of the tournament, held at Wembley, was a dreadful one; the most arid of goalless draws between England and Uruguay. The Uruguayan tactics had been predictable from the beginning; *catenaccio* defence and minimal ambitions. In the circumstances, Ramsey's own tactics and team selection were curiously obtuse. Connelly *did* play instead of Peters, but far from guaranteeing the attacking game Viera had expected it simply meant that England, with only one winger, Bobby Charlton out of form, and neither Hunt nor Greaves making much impression on Uruguay's solid, contemptuously resourceful defence, had little chance of a goal.

Brazil's beginning, at Everton, was better; they beat Bulgaria 2–0, thanks to two fulminating goals from free kicks, one in the first half by a splendid Pelé, one in the second by Garrincha.

At Old Trafford their rivals, Portugal and Hungary, played, and an injury to Szentmihalyi, Hungary's goalkeeper, only a few seconds after the kick-off, tipped the balance. José Augusto's first goal soon followed, Szentmihalyi missing a corner, and all Hungary's clever, furious attacks came to naught. Playing with a novel formation, three midfield men breaking splendidly to support Bene and Farkas up front, they twice hit the bar. At last Bene equalised, after sixty-one minutes, but six minutes later, with Szentmihalyi again at fault, Augusto made it 2–1. Torres got the third goal from an 'impossible' angle with almost the last kick, giving Portugal a 3–1 win which ridiculed the actual play.

In Sheffield the Swiss collapsed 5–0 before the West Germans, Beckenbauer gliding through for a couple of fluent goals. At the last moment Switzerland had dropped two of their best players. Leim-gruber and Kobi Kuhn, for breaking curfew. The punishment seemed rather severe, both for team and players.

At Villa Park, Argentina, who had lost 3–0 in Italy on the way to England, beat Spain 2–1 in a disappointing game, twice cruelly hacking down Suarez, early on. Artime, sharply exploiting Onega's clever suggestions, scored both goals for Argentina, while Pirri, in his first international, replied with a curious, looping header for Spain. Argentina had the blond Silvio Marzolini again as one of their two overlapping full-backs, Roberto Perfumo as a composed and elegant sweeper.

At Middlesbrough the North Koreans, who would be taken to the hearts of the Ayresome Park crowd, referred to lovingly as 'us', for all their exotic remoteness, began badly. Russia, physically much too powerful, brushed their over-cautious team aside, 3–0, Malafeev and Banichevski, the big strikers, getting the goals. There still seemed no reason to believe that the Koreans could do anything.

Italy, at Sunderland, laboriously beat Chile 2–0 with an early goal and a late goal. Something strange had happened to them since their string of 'friendly' victories; the cynical would whisper afterwards of the effects of strict drug control. The players seemed tense, reflecting the tension of little Fabbri, which seemed unassuaged by the fact that the Italian Federation had extended his contract to 1970.

The French, meanwhile, ensconced at Welwyn Garden City, began badly with a draw against Mexico, whose goal was scored by the alert Enrique Borja. The bone of contention was Lucien Muller, an ex-perienced midfield player now with Barcelona, who had been brought from Spain but would not play a match.

Succumbing 2–1 to Uruguay at White City, the French thus lost all chance of qualifying; they could hardly hope to beat England.

## Hungary v. Brazil

The second round of matches brought a glorious game between Hungary and Brazil at Everton, worthy of standing with the best the World Cup has ever produced. It was exciting, dramatic, full of fine goals and delightful football, played at extraordinary speed. It also represented the first defeat of Brazil in a World Cup since 1954.

Pelé, let it be said at once, could not play, his place being taken by young Tostao. Gerson replaced Denilson, essentially a half-back, in midfield, while the veterans Djalma Santos and Garrincha were most unwisely committed to their second match in a few days. The Hun-garians made several changes, including Gelei for Szentmihalyi in goal.

It was Albert, however, who dominated the field, left to wander at will by the Brazilians, orchestrating Hungary's flowing attacks, now running beautifully with the ball, now passing cleverly, always willing and able to beat his man, consummately versatile. At the end of the remarkable match, when he stood by the tunnel in the rain taking a pull from a bottle of water, the Everton crowd were chanting, 'Al-*bert*, Al-*bert*!' paying a great performance the tribute it deserved.

After only three minutes, little Bene was wriggling in from the right, infiltrating Brazil's ponderous defence, and striking his shot from the narrowest of angles past Gilmar. From that moment, Hungary had the bit between their teeth. Their defence was excellent, the prematurely grey Matrai sweeping diligently behind the muscular Sipos and Meszoly, with Sipos always ready to go forward. The attack, marvellously fast and fluid, struck now from this angle, now from that, as midfield players and even defenders dashed into the open spaces left by the clever two front runners.

Brazil were reprieved when, after fifteen minutes, Lima's free kick rebounded to Tostao, who whipped it smartly home, but the half-time score of 1–1 was illusory. Hungary finally regained a lead they would not lose with an exhilarating goal by Farkas. Albert's clever run and pass exposed the Brazilian defence again, sending Bene flying down the right. Bene pulled back a fast, low cross which Farkas met with a ferocious right-footed volley on the near post, a goal which left the crowd first breathless, then exultant. Ten minutes later a penalty by Meszoli, conceded by an overplayed Brazilian defence, fouling Bene, knocked the last nail in the Brazilian coffin.

### Portugal v. Brazil and Italy v. Russia

Pelé came back for the final throw against Portugal, but he was obviously not fit, and the match was lost and won long before a brutal, inexplicable double foul by Morais put him out of the game. In the panic after the match with Hungary, Brazil made seven changes, ejecting the veterans Gilmar, Bellini, Djalma Santos and Garrincha, yet restoring the veteran Orlando for his first World Cup match since 1958. Manga, a tall, agile goalkeeper nicknamed 'Frankenstein' for his bizarre appearance, replaced Gilmar, and crossed himself anxiously as he emerged from the tunnel; all nerves, despite his excellence on a tour of Europe the previous year.

After fourteen minutes he had given away a goal, feebly punching out Eusebio's centre for Simoes, who had begun the move, to head in. After twenty-five minutes, another goal: Coluna, Portugal's splendid black captain and left-half, a beautiful striker of the ball, sent over a free kick which Torres nodded back from the far post. Eusebio headed in again.

The game was in Portugal's pockets, and there was no excuse, not even that of cynical necessity, for Morais to chop down Pelé. Later, Pelé would say that it was only when he saw the incident on film that he realised how bad it was. He would swear, then, never to play in a World Cup again. The indulgent, flaccid English referee, George McCabe, allowed Morais to stay on the field, so that now Portugal were virtually playing against ten men. Silva, Brazil's new centre-forward, had also been hurt, while even at full strength they had been quite unable to curb a rampant Eusebio, whose speed and flexibility were a dreadful torment to their defenders.

The second half was curiously barren of goals until, after sixty-four minutes, Rildo, the young, attacking left-back, gave Brazil false hope with an enterprising run and goal. Five minutes from time, Eusebio appropriately ended such illusions when, after a right-wing corner, he thrashed the ball back into goal.

Brazil were out, and with both Hungary and Portugal defeating Bulgaria, these two passed into the quarter-finals.

England's group went on its weary way. Calderon, Mexico's goal-keeper, knelt in prayer beneath his crossbar before the kick-off of another tiresome game, against England, ruined by a Mexican team which kept nine or even ten men in defence. At last, with the crowd chanting, 'We want goals!'—it was a crowd immeasurably more vocal than in Winterbottom's reign—Bobby Charlton obliged them. Seven minutes from half-time, from well outside the area and at a sharp angle, he struck a memorable right-footed cross shot past Calderon. In the second half, his excellent pass sent Greaves through, for Hunt to put in the rebound, but though Peters had been added to the mid-field and Terry Paine tried at outside-right, the team was still creaking. Stiles, whatever his inspirational function, gave nothing in creativity, and seemed in these games, when goals had to be scored, no more than a testimony to Ramsey's penchant for counter-attacking football and at least one 'hard man'.

A crisis was reached in the subsequent game against France, again won 2–0, laboriously, against a French team which played most of the match with the injured Herbin at centre-forward. The English players complained afterwards that opponents spat at them. Be that as it may, Stiles' foul on Jacky Simon late in the game seemed a gross one. Two officials of the Football Association insisted that Ramsey withdraw him from the team. Ramsey, loyal to his players and his somewhat contentious ideology, said that if Stiles went, so would he. Stiles, inevitably, remained.

This, however, was the only match after which Ramsey reproached his team. Once back at the Hendon Hall Hotel, their headquarters, he castigated them for sins of presumption, though exempting the hard-working Roger Hunt, who had scored both goals. To the onlooker, England's performance had seemed, if anything, rather better than in the previous two games. The match was significant for an injury to Greaves which allowed him to be gently discarded, and Ramsey's last attempt to play with an orthodox winger, Ian Callaghan of Liverpool. It must also have convinced him of the value of the absent Ball.

If Calderon had prayed, Carbajal, after Mexico's 0–0 draw with Uruguay, kissed both goalposts. It was the thirty-seven-year-old 'keeper's final match, in his fifth World Cup; and a most satisfactory one for his country. This time it was the Uruguayans, cynical and negative, masters of the 'tactical' foul, who shut up shop, knowing that a draw would take them into the quarter-final.

More cynical and provocative still were their Argentinian neighbours, in a deplorable, goalless match against West Germany at Villa Park. This time the Germans could not frolic as they did against the Swiss, Beckenbauer being much too concerned with countering the clever, inventive Onega. Albrecht, who had outrageously rugby-tackled Haller, was sent off after sixty-five minutes for another bad foul, on Weber, but still the Germans played it close to the chest; though Perfumo, acrobatic and resilient, cleared from beneath his own bar.

These two now proceeded to qualify, Argentina beating the Swiss 2–0 with goals by Artime and Onega, Germany defeating Spain 2–1 at Birmingham in a very tight match. A powerful shot from an astonishing angle by the hefty Emmerich, their left-winger, gave them the lead, but Fuste equalised, and Seeler won the match only six minutes from time.

Meanwhile the travails of Italy continued—and multiplied. Fabbri, in an evident state of alarm, put out a curiously unbalanced, hitherto untried, team against Russia at Sunderland, dropping Gianni Rivera and both wingers, choosing Giacomo Bulgarelli of Bologna, despite a knee injury.

With the vastly tall Giacinto Facchetti of Inter, essentially an over-lapping full-back, helpless against clever Chislenko, Russia's outside-right, the Italians never found a rhythm, never made adequate chances for their chief bombardier, the slender but incisive Sandrino Mazzola, son of Valentino. A goal by Chislenko in the second half settled the match. Some critics remarked on the officiousness of the referee, a tiny, bald, dark West German called Herr Kreitlein, of whom more would be heard.

### Italy v. North Korea and Russia v. Chile

So to the ultimate Italian trauma: Middlesbrough, and the match with

North Korea. Finding confidence, the little Koreans had come out of their shells against Chile and, to the delight of the friendly Middlesbrough crowd, gained a draw which could have been something better. Speed, in Fabbri's view and that of others, was the North Koreans' only real weapon; it was generally agreed that quick, flexible men were required to counteract it. Fabbri, however, surprisingly chose for his defence two slow players in Janich and Guarneri. Worse still, he called up again the manifestly unfit Bulgarelli, who was out of the game in half an hour after attempting to foul an opponent and definitively injuring his knee.

The Koreans played with splendid spirit and refreshing sportsmanship: the kind of 'professional' foul to which the World Cup exposed them clearly filled these straightforward little men with pained surprise. After forty-two minutes their inside-left, Pak Doo Ik, tackled Rivera—who was back in the team—advanced, and beat Albertosi with a searing cross shot. There were no more goals, and for many months the mocking cry of 'Ko-re-a!' would echo over Italian stadiums when Fabbri or any of his World Cup men appeared. He himself in a volley of accusation and counter-accusation, would lose his job.

Russia, beating Chile 2 1 at Sunderland with a couple of goals by a new left-winger, Porkujan, maintained a one hundred per cent record, and passed into the quarter-finals, against Hungary, on the same ground.

### The Quarter-Finals   England v. Argentina

In this round, run again on a knock-out pattern, the most brilliant and exciting match was unquestionably that between Portugal and North Korea at Everton, while it would be hard to decide which was the more turbulent—Wembley's England v. Argentina, or Sheffield's West Germany v. Uruguay.

The Wembley match, or fiasco, would reverberate for years to come, would polarise European and South American football, evoking almost paranoic reactions from the River Plate. The Brazilians were already away, arriving by train at Euston with the faces of condemned men, muttering, not without justice, of the inadequacies of English referees. Now Argentinian cynicism and provocation met the authoritarianism of Herr Kreitlein; and all was chaos.

Scarcely had the game begun than the Argentinians embarked on a maddening series of deliberate fouls so that England—who had left out Greaves and brought in Hurst for his first game—found every attack choked at birth. Herr Kreitlein rushed hither and thither, an exacerbating rather than a calming influence, inscribing names in his notebook with the zeal of a schoolboy collecting engine numbers. Where

Herr Kreitlein's tiny form perambulated, there generally followed the much larger form of Rattin, looming above him like a tree in the cork forest he was supposed to own, arguing, protesting, provoking. When he was booked, ironically, it was for a trivial foul on Bobby Charlton, but his whole attitude was one incompatible with the proper running of the game.

At the same time his large, loping figure was at the centre of Argentina's elaborate web of short passes, of the occasional attacks which once caused Banks, unsighted, to dive vigorously to a sudden shot by Mas.

Nine minutes from half-time, however, objecting to the 'booking' of a colleague, Rattin was sent off; and refused to go. The incident itself may, in isolation, have been unexceptional, but cumulatively things had gone too far. Herr Kreitlein, bald head gleaming in the sunlight, had had enough. He said the day after that though he understood no Spanish, the look on Rattin's face was enough.

For ten long minutes there were arguments, petitions, appeals. Albrecht at one point seemed to beckon his whole team off. The tall, de Gaulle-ish figure of Ken Aston, victim of Santiago and now chief of the World Cup referees, appeared by the touchline to intercede. And at last, slowly and with huge reluctance, Rattin went, making the long, long circuit of the pitch, accompanied by his trainer, exchanging insults with the crowd, pausing now and then to watch as the game went on, like some reluctant phantom.

The ten Argentinians held out astonishingly well, harshly exposing England's bankruptcy in midfield, where there was no one with Onega's subtlety. Hurst, playing his first competitive match since Copenhagen, found the going quite exhausting at first, but his was the first really dangerous English shot of the match, a reward for his power and perseverance. Four minutes after the interval, Wilson, receiving from Moore, dropped a centre over the defence. Hurst seemed almost surprised when it bobbled beneath his feet on the far post, but he recovered in time to strike an immensely strong shot. Roma, with a jackknife dive of fabulous agility, got a hand to it, and turned it round the post.

Argentina, when they did break, were dangerously effective, with Artime and Mas so quick on the turn, the full-backs so keen to overlap, Onega so inventive. Thirteen minutes from the end, however, Wilson found Peters, whose high cross curled in from the left was met by Hurst, this time at the near post, with a prodigious jump, a header glanced beautifully into the right-hand corner. Mas, having cuffed a small boy who ran on to felicitate Hurst, was nearly through to score from the kick-off, but England were in the semi-final.

## Uruguay v. West Germany

Meanwhile, at Hillsborough, Sheffield, two Uruguayans were sent off and West Germany won, 4–0. Neither side was blameless; much went on which escaped notice at the time. Uruguay, beginning well, should have scored early on, but instead fell behind, Haller flukily diverting a shot by Held past Mazurkiewiecz. The flashpoint came when Uruguay believed Schnellinger to have handled on the line. When Emmerich painfully kicked Troche, the Uruguayan captain, Troche kicked him back in the stomach, and was sent off, slapping Seeler's face on the way for good measure.

To those who accused the Germans in general, and Haller in particular, of 'acting', it might be pointed out that when Haller at one point collapsed and writhed, it was because a Uruguayan had seized his testicles, and that night he was oozing blood.

Troche had gone five minutes after half-time. Five minutes later, Jim Finney, the English referee, expelled Silva, the Uruguayan inside-forward, for chopping down Haller.

The nine surviving Uruguayans resisted with the determination for which their football is famous, but it could not last. With Beckenbauer able now to go fluently forward as he had not done since the Swiss match, the writing was on the wall; even if it was twenty minutes from time before Beckenbauer brought off a one-two with Seeler, casually dribbled round Mazurkiewiecz, and scored. Seeler and Haller added two more.

## Russia v. Hungary and Portugal v. North Korea

Hungary, after their excellence against Brazil, now blew up, losing, as they so often have done, to the Russians' greater physical power. Albert was consigned to the obsessive care of Voronin, who forsook, for the occasion, his usual constructive game to take part in the man-to-man marking. Sabo—ironically himself Hungarian by origin—outshone Albert as a general, splendidly abetted by Chislenko, who had begun the World Cup so well, and would finish so depressingly. He it was who exploited yet another in the series of Hungarian goalkeeping errors which had followed the going of Grosics, Gelei dropping an easy ball after only six minutes.

Porkujan, two minutes after the interval, made it 2–0, at a corner Gelei did not catch, little Bene replied, and hope revived; only for the energetic Rakosi, ten minutes from time, to miss the equaliser. A marvellous save by Yachine from Sipos' thumping free kick; and the Russian steamroller rolled on.

At Everton, the beginning of Portugal v. North Korea was sensational; a goal in a minute, followed by a second and a third; and all for North Korea. Their opening was extraordinary, a thunderclap of dazzling, attacking football, Pak Seung Jin driving home after a cutting right-wing move.

Portugal had some twenty minutes to ride the punch, but could not do so, Li Dong-Woon scoring a second, Yang Sung Kook, the outside-left, a third. The Portuguese team, conquerors of Brazil, seemed now quite *bouleversés*. It would take genius to revive them; and Eusebio provided it, running, shooting and fighting with indomitable flair, long legs threshing past the little Korean defenders.

After twenty-eight minutes Simoes put him through for his first goal. Three minutes from half-time a Korean brought Torres tumbling like a forest giant. Eusebio belted in the penalty, then urgently picked up the ball and galloped back to the centre-spot, to be intercepted and upbraided by an obscurely outraged Korean.

Eusebio would, in the event, have the best of the argument. Fifteen minutes from half-time, he sprinted through again to equalise, then, after another of his exhilarating left-wing runs, in which he negotiated tackles with electric ease, he was hacked down—and scored another penalty. At a corner kick Augusto got the fifth, and the Koreans, too generous and ingenuous to sit on their lead, were out. Alas, they would sink back into their strange isolation, leaving us with memories of their courage, their talent, their generosity.

## The Semi-Finals   Germany v. Russia and England v. Portugal

The semi-finals pitted West Germany against Russia at Everton; England against Portugal at Wembley. The first match, played a day earlier, was a wretched parody of football; the second, if it fell short of the glories of Hungary v. Brazil, a tribute to the game.

The Germans and the Russians produced a sour, ill-tempered, impoverished match, refereed without illumination by the handsome, obtrusive Sicilian, Concetto Lo Bello. Sabo, stupidly trying to foul Beckenbauer and laming himself in the process set the tone, and it was only the majestic goal-keeping, the immaculate sportsmanship, of Yachine that gave the game any distinction. It was especially ironic that afterwards he should be blamed by Morozow, the team manager, for conceding a goal, when he had kept Russia afloat for so long.

A minute from half-time Russia found themselves in still worse plight. A powerful tackle by Schnellinger robbed Chislenko, and hurt him in the process. The left-back ran on to send a perfect crossfield ball to the blond Haller, who ran on to it and scored. Russia then ill-advisedly brought the hobbling Chislenko straight back on to the field.

He at once lost the ball to Held and, in his pain and frustration, kicked him. Lo Bello instantly sent him off; and then there were nine.

These nine the Germans treated with extraordinary respect and caution. They scored only once more, with a remarkable left-footed shot, curling from outside the box around the Russian wall and in at the far post, by Beckenbauer. But with Voronin and Khusainov fighting bravely and skilfully the Russians actually managed a goal of their own. A couple of minutes from the end Tilkowski, always vulnerable in the air, dropped a left-wing cross under pressure, and Porkujan put the ball in. It was a meagre victory.

England won much more handsomely, though the score was the same, in a game which they should have won with ease, but nearly allowed to slip away from them, a game in which Eusebio, the tournament's leading scorer, was simply blotted from sight by the tenacious Stiles, who also found time to exhort, upbraid and castigate his own defence.

Bobby Charlton had much his best game of the World Cup, perhaps the best he ever played for England, his distribution for once being quite the equal of his fine running and shooting. When, after half an hour, Ray Wilson cleverly sent through Hunt, and Pereira could only block the shot, Charlton coolly drove it back into the net. At half-time, with Ball running like a Zatopek or a Zagalo the score 1-0 remained, and England had missed a dangerous number of chances.

For a quarter of an hour after the break, Portugal's gifted forwards pressed, only to find a defence in which the tall, blond Moore and Jackie Charlton, the faultless Banks, the galvanic Stiles, defied them, too compact to be breached.

So England regained ascendancy, and eleven minutes from the end they at last scored again. Hurst forcefully shook off Carlos' challenge, went to the right-hand goal line, pulled the ball back, and Bobby Charlton's right foot struck a fulminating goal.

Portugal again revived, driven on by the muscular, tireless Coluna. In another three minutes, Simoes had curled the ball over from the right, Torres rose to it above the defence and headed over Banks, Jackie Charlton punched it out, Eusebio scored still another penalty.

Now Portugal assailed the English goal, and only Stiles' fine covering tackle thwarted Simoes, after which Stiles turned on his defence with a wealth of outraged gesture. Bobby Charlton let fly a left-footed shot which Pereira smothered but again could not hold, and Banks had to tip over a raking, right-footed shot by Coluna. Then it was time; England had reached the Final.

### The Final   England v. Germany

They had reached the Final without Greaves, and the question now was whether he would return. To Greaves himself, it was one of absolute importance; this was the match on which he had set his heart. Hurst, who had replaced him, was obviously playing far too well to be dropped; if anyone went it would plainly be Roger Hunt, diligent but mediocre, a selfless and intelligent runner, a more than adequate finisher, but never a forward of true international class.

The Germans had two problems: goalkeeper and outside-left. They were not satisfied with Tilkowski's performances, above all when it came to dealing with high crosses, and he had injured his shoulder against Russia. Helmut Schoen, their team manager, would have liked to replace him with the fair-haired Bayern Munich goalkeeper Sepp Maier; but Maier was himself injured.

Then there was the question of Lothar Emmerich, the Bundesliga's most prolific scorer, a tall, strong player with a ferocious left foot who had got that important goal against the Swiss, but was not renowned for his audacity. The temptation was to drop him; the fear was that should Germany then lose, fury would break about Schoen's head. He chose Emmerich.

Ramsey, following a strangulated Press conference on the Bank of England grounds at Roehampton at which, after agonised reflection, he reaffirmed that England would win the World Cup, chose Hunt.

So, after a meaningless third-place match in which Portugal, with yet another penalty by Eusebio, beat Russia 2–1, the lines of battle were drawn.

History spoke firmly in England's favour. After sixty-five years they had yet to lose to Germany, whom they had been beating regularly since a team of amateurs overplayed them 12–0 at Tottenham in 1901. The Germans, now esconced at Welwyn Garden City, were all too cognisant of the fact. To beard the lion in his den was no joking matter. Perhaps if the match had been played elsewhere, Schoen would have been more enterprising than to sacrifice Beckenbauer to the ungrateful task of 'policing' Bobby Charlton. The Germans would in fact again play a flexible version of *catenaccio*, with the robust Willy Schulz as sweeper, Weber at centre-back, Haller and Overath in midfield, Seeler, Emmerich and the rapid Held up front.

Ramsey had hoped to exploit the relative slowness of Schnellinger by getting Ball to draw him into the middle. In fact this slowness would be much more fully and logically exploited out on the wing, where Ball would show an unsuspected talent for beating his man, than leaving him standing.

England, however, made a bad beginning. After only thirteen inconclusive minutes Ray Wilson, most uncharacteristically, headed Held's left-wing cross straight to the feet of Haller on the far post. Haller crisply controlled the ball and drove it low and wide across Banks into the left-hand corner. The banners waved in triumph.

It took England, morale as high as ever, only six minutes to equalise. Tilkowski had already looked unhappy on crosses, had already needed treatment after a collision in the air with Hurst. Handsome and anxious, he fretted on his goal-line; alas, certainly no Turek.

Now, when Overath fouled Bobby Moore, the English captain took the German defence unawares with a quick, long, accurate free kick from the left. Hurst, timing his run immaculately, ran in from the right to glide the ball with his head past Tilkowski, who exchanged recriminations with his colleagues.

The match was open again—in both senses of the word, for though Beckenbauer's fluent excursions into midfield to link up with Overath were inevitably limited, the Germans were certainly not committed to mere defence. With Held running forcefully on the left, Seeler finding space on the right, Haller lurking slightly behind the strikers, they were flexible and dangerous, a different team from the grim company that beat the Russians.

Tilkowski's weakness showed again when he could only palm out Hurst's gentle header, and Ball whipped it across an empty, tempting goal. Germany soon struck back, twice. Held, strongly tackled on the goal line by Jackie Charlton, took the corner himself. It was weakly headed out, Overath drove it back again, Banks blocked, Emmerich, still nearer, shot again, and again Banks saved. His mind was indeed not wandering.

Three minutes from half-time Hunt's preference to Greaves was put severely in question. When Wilson brought off yet another of his overlaps and well-judged crosses, Hurst outjumped the German defence and glided the ball to Hunt on the left-hand post. Greaves would surely have put the chance away, but Hunt's left foot was his 'swinger'. Tilkowski raised his arms like a man in prayer, and his prayer was answered as the ball struck him and bounced loose. There was time for a shot by Seeler, a tip-over by Banks, then a pleasing, inconclusive half was at an end.

The second half began with a heavy shower, and two intricate, fine pieces of control on the right by Ball who, in the first half, had been tirelessly pulling Schnellinger across the whole face of the forward-line. Then came a period of stalemate, phoney war, in which no chances were made. Each defence had the measure of its opposing attack, and if Bobby Charlton still ran gracefully, there was a gaping space on England's left wing unless Wilson filled it.

Only twelve and a half minutes remained when England broke the deadlock. Ball thumped into Tilkowski, bundling him over the goal-line for a left-wing corner which he then took. The ball ran loose to Hurst, who shot, Weber lunged in to block and the ball rose tantalisingly into the air as though on a jet of water in a shooting gallery. It was Peters who shot—and scored.

After the hugging, the congratulations, Stiles and Wilson turned to the touchline, eyebrows questioningly raised, fingers upstretched, as if they had some premonition of what was in store.

With four minutes left England spurned a handsome chance to finish the job. With Germany now desperately committed to seeking the equaliser they broke away, a superb through pass by Ball cutting the defence to shreds and putting Hunt quite clear. On his right he had not only Bobby Charlton but Geoff Hurst, while in front of Tilkowski there was only Schulz; a *three* to one situation which should automatically have produced a goal. But for the second time in the match Hunt blundered, making his pass to Charlton too soon, before Schulz was fully drawn; too shallow and too square. This haste communicated itself to Charlton, who sliced wildly at the ball and hit it wide.

For this England paid heavily. There was less than a minute left when Held and Jackie Charlton jumped for a header. Many thought Held had backed into Charlton. Herr Dienst, the Swiss referee, was of the view that Charlton had fouled Held. He gave a free kick on the left, just outside the penalty area, which at last allowed the hesitant Emmerich to justify his choice. His strong, left-footed shot hit Schnellinger in the back, was sent across the goal-mouth by Held, and there was driven home past the lunging Wilson and the plunging Banks by another defender, Weber. There would now be extra time.

Exhausted by the drama, the tension of it all, as much as by the running, the players sprawled about the grass. Ramsey, in his bright blue tracksuit, marched onto the field and told the England team that they had won the World Cup once; now they must win it again. 'Look at them!' he said, indicating the weary Germans. 'They're finished!'

Alan Ball was anything but finished. Within ninety seconds he was tearing down the right wing yet again, a miracle of perpetual motion, far too much for heavy Schnellinger, letting go a shot which Tilkowski turned over the bar.

England had the wind in their sails. Jackie Charlton came up and passed to his brother, whose blistering left-footed shot Tilkowski—a new goalkeeper, now—turned full stretch on to the post. After a hundred minutes, however, a long, excellent pass to the right wing by Stiles found Ball again. Ball would later write that he thought, 'Oh, no! I can't get that one! I'm finished!' He had already, he said, 'died twice', but once more he found the energy to leave Schnellinger standing, then centre on the run.

This time, Geoff Hurst met the ball on the near post with a furious right-footed shot. Tilkowski had no chance with it; it tore past him, hit the underside of the bar and bounced down. Roger Hunt stood with arms joyfully raised, not troubling to apply the *coup de grâce* which, in retrospect, would have avoided so much controversy. Clearly he was sure the ball had crossed the line.

Herr Dienst was not. Besieged by protesting German players, he marched to the right-hand touchline to consult his Russian linesman, Bakhramov. He, a tall, silver-haired, distinguished figure, reminiscent of a chess-player or a violinist rather than a referee, quickly ended the poignant hiatus, jerking his flag with the utmost emphasis towards the centre spot. For the English crowd, the England players, it was a moment of ecstatic catharsis. The goal stood; the World Cup was clearly theirs.

Once more the Germans threw their men into unbridled attack; once more their defence broke down in consequence. It was in the last seconds that Moore's long pass, capping an immaculate performance, sent Hurst through, and this time there would be no erring. As joyful small boys dashed on to the pitch, anticipating the goal, the final whistle, he carried on alone, blew out his cheeks, and beat Tilkowski with a terrible left-footer. He was the first man to score three in a World Cup Final; and the Cup itself had at last come to the country where football began.

# RESULTS: England 1966

## Group I

England 0, Uruguay 0 (HT 0/0)
France 1, Mexico 1 (HT 0/0)
Uruguay 2, France 1 (HT 2/1)
England 2, Mexico 0 (HT 1/0)
Uruguay 0, Mexico 0 (HT 0/0)
England 2, France 0 (HT 1/0)

| | P | W | D | L | GOALS F | A | Pts |
|---|---|---|---|---|---|---|---|
| England | 3 | 2 | 1 | 0 | **4** | **0** | 5 |
| Uruguay | 3 | 1 | 2 | 0 | **2** | **1** | 4 |
| Mexico | 3 | 0 | 2 | 1 | **1** | **3** | 2 |
| France | 3 | 0 | 1 | 2 | **2** | **5** | 1 |

## Group II

West Germany 5, Switzerland 0 (HT 3/0)
Argentina 2, Spain 1 (HT 0/0)
Spain 2, Switzerland 1 (HT 0/1)
Argentina 0, West Germany 0 (HT 0/0)
Argentina 2, Switzerland 0 (HT 0/0)
West Germany 2, Spain 1 (HT 1/1)

| | P | W | D | L | GOALS F | A | Pts |
|---|---|---|---|---|---|---|---|
| West Germany | 3 | 2 | 1 | 0 | **7** | **1** | 5 |
| Argentina | 3 | 2 | 1 | 0 | **4** | **1** | 5 |
| Spain | 3 | 1 | 0 | 2 | **4** | **5** | 2 |
| Switzerland | 3 | 0 | 0 | 3 | **1** | **9** | 0 |

## Group III

Brazil 2, Bulgaria 0 (HT 1/0)
Portugal 3, Hungary 1 (HT 1/0)
Hungary 3, Brazil 1 (HT 1/1)
Portugal 3, Bulgaria 0 (HT 2/0)
Portugal 3, Brazil 1 (HT 2/0)
Hungary 3, Bulgaria 1 (HT 2/1)

| | P | W | D | L | GOALS F | A | Pts |
|---|---|---|---|---|---|---|---|
| Portugal | 3 | 3 | 0 | 0 | **9** | **2** | 6 |
| Hungary | 3 | 2 | 0 | 1 | **7** | **5** | 4 |
| Brazil | 3 | 1 | 0 | 2 | **4** | **6** | 2 |
| Bulgaria | 3 | 0 | 0 | 3 | **1** | **8** | 0 |

## Group IV

Russia 3, North Korea 0 (HT 2/0)
Italy 2, Chile 0 (HT 1/0)
Chile 1, North Korea 1 (HT 1/0)
Russia 1, Italy 0 (HT 0/0)
North Korea 1, Italy 0 (HT 1/0)
Russia 2, Chile 1 (HT 1/1)

| | P | W | D | L | GOALS F | A | P |
|---|---|---|---|---|---|---|---|
| Russia | 3 | 3 | 0 | 0 | **6** | **1** | |
| North Korea | 3 | 1 | 1 | 1 | **2** | **4** | |
| Italy | 3 | 1 | 0 | 2 | **2** | **2** | |
| Chile | 3 | 0 | 1 | 2 | **2** | **5** | |

## Quarter-finals

*Wembley*

| **England 1** | **Argentina 0** |
|---|---|
| Banks; Cohen, Wilson; Stiles, Charlton, J., Moore; Ball, Hurst, Charlton, R., Hunt, Peters. | Roma; Ferreiro, Perfumo, Albrecht, Marzolini; Gonzalez, Rattin, Onega; Solari, Artime, Mas. |

SCORER
Hurst for England
HT 0/0

*Sheffield*

| **West Germany 4** | **Uruguay 0** |
|---|---|
| Tilkowski; Hottges, Weber, Schulz, Schnellinger; Beckenbauer, Haller, Overath; Seeler, Held, Emmerich. | Mazurkiewicz; Troche Ubinas, Gonçalves, Manicera, Caetano; Salva, Rocha; Silva, Cortes, Perez. |

SCORERS
Held, Beckenbauer, Seeler, Haller for West Germany
HT 1/0

*Everton*

| **Portugal 5** | **North Korea 3** |
|---|---|
| José Pereira; Morais, Baptista, Vicente, Hilario; Graça, Coluna; José Augusto, Eusebio, Torres, Simoes. | Li Chan Myung; Rim Yung Sum, Shin Yung Kyoo, Ha Jung Won, C Yoon Kyung; Pak Seun Jin, Jon Seung Hwi; Han Bong Jin, Pak Doc Ik, Li Dong Woon, Yang Sung Kook. |

SCORERS
Eusebio (4) (2 penalties), José Augusto for Portugal
Pak Seung Jin, Yang Sung Kook, Li Dong Woo for North Korea
HT 2/3

| **Russia 2** | **Hungary 1** |
|---|---|
| Yachine; Ponomarev, | Gelei; Matrai, |
| Chesternijev, Voronin, | Kaposzta, Meszoly, |
| Danilov; Sabo, | Sipos, Szepesi; Nagy, |
| Khusainov; Chislenko, | Albert, Rakosi; Bene, |
| Banichevski, Malafeev, | Farkas. |
| Porkujan. | |

SCORERS
Chislenko, Porkujan for Russia
Bene for Hungary
HT 1/0

## Semi-finals

*Everton*

| **West Germany 2** | **Russia 1** |
|---|---|
| Tilkowski; Hottges, | Yachine; Ponomarev, |
| Weber, Schulz, | Chesternijev, Voronin, |
| Schnellinger; | Danilov; Sabo, |
| Beckenbauer, Haller, | Khusainov; Chislenko, |
| Overath; Seeler, Held, | Banichevski, Malafeev, |
| Emmerich. | Porkujan. |

SCORERS
Haller, Beckenbauer for Germany
Porkujan for Russia
HT 1/0

*Wembley*

| **England 2** | **Portugal 1** |
|---|---|
| Banks; Cohen, Wilson; | José Pereira; Festa, |
| Stiles, Charlton, J., | Baptista, José Carlos, |
| Moore; Ball, Hurst, | Hilario; Graça, Coluna, |
| Charlton, R., Hunt, | José Augusto; Eusebio, |
| Peters. | Torres, Simoes. |

SCORERS
Charlton, R. (2) for England
Eusebio (penalty) for Portugal
HT 1/0

## Third place match

*Wembley*

| **Portugal 2** | **Russia 1** |
|---|---|
| José Pereira; Festa, | Yachine; Ponomarev, |
| Baptista, José Carlos, | Khurtsilava, Korneev, |
| Hilario; Graça, | Danilov; Voronin, |
| Coluna, José Augusto; | Sichinava; Metreveli, |
| Eusebio, Torres, | Malafeev, Banichevski, |
| Simoes. | Serebrianikov. |

SCORERS
Eusebio (penalty), Torres for Portugal
Malafeev for Russia
HT 1/1

## Final

*Wembley*

| **England 4** | **West Germany 2** |
|---|---|
| (after extra time) | |
| Banks; Cohen, | Tilkowski; Hottges, |
| Wilson; Stiles, | Schulz, Weber, |
| Charlton, J., Moore; | Schnellinger; Haller, |
| Ball, Hurst, Hunt, | Beckenbauer, Overath; |
| Charlton, R., Peters. | Seeler, Held, |
| | Emmerich. |

SCORERS
Hurst (3), Peters for England
Haller, Weber for Germany
HT 1/1

# Mexico
## 1970

## The Challenge of Mexico

The 1970 World Cup, played, inexplicably and inexcusably, in Mexico, was gloriously won by Brazil. For all the appalling problems of heat and altitude, all the preceding threat of violent, negative play, they triumphed with a panache, elegance and enterprise which raised new hope for attacking football. It was especially suitable that in the Final they should thrash an Italian team which stood for all that was most cautious and destructive in the contemporary game.

The decision to make it Mexico, rather than Argentina, had been taken by FIFA at their Congress in Tokyo during the 1964 Olympic Games, thus following the dubious example of the Olympic Committee which had decided to hold the Games in Mexico City in 1968. What may euphemistically be described as lobbying by the interested parties was particularly fierce. Several delegations, including that of the Football Association, whose Secretary had personal experience of conditions in Mexico City, opposed the choice of Mexico. What possibly swayed the final choice was the inconsistency of Argentina's support for the World Cup, and their tenuous economic situation.

The displeasing machinations in Tokyo one delegate admitted that his fare had been paid by an aspirant World Cup host—the whisperings in hotel corners and corridors, prompted Sir Stanley Rous to cry 'Enough!' Mexico, as it was, prevailed by fifty-six votes to thirty-two, with seven abstentions, but he, and others, wanted no more of such gerrymandering.

The intense heat of the Mexican summer—rising to well over ninety degrees—and the breathing difficulties experienced at heights of over seven thousand feet, in Puebla, Toluca, Mexico City and the rest, were problems enough. To make matters worse, the World Cup Committee entered a lamentable agreement with international television to begin their Sunday matches—including the Final—at twelve noon. In almost every one of the chosen venues noon is an hour at which it is inadvisable even to walk about. To attempt to play football, and World Cup football at that, was both ludicrous and potentially dangerous. It was particularly difficult for teams from northern Europe; the holders, England, would find themselves melting in the torrid ninety-eight degrees of Guadalajara, when up against Brazil, and finally succumbing in the still stickier heat of Leon.

In retrospect, the decision to play in Mexico, and to play frequently at noon, looks as shameful as it did in prospect. The World Cup of 1970 ultimately succeeded in spite of the abominable conditions, and one hopes, though without any great confidence, that the lesson has been learned.

## Acclimatisation

One inevitable effect, just as in the case of the 1968 Olympiad, was a huge increase in the cost of preparation. Though medical opinions varied sharply on the best means of acclimatisation and the optimum period of adaptation, there was no doubt that such a period was essential. The Olympic soccer tournament of 1968, in which Mexico's team of young League players was well beaten by France and Japan, showed that teams from sea level could settle down quite happily after three weeks or so. The Final, after all, had been between Hungary and Bulgaria.

## The Contenders    Brazil

Brazil's preparation, heavily and generously underwritten by the President of their Sports Confederation, João Havelange, was a protracted one, extending over some three months. Their prospects, however, were seriously compromised by a sudden change of horses in mid-stream when, in March 1970, João Saldanha, the team manager, was replaced by Zagalo. It was a situation heavy with irony, for Zagalo, Brazil's left-winger in the victories of 1958 and 1962, had been a protégé of Saldanha when he was managing Botafogo.

With his intelligence, enthusiasm, and vigour, Saldanha gave the national side new direction and allure. It did not look terribly impressive when it scraped through 2–1 in the Maracanà against England in June 1969, with late goals by Tostao and Jairzinho, but the following August, with Tostao scoring abundantly, it swept through its qualifying group against Colombia, Paraguay and Venezuela, uniting the vast country behind it.

Saldanha, intellectual and revolutionary, dialectician and, we were to understand, master of unarmed combat, departed for Europe trailing clouds of glory, saw seven international games, locked horns with the dour Alf Ramsey in a television interview; and returned to Brazil a changed man. Something had happened; something at once radical and puzzling. Now Saldanha's policies, always unexpected and spectacular, became frenetic and bizarre. In November 1969, without an international match being played for four months, he suddenly dropped four defenders, including both goalkeepers, and called up five new men.

There was instant outrage and protest, compounded the following February, when Toninho and Scala were, on medical grounds, sent back from training camp to their clubs by Dr Toledo, the Brazilians' medical adviser, only to be pronounced perfectly fit by their own infuriated clubs. On March 4, Brazil played at Porto Alegre, and lost to Argentina, who had already been eliminated from the World Cup by Peru. Four days later, Saldanha committed the ultimate and unforgivable crime: he contemplated dropping Pelé, with whom he had for some time been embroiled in a struggle for power. The heavens opened, Saldanha disappeared, Zagalo took over.

Thorough, calm, reputedly and invariably 'lucky' in all that he did, Zagalo made certain small but vital changes. The most important of them was using Rivelino, a powerfully built inside-left with a magnificent left foot, the equal of the celebrated Gerson's, as a nominal left-winger. This, at one blow, solved the problem of incorporating both these splendid talents in the team and also relieved Rivelino of the necessity to play flat out for ninety minutes. His previous appearances had been distinguished but insufficient, falling away after one dazzling half.

Zagalo's famous luck was confirmed by the recovery of Tostao from a severe eye injury. Suffered in training, when a ball hit him, all unaware, and detached the retina, it had necessitated two operations in Houston, Texas. Since his brief appearance in the 1966 World Cup, Tostao had developed into a player of glorious technical skill, great subtlety and considerable courage. Certainly the lack and loss of him had clipped the wings of Saldanha's Brazil; but now he was back.

Back, too, though less significantly, came the little Fluminense goalkeeper, Felix, first called up and then jettisoned by João Saldanha. Felix would play every game in Mexico, but his performances, his vulnerability to the high cross, would, *mutatis mutandis*, recall the old, cruel Harry Truman joke; that indeed, 'anybody' could be President; 'any' goalkeeper could win a World Cup medal. A far cry, this, from the immaculate, imperturbable Gilmar.

Brazil were assigned to the same qualifying group as England, Guadalajara, together with Romania and Czechoslovakia. They arrived there with an evident, shrewd policy of 'beads for the natives'. Clearly they knew their Mexicans. Distributing flags, smiles and pennants, full of protestations of good will, admiration and affection for the local populace, they had done a thorough job of seduction by the time they took off for their training redoubt at Guanajuato. On their return, they ran their training camp, outside Guadalajara at the Suites de Caribe, like a fortress, even obliging journalists to obtain and produce a separate identity card from that required and issued by the World Cup Committee. It did not matter. Good will had been shown and reciprocated. It would cost England dear.

## England

It was clear at the time, and is still clearer now, that the confrontation between Ramsey and the Mexicans, ultimately so disastrous for his team, should have been mediated. Indeed, it was quite clear on England's exploratory tour in 1969. It was Sir Alf's hope and ambition, frequently and fervently expressed, that England in 1969 would make friends, and create the climate they required for success in 1970. In these circumstances, his own performance was sometimes a little surprising.

After the goalless draw between Mexico and England in the Azteca Stadium in May 1969, he gave a short Press conference outside the dressing-rooms, and was asked if he had anything to say to the Mexican Press. 'Yes,' he replied. 'There was a band playing outside our hotel till five o'clock this morning. We were promised a motor cycle escort to the stadium. It never arrived. When our players went out to inspect the pitch, they were abused and jeered by the crowd. I would have thought the Mexican public would have been delighted to welcome England. Then, when the game began, they could cheer their own team as much as they liked. But'—a happy, hasty, afterthought—'we are delighted to be in Mexico, and the Mexican people are a wonderful people.'

In Guadalajara a few days later, after an England xi had thrashed a Mexican xi 4–0, there were further solecisms. When the game was over, the Governor of the state of Jalisco made a presentation to Ramsey, and was then escorted into what were then, before the building of the World Cup stadium, the underground dressing-rooms. After them scuttled a flock of Mexican journalists, who re-emerged almost instantly, chivvied by an irate Sir Alf, very much like the money-changers being driven from the temple. '*You've* got no right in here!'

Whatever Ramsey's many solid qualities, diplomacy was scarcely one of them, and in the difficult circumstances it was of the essence. Instead, apparent xenophobia was compounded by his well-known aversion to the Press; one which had by now been widely reciprocated. It was no use explaining to Mexican journalists that they were being treated no more brusquely, no more indifferently, than their English counterparts. The Mexican capacity for self-hatred, wounded feelings, is large; the seed fell upon ground already dangerously fertile.

England, indeed, had clearly become the team the Mexicans loved to hate: 'a team of thieves and drunks', as one local newspaper amiably put it. There had been Ramsey's indifference to the Press, Bobby Moore's absurd persecution in Colombia, and the arrival of Jeff Astle,

most nervous of air travellers, at Mexico City airport in a state of some
disarray.

Moore's astonishing, impregnable calm, that icy self-possession
which had made him such a force in the England defence, had never
been so impressively manifest as it was in his Colombian tribulations.
While the England team were staying at the Tequendama hotel in
Bogotà, he and Bobby Charlton visited the Green Fire jewellery shop
inside the hotel. While they were afterwards sitting just outside it, they
were approached, and asked to explain the alleged disappearance of a
bracelet. Both were naturally astonished, unaware of the well-
established Colombian pastime of thus accusing visiting celebrities.
Indeed, when the news of Bobby Moore's subsequent arrest and
detention broke upon the world, a rash of similar cases was exposed,
their victims ranging from singers to bullfighters.

England, despite the eight thousand-foot altitude, won easily against
Colombia in Bogotà—as did their second eleven, on the same night—
then travelled for two similar matches in Quito, Ecuador (nine
thousand feet), both of which they also won, Moore behaving through-
out with his customary poised detachment. On arriving once more in
Bogotà, on the way back to Mexico City, he was arrested by the
Colombian police and put under house arrest in the care of the
President of the Millonarios Football Club.

Accusations were made against him by the proprietor of the jewellery
shop, the shopgirl, and a mysterious 'witness', whose background
would turn out to be, at the least, equivocal, and who would ultimately
disappear. Following diplomatic intervention, Moore was 'bailed' to
play in the World Cup, played superbly, and was persecuted for a few
months more with threats of further charges before the case died a
belated, murky death. Plainly it was a fabrication from the start (its
perpetrators were charged for conspiracy in 1972), but this cannot
detract from the extraordinary qualities of resilience shown by Moore,
whose 1970 performances outstripped even those of 1966.

England's hopes of keeping the World Cup seemed quite substantial, for all the oppressive conditions. Though Cohen and Wilson,
the full-backs, Nobby Stiles, Hunt and Jackie Charlton had dropped
out of the 1966 side (Stiles and Charlton remaining in the 1970 party)
morale was excellent. New stars had been discovered. A most useful
aid, slow sodium, had been adopted. Of the old brigade, Bobby Moore,
Gordon Banks and Geoff Hurst seemed better than ever. Terry Cooper,
a small, strong, immensely mobile left-back who had begun with Leeds
as a left-winger, was the perfect man for an overlap, full of pace, control
and enterprise. Alan Mullery, a cheerful Londoner, had efficiently
succeeded Stiles. He was a solid, all-round player who, though scarcely
an artist, was technically better endowed than his predecessor, even if

he lacked Stiles' galvanising qualities. Both he and Manchester City's lean inside-right, Colin Bell, had excelled on the 1969 Latin American tour.

Francis Lee, the blond, stockily-built Manchester City striker, had come into the team at outside-right in 1968 and shown a heartening response to the great occasion. An explosive runner with a strong shot, especially happy when operating on the left flank, he was a most useful ally for the muscular, self-sacrificing Hurst, whose positional play now equalled his admirable finishing.

Perhaps the team had no great flair; it had gone out to Yugoslavia in the violent semi-final of the 1968 European Championship, had continued to exalt effort over talent. Nevertheless, it was respected and feared.

Some World Cup countries perhaps took caution too far—England among them. The English players arrived in Mexico early in May, the best part of a month before their first game. The West Germans, who would ultimately beat them, arrived weeks later.

## Germany

West Germany, playing in the group at Leon—a small, hot, rather squalid city north-west of Guadalajara—were moderately fancied. They could again call on the gracefully inventive Franz Beckenbauer and Wolfgang Overath in midfield, not to mention the resilient Uwe Seeler, playing his fourth World Cup. Moreover, there was a new and formidable threat in the person of Gerd Muller, the young Bayern Munich centre-forward. Short, dark-haired, with heavy, powerful thighs, Muller was a finisher *par excellence*, deadly in the box, a splendid volleyer.

How, then, could he be reconciled with that other fine centre-forward, the veteran Seeler? Helmut Schoen, though violently and vociferously criticised by his lieutenant of 1966, little Dettmar Cramer, resolved the question masterfully. First, Pozzo-like, he set Seeler and Muller to share a hotel room. Secondly, he decided to play Seeler in midfield; an inspired choice.

West Germany had strong rivals in Peru, whose ebullient, inventive, highly adventurous team had put out dour Argentina. Skilfully managed by Didì, the old Brazilian general of 1958 and 1962, the Peruvians scorned negative methods—even in their last, decisive quali-fying game in Buenos Aires, when they had daringly used two wingers in a 4-2-4 formation, forced a draw, and come through. Though star players had been suspended for violence perpetrated in that elimina-ting series, there was talent to burn: the black, effervescent, twenty-year-old Teofilo Cubillas at inside-forward; the powerful, adventurous

Chumpitaz, with his mighty right foot; the experienced black striker, Gallardo.

## Italy

The Italians, drawn in the high altitude Puebla-Toluca group with Israel, Uruguay and Sweden, were placing almost messianic hopes in Luigi Riva. Long before they flew off to Mexico, it was clear to any visitor that the country was burdening the Cagliari forward with a responsibility and a mission he could scarcely hope to discharge.

Of Riva's great, goal-scoring talent, of his control, acceleration, his mighty left foot, his courage, there was no doubt. Yet his very fame and presence were enough to confirm Italy in their dreadfully sterile addiction to *catenaccio* tactics; enough to lull them into a belief that if ten men stayed in defence and Riva was upfield, it was sufficient to guarantee goals. On top of this, and the North Korean complex which exacerbated it, there was the contretemps of Rivera and Mazzola, which threatened to split the team asunder before ever a ball was kicked.

We are familiar by now with both players. Gianni Rivera, as poised, elegant and economical as ever, captain and orchestrator of Milan, was now a ripe twenty-six, playing in his third World Cup, chosen as European Footballer of the Year. Sandrino Mazzola, who had made his name as a scoring centre-forward or striker, had in 1968, when Rivera was injured, used the Nations Cup final against Yugoslavia, in Rome, to affirm himself as a superb midfield player. Finals, indeed, seemed to bring out the best in him, for he played heroically well in Mexico City.

If the Italians were haunted by nightmares of North Korea, at least the North Koreans were not there to trouble them in person. After their mysterious and remarkable presence in England, they had characteristically withdrawn from the 1970 World Cup, refusing to play qualifying games against Israel. The Israelis, in consequence, were able to win in an immensely far-flung group, including South Korea and the ultimate runners-up, Australia. Their team had already played, and played well, in Mexico in the 1968 Olympics, and had an excellent inside-left in Mordecai Spiegler, an Israeli of Russian birth.

This time, there was both an African and an Asian entrant, for the Afro-Asians had had their way, the groups had been separated and a displeasingly anomalous situation thus created. De-zoning alone could at once content the Afro-Asians and see to it that Europe had a proper representation. As it was, Morocco and Israel qualified, while such teams as Scotland, Yugoslavia and Spain did not.

## Belgium

Group I, in Mexico City, had the Mexicans themselves, the mathematical and solid Russians, El Salvador—whose elimination of Honduras had provoked a short and bloody war—and Belgium, greatly favoured. Discovering a fine midfield player in Odilon Polleunis, reaffirming the talents of Paul Van Himst, 'motivated' by a forceful coach in Raymond Goethals, they had surprisingly put out both Yugoslavia and Spain, though they had flagged towards the close. Alas, they would disappoint everybody with their wretched performances in Mexico.

## The Opening Games

The tournament opened with a ploddingly dull midday game between Mexico and Russia at the immense, vertiginous Azteca Stadium. No goals were scored, little drama was distilled. Mexico did not choose their admirable striker, Enrique Borja, who had been enmeshed in the coils of their tangled football politics, transferred from Universidad to America and mysteriously kept on sidelines. Russia, with their big captain, Albert Chesternijev, sweeping up in his diligent, crouching bird dog's manner, obviously suffered from the great heat, and showed scant initiative. The most passionate moment was evoked by the appearance of the Union Jack in the parade before the game; it was fervently and ferociously whistled.

If the Mexico-Russia game was notable for anything, it was for the fussy, officious refereeing of West Germany's Herr Tschenscher. Strong in what to many of us seemed the equivocal experience of the Olympic tournament, the FIFA Referees' Committee had once more put its trust in the flourishing of coloured cards, and in Draconian instructions to its officials. Herr Tschenscher, all too keenly conscious of the occasion, 'booked' a succession of largely inoffensive Russians, dealt much more leniently with the Mexicans, and was partly responsible for the tedium of the occasion, which was to a certain extent redeemed by a fine save in each half by the Russian goalkeeper, Kavazashvili. Mexico certainly felt the unlucky loss of their midfield player, Onofre, who had broken a leg in training only a few days previously.

That Herr Tschenscher's interpretation of the new refereeing dispensations was largely personal was shown the following Tuesday, when England opened their series against Romania in Guadalajara. Mocanu, the Romanian left-back, committed at least three brutal, crippling fouls, swinging knee-high kicks which lamed two English players, yet was so indulgently treated by M. Loraux, the Belgian referee, that he did not even have his name taken.

England, winning with a goal smartly and powerfully taken by Geoff Hurst's left foot in the second half, certainly deserved their victory. The star of the afternoon was unquestionably Terry Cooper, who exploited Romania's defensive tactics to overlap, on both flanks, with high spirit and effectiveness.

Meanwhile, the Brazilians had begun more impressively with their 4–1 victory over the Czechs, featuring the prodigies of Pelé, Jairzinho, Gerson and Rivelino. As so often in the past, the Brazilian defence had not looked remotely equal to the attack, yet it had not mattered. Perhaps it would have done had the Czechs been less prodigal with their chances. 'They played basketball football,' said Ball scornfully. 'As soon as the Brazilians got the ball, they all ran back, seven of them. The midfield was wide open.'

Petras, the stalwart, blond Czech centre-forward, swept easily past Brito to give his side the lead, and might in that opening period have had at least one other goal. One of Rivelino's swerving, fulminating, celebrated free kicks brought an immediate equaliser, and just after half-time Pelé got the second. He immaculately caught a long, high pass from Gerson's superb left foot on his chest, before volleying in.

The tall Kvasniak, a star of the 1962 World Cup Final, who had come on as a slow substitute, missed a palpable chance to equalise, after a corner, and the error was punished at once, Jairzinho breaking away to score from what might have been an offside position. There could be no doubts, however, about his and Brazil's last goal. Running with marvellous control and power, shaking off three defenders and an attempted foul, he cut in to drive the ball home with his strong right foot.

Didì, their black master spirit, and strategist of two World Cups, meanwhile took his gifted Peruvians into action. The omens and the beginning could scarcely have been more depressing. A minute's silence was observed in Leon for the appalling Peruvian earthquake. No doubt the psychological reaction had something to do with the fact that the Peruvians quickly went two goals down to Bulgaria, who cleverly exploited a couple of free kicks. But then, bringing on substitutes, in Campos to tighten the defence and the coloured Hugo Sotil to enliven the attack, Peru hit back. The elusive dribbling of Cubillas, the powerful breaks from the back four of Hector Chumpitaz, the running of Sotil and Gallardo, turned the tide. Gallardo, once an unsuccessful Milan player, later with Cagliari, answered Bonev's goal quickly with a cross shot. In the second half, Chumpitaz's mighty right foot scored from a free kick for Peru, by way of revenge, and Cubillas ran on to the impressive Mifflin's pass to get the winner.

The following day, on the same ground, the untrumpeted Moroccans gave West Germany an appalling fright. Who would have expected these minnows to come out and attack furiously for the opening twenty minutes? Not the puzzled Germans, whose *catenaccio*, Schulz, sweeping up again, was overcome when Hottges headed weakly back to his blond goalkeeper, Sepp Maier, and the ball fell as a gift before Houmane, who scored.

For the first but by no means the last time in this tournament, Grabowski came on as substitute, with telling effect. This was, indeed, the first World Cup in which substitutes had been allowed—two for each side, at any juncture of the game, the formality and fiction of being able to replace only an injured man having been abandoned. Ironically, as we shall see, the Germans would later be hoist with their own petard. Meanwhile, Helmut Schoen made his first good use of Grabowski, a fair haired right-winger of pace, initiative and subtle control, who replaced Helmut Haller and created the winning goal.

Not until eleven minutes after half-time did the anxious Germans equalise, and Schoen must have been particularly pleased that it should come from the co-operation of Seeler and Muller, the old war-horse driving home Muller's pass. Twelve minutes from the end, Grabowski got away on one of his characteristic runs, Loehr, the other winger, headed against the bar and Muller, forever in the imminent, deadly breach, scored the first of his ten World Cup goals.

The second game in Group i saw Belgium's talented team make a good enough start, easily defeating, 3–0, an El Salvador side which clearly had no real business to be there; indeed, would not have been, had Mexico's status as hosts not exempted them even from their custo-mary facile passage to the finals. Wilfried Van Moer, the sturdy and dynamic little Standard Liège midfield player, scored two of the goals, Raul Lambert, the powerful Bruges striker, the other. With Van Himst and another fine opportunist in Devrindt also in the attack, goals seemed potentially abundant. In fact, this was the merest flash in the pan.

The Puebla-Toluca Group ii produced a couple of deadly dull games. Uruguay made very heavy weather of winning 2–0 against a determined Israeli team. Worst of all, their splendid midfield inside-forward, the lithe, dark Pedro Rocha, hurt himself so badly after twelve minutes that he would take no further part in the competition.

The Italians, in all their three opening games, played in a lather of foreboding, as if defeat would result in execution. In the first match, against Sweden at Toluca, they scored through Domenghini after eleven minutes, with a shot that might have been saved, then sat on their lead. Domenghini's was the only goal Italy would get in their group matches.

The remaining games, against Urugay and Israel, were both of them grim and goalless. Not unexpectedly, the exaltation of Riva had inhibited the functioning of the team; for what star footballer, used to earning his 40 million lire a year, takes kindly to being reduced to a kind of water carrier?

Uruguay were lucky to join Italy in the quarter-finals, for they lost 1–0 to the Swedes in the final game, Grahn heading the only goal. Previously, they had been held to a draw by the determined Israelis, who had surpassed themselves in their results and their competent displays.

## Meeting of Champions    Brazil v. England

The meeting of England, the holders, with Brazil, for former holders, was without doubt the *pièce de résistance* of the qualifying rounds. The conditions would certainly favour Brazil, but news that Gerson, with an injured thigh, would probably miss the game, threw it open.

On the previous afternoon, Romania beat the disappointing Czechs 2–1, though Petras, with a fine, glancing header, got his customary early goal. Petras ran powerfully and dangerously on either flank, but the Romanians came back into the game, equalised through Neagu after half-time, and won through a penalty by the blond, talented Florea Dumitrache.

As in 1958, England had elected to stay at an hotel in the middle of town, and now it would cost them still dearer. The previous year, on their arrival from Mexico City on their tour, to them the Guadalajara Hilton, with its swimming pool, its sham-colonial style, had seemed a quiet haven. What no one had been percipient enough to realise was that it would be flooded with supporters, and within easy access of the malevolent.

Day by day, as the rows of half-naked bodies formed around the swimming pool, the England players in their blue tracksuits looked like wistful trusties out on parole, denied the benefits of sun and still water. Considerably worse was to befall them on the eve of the Brazilian match.

From quite early in the evening, the advance guard of the besieging army began to arrive; on foot, in cars, on motor cycles, shouting, honking and chanting. The chant was largely for '*BRA-sil, BRA-sil!*' though its intention was fundamentally hostile to England. Round and round the hotel drove the cars and motor cycles, honking obscenely and provocatively, while the crowd in front of the hotel steadily grew.

There was to be no remission. As the night wore on, so the noise increased—now an obvious, malign attempt to disturb the English players' slumbers. It succeeded and many of the English team were forced to add the effects of a broken night to the already formidable hazards of the next day's game.

Ramsey made only one change for the match. Mullery would again look after Pelé; Brian Labone, the strong Everton defender, would play stopper. At right-back, however, Keith Newton, who had been one of those kicked by Mocanu, was replaced by Tommy Wright of Everton. 'He can beat you,' Ramsey warned Wright of Paulo Cesar, who played on Brazil's left wing; and he did. He was picked to replace Gerson, to advance from deep positions and give help in midfield to Rivelino and the young right-half Clodoaldo, a player who would not come fully into his own till later on.

'It's when they get to the eighteen-yard box,' said Bobby Charlton of the Brazilians, 'if you *let* them get to the eighteen-yard box.' He himself had shown greater fire and efficiency against Romania than he had for a long time—the unquestioned prince of midfield, where only a year before he had been threatened by the excellence of Colin Bell. Though Bell would substitute him in both this match and against the West Germans, he would never show the form he had shown the previous year, when he played so hearteningly well, with such stamina and versatility.

Many have seen the England versus Brazil game as the 'real' Final, England as the 'real' runners-up, and there is no doubt that they gave Brazil a far more courageous and substantial fight than craven Italy. Yet the absence of Gerson cannot be discounted, while if England missed a couple of fine chances, then only Gordon Banks could have made the miraculous save from Pelé's header that came in the tenth minute of the game.

The groundwork was done by Jairzinho, confirming fears that Cooper would not be able to hold him, nor be able to attack as he had done against largely wingless Romania. Brushing past the left-back with all the strength and acceleration of his predecessors, Garrincha and Julinho, Jairzinho dashed to the line and centred perfectly. Pelé headed the ball down hard, on the bounce, inside the left-hand post, and was already shouting, 'Goal!' when Banks, with incredible, gymnastic agility, somehow launched himself across his goal from the opposite post, to flail the ball, one-handed, over the bar.

With the dry, blazing heat reaching ninety-eight degrees, it was extraordinary, even with their slow sodium tablets, that England resisted as they did. No English player lost less than ten pounds in weight, and their doctor pointed out that an American Army manual forbade even training to be done when the thermometer exceeded eighty-five degrees. The World Cup Committee had prostituted their tournament and sacrificed its players to the demands of European television.

England threw away a couple of good opportunities in each half. In the first, Geoff Hurst, clear through the Brazilian defence, made the elementary mistake of presuming himself in an offside position, hesitating, and at length shooting hastily and feebly. Francis Lee, when a right-wing cross by Tommy Wright put the goal at his mercy, contrived to head straight at Felix.

The goalkeeper again betrayed his fallibility with high centres, but England's long inimicality to orthodox wingers meant that he was not often under pressure. It was only late in the game that Ramsey at last sent on the tall Jeff Astle, whose greatest strength was in the air, while Charlton gave way to Bell. Astle, though he would miss horribly, at once set the Brazilians problems; but by this time England were a goal down.

It came after fourteen minutes of the second half, and Tostao was its motivating force. His splendid dribbling on the left took him past three English defenders; though he certainly pushed off Bobby Moore, who played throughout with superb aplomb. Finally, he passed to Pelé in the goalmouth, and Pelé, without ado, laid the ball off beautifully to his right, for Jairzinho to dart in and score.

A cross headed down by Astle gave Alan Ball a chance which he squandered; Astle himself contrived to shoot over the bar when a panicky defender headed the ball straight to his feet, and another shot by Ball clipped the bar. Brazil, however, held out. It had been a magnificent, enthralling display of football, admirably refereed by the obscure Israeli referee, Abraham Klein; an inspired appointment. In the English defence, Alan Mullery had played Pelé as cleanly and resourcefully as he had a year before in Rio. Next morning, Ball sat disconsolate by the swimming pool: 'How could Jeff miss that chance?'

## Towards the Finals

In Group 1, the Russians suddenly cut loose against a surprisingly feeble Belgium, thrashing them 4–1. Two of the goals went to the Dynamo Kiev striker, Bychevetz, and the Russian midfield functioned sweetly with another Kiev player, the elegant Muntijan, in incisive form.

Mexico then disposed of El Salvador 4–0, though they owed their first goal to an abominable refereeing error; one which presaged the decision which would win them their match against Belgium. El Salvador in fact began well, Rodriguez, in the ninth minute, hitting the post, then Calderon with successive shots. A couple of minutes from half-time, however, Hussain Kandil, the Egyptian referee, gave El Salvador a free kick. It was promptly taken by Perez of Mexico, who pushed to it Padilla. The latter centred, Valdivia scored, and Kandil gave a goal. In vain did the El Salvador players argue, weep and lie on the ground; the goal, disgracefully, stood. Mexico went on to score three more against a demoralised side.

So to Belgium, a crowd of 112,000 in the immense Azteca, and another gravely dubious goal. This time it was the only one of the game; a penalty, given after fifteen minutes. Jeck cleared the ball, Valdivia, rushing onward after the event, fell over his leg. Señor Coerezza, of Argentina, gave a penalty kick. Despite two minutes of Belgian protests, Pena took it and scored, and Mexico narrowly survived the remainder of the game. 'The penalty,' said Goethals, Belgium's manager, 'was the worst I have ever seen, nor have I ever experienced such a hostile, biased crowd.' So Mexico attained the quarter-finals for the first time in their long World Cup career.

Russia beat El Salvador 2–0 in the ante-penultimate game.

In Leon, Peru, with a couple of goals from the exciting Cubillas, disposed of Morocco 3–0, while the West Germans thrashed a flaccid Bulgaria 5–2, Gerd Muller scoring three, one from the penalty spot. The blond Karl-Heinz Schnellinger, playing, like Seeler, in his fourth World Cup, took over from Willie Schulz as sweeper.

It was plain that Brazil would win Group III, probable that England would accompany them. The Brazilians put out a diminished team against Romania, lacking both Rivelino and Gerson, pushing Piazza into midfield, and winning only by 3–2. Pelé got a couple of crisp goals, Jairzinho the other when Paulo Cesar—again emphasising what Brazil could do and wingless England could not—went to the by-line and pulled the ball back. The Romanians, after a poor start, played brightly, Dumitrache once more casting doubt on Brazil's central defence with his first-half goal, Dembrowski heading a second near the end. Felix again looked vulnerable, but Brazil were hardly extended.

England, next day, looked quite abysmal. Drafting in a bevy of reserves, they struggled pitifully to find rhythm against the Czech team who, as Keith Newton ruefully observed, never stopped running, and ridiculed their previous form. Allan Clarke, far from a success, scored the only goal of the match early in the second half, from a penalty so dubious that even the French referee, M. Machin, gave a mysterious explanation. When Kuna tackled Bell he appeared to fall on the ball and handle it, yet Machin said afterwards he had given the penalty for tripping. With Jackie Charlton sadly at sea in defence, Astle easily mastered in the air and ineffectual on the ground (the Czech defence was not Brazil's), the English display was embarrassing. Indeed, the enterprising Czech right-back, Dobias, almost equalised with a shot which deceived Banks but hit the bar. As against that, Ball hit the bar, for England.

**The Quarter-Finals**    Italy v. Mexico

The quarter-finals drew West Germany against England in Leon, Brazil against Peru in Guadalajara, Italy against Mexico on the heights of Toluca, Uruguay against Russia in Mexico City, where the rejoicing at the home team's success had reached frightening proportions. Santiago, eight years before, was almost docile by comparison, as the mobs gave vent to their fearful joy.

It would not last long. Freed at last from the Korean complex, Italy and Riva came out of their shell; their extravagantly talented players, for once allowed to express themselves, swept the weak Mexican team aside.

Though Riva scored two goals, it was Gianni Rivera's day. Valcareggi's compromise was to play Mazzola for the first half, Rivera in the second, and it was with Rivera's arrival that Italy took charge of the game. At half-time, the score was 1–1, Gonzalez giving the Mexicans a false dawn with a goal in twelve minutes, which was equalised when Domenghini's shot was deflected home. In the second period, Rivera ruled the field.

Exchanging passes with the clever little Picchio De Sisti, Rivera crossed to Riva, who burst past two defenders, then beat Calderon from a sharp angle. Next his shot, then Domenghini's, were blocked, but Rivera drove the second rebound home. Finally, Rivera's immaculate pass sent Riva through for the fourth. There would be no more rowdy rejoicings in Mexico City.

## Uruguay v. Russia

The Azteca Stadium confirmed its recent reputation for dubious goals when Uruguay defeated Russia 1–0 in the last seconds of extra time. As little, dark Cubilla, the serpentine Uruguayan right-winger, pulled the ball back, it seemed quite clearly to have crossed the goal-line. But neither the referee nor his linesman thought so, and when Esparrago scored the goal stood. So the Russian team, purportedly fed up that promises to pay them a large bonus had not been kept, went out of the Cup. Their attack had again lacked flair and punch, but disappointment may have had something to do with that.

As for the Uruguayans, their achievement in reaching the semi-finals without Rocha had to be saluted. Apart from the experienced Cubilla, who had not long since returned from playing in Buenos Aires for River Plate, their stars were in defence; Ancheta, the big, dark, young centre-half, splendid on the ground and in the air, and of course the famous Mazurkiewiecz, keeping a superb goal in his third World Cup.

### Brazil v. Peru

In Guadalajara, Brazil, still the darlings of the crowd, accounted for Peru in a spectacular and effervescent game, a game in which both sides delighted in attack and scorned caution. That Peru's defence was very far from the equal of their shining attack had been plain in their concluding group game with West Germany. Again, the persisting importance of wingers was shown as the Germans, despite their *catenaccio* formation, used Libuda—then Grabowski—and Loehr wide on the flanks, to pour out a cornucopia of centres. Gerd Muller, seldom troubling to move out of the middle, as his future opponent Brian Labone remarked, made superb use of them, scoring three times; once with a magnificent header. Indeed, despite his lack of height, or perhaps because of its lulling effect on opposing defences, he was surprisingly dangerous in the air. Curiously enough, he also missed a very good chance, when the score was still 0–0, and the subtle Beckenbauer lobbed a free kick above the wall to find him unguarded. Peru scored just before half-time, and had the better of the second half, when the height and heat seemed to have sapped the Germans and given the Peruvians the advantage their native conditions implied. But there were no more goals, and a dull 1–1 draw between Bulgaria and Morocco completed the group.

Now, against Brazil, Peru played with dash and spirit but ultimately with little hope. Brazil had Gerson back again; and Rivelino, with his thumping left foot and his bandit's moustache. Both left feet, indeed, thumped to excellent purpose, with Rivelino often working alongside Gerson in midfield. Peru brought back their black winger, Baylon, of whom so much had initially been expected, but though Brazil had to use the young Marco Antonio in place of the injured Everaldo, Baylon got little change out of him. On Brazil's right wing the muscular Jairzinho was ill, and even though he scored Brazil's fourth from Tostao's insidious pass, was not the force he had been in the group matches.

Brazil went ahead after eleven minutes with a goal which emphasised their quick thinking and equally swift reflexes. When Campos, trying to breast the ball down, slipped, Tostao instantly found Rivelino, whose deadly left foot struck again. The ball beat Rubiños, to go in off the post. Hard on the heels of that Tostao, now moving with all his old provocative sleight of foot, feinted right to unbalance an opponent, then beat Rubiños with his left.

Peru, inevitably depressed, were allowed to come back into the game on the half-hour, with the complicity of Felix, who totally misjudged Gallardo's long spinning cross from the left.

It didn't matter. Just after the interval, Pelé's long shot was deflected home by Tostao. Again Peru reacted, Sotil, who had replaced Baylon as he did in their first match, having a shot which Brito could not clear, Subillas driving in from twenty yards. Then came Brazil's fourth, from Jairzinho.

## West Germany v. England

At Leon, it may with hindsight be said that England lost the match at the moment when Gordon Banks drank a bottle of beer. 'The world's best goalkeeper!' his colleagues had jokingly been calling him throughout the tour, but it was no more than the truth. On the Saturday, however, he was taken ill, and on the Sunday morning, on the large green lawn of the English team's hotel in Leon, he was to be seen hobbling, white and manifestly sick, on the arm of the England team doctor, Neil Phillips. There was plainly no hope of his playing and so it might be said, a little callously, that his place went to Peter Bonetti and the match to West Germany.

That it was by no means so simple as this is shown by the controversy which has surrounded the game ever since; not the kind of controversy evoked by Hurst's goal in the two teams' previous World Cup meeting, but by the question of tactics, the question of Ramsey, the question of Bonetti's fallibility. Was it an oversimplification, too easy an escape for Ramsey, to say that if Banks had played England would have won—or had his mistaken tactics, his ill-handled substitutions, been fundamentally responsible?

What is quite beyond doubt or argument is that England, forty minutes from the end, were leading 2–0, and that they finally lost, in extra time, 3–2.

The match, in prospect, had several fascinating attributes. In the first place, it included the teams which had contested the 1966 Final. In the second, West Germany had at long last broken their protracted run of defeats against England; a run which had begun in 1901 with the visit of the first German team to play in England. Admittedly, the crucial victory had more extrinsic than intrinsic significance, for West Germany's 1–0 win against England in Hanover in May 1968 was a trivial one. The England team was below strength, the standard low, the occasion tedious. Nevertheless, after sixty-seven years, a win was a win.

The West Germans, however, looked strong favourites. After their dull beginning against Morocco they had swept aside Bulgarians and Peruvians in a flurry of goals, Wolfgang Overath, with his splendid, long, 'quarter-back's' left-footed passes, combining with Seeler and the matchless Beckenbauer in midfield, to make the bullets for the formidable Muller to fire. The wingers, all three of them, had been fast and dangerous, ideas had been many. By contrast, England had scored only a couple of goals, and though admittedly below full strength had looked dreadful against the Czechs. Their 4-4-2 plan, described by the Manchester City manager and former England left-half, Joe Mercer, as 'cruelty to centre-forwards', had been neither effective nor entertaining. Later, the handsome, multilingual Romanian World Cup captain, Mircea Lucescu, an anglophile and an admirer of British football, would complain that England had come to Mexico with the too narrow ambition of keeping the World Cup rather than of playing good football.

Among England's senior players there had been a rumble or two; some would have preferred a more active policy against the Brazilians. But Ramsey, putting Lee back into the team alongside Hurst, was unshakeably committed to 4-4-2, and it was only to be hoped that the full-backs' overlap would compensate for the lack of wingers, that Martin Peters would at last rediscover his 1966 form in midfield and around the goal area, and that Bobby Charlton would do something special in his record-making 106th appearance.

Bonetti, Banks' replacement, was no tyro. A vastly agile, slim, spectacular keeper, he had made his debut just before the 1966 World Cup, and in his sporadic games for England had always shown a fine response to the occasion. But he had never played in so important a match before, and he had not taken part in a competitive game for a month.

Yet for an hour England played quite splendidly, showing strength, pace and invention, together with a finishing power quite absent in their previous games. The two goals came, but they were not enough.

The first was scored after half an hour; a goal transcendently Mullery's from start to finish, in conception and execution. First giving and taking passes with Lee, he hit a splendid crossfield ball out to Newton on the right. As the full-back made ground, Mullery raced diagonally towards the far post, getting there, meteoric and unexpected, exactly with Newton's centre, which he drove past Maier.

Five minutes after the interval Geoff Hurst, tirelessly unselfish, set Newton off again. Once more the run finished with an excellent cross, and this time it was Martin Peters, in his best 1966 manner, who popped up, to score.

It was just after this that Schoen took off Libuda and put on Grabowski; and the game changed. In a nutshell, Grabowski was fresh and full of running, Cooper exhausted by the killing heat and unaccustomed altitude. From being one of England's most effective players, he now degenerated into one of their most vulnerable; and was not substituted. It was the second German substitution, for Willi

Schulz had come on instead of Hottges at half-time to take over the marking of Hurst, who had been rather too much for Fichtel.

Grabowski's pace and enterprise gave the Germans new heart, and it is significant, given the subsequent theory that all went awry when Charlton departed, thus allowing Beckenbauer to come forward, that Beckenbauer scored his vital goal *before* Charlton was replaced. It came when he advanced, picked up a rebound, and sent a low, right-footed, unexceptional shot towards the left-hand corner. Bonetti went down too late, the ball ran under his dive, and the score was 2–1.

Now Bell came on for Charlton, who had been showing certain signs of wear; though hardly as obviously as Cooper. On, too, subsequently and quite inexplicably, came the hard-tackling, quintessentially destructive Norman Hunter of Leeds in place of Peters. Thus, almost at a stroke, the English midfield had been radically altered. Moreover, the obvious inference that Hunter had been brought on to stiffen the defence was proved wrong when he began to run wild and free; even, at one moment, taking a corner.

England were far from recumbent. Ball unleashed Bell, to whose low, near-post centre Hurst—who had had far too few of them—stooped in his most effective manner. The ball flew across the goal, beating Maier, but passed just outside the far post.

So Germany, with an extraordinary headed goal by Uwe Seeler, were able to equalise. A weary Labone cleared out of the goalmouth straight to Schnellinger, who lobbed back again. The English defence had not moved up quickly enough to put Seeler offside, and the stocky little forward, leaping mightily with his back to goal, managed to send the ball in a remarkable, tantalising parabola over the head of Bonetti, who was off his line and in limbo.

Thus there was extra time, and the initiative was now palpably Germany's. England's last chance went when Lee wriggled past Schnellinger on the right-hand goal-line, delivered one of the few perfect, pulled-back crosses which England produced in the series, and Hurst drove it in. The goal was disallowed for no evident reason; neither English player could have been offside, and Lee had certainly not fouled Schnellinger. So Muller, with a thundering volley, knocked the last nail into England's coffin. Inevitably, the goal derived from Grabowski's mastery of Cooper. Beating him again, he crossed, Loehr headed the ball back from the left, and once more Bonetti was out of the picture.

It was a splendid recovery by West Germany, a harsh blow to England, whose exhausted players sprawled in the sunshine on the lawn of their hotel like the casualties of a war. The burden placed on their overlapping full-backs in such cruel conditions had finally worn them out; and yet it had been such a close thing.

### The Semi-Finals   Brazil v. Uruguay

The semi-finals pitted those old foes, Uruguay and Brazil, against each other at Guadalajara, and Italy against West Germany in Mexico City. The Uruguayans were highly displeased to be playing on what was by now Brazil's home from home ground. They maintained, not without some logic, that the game should take place in Mexico City, arrived late in Guadalajara, and snubbed the Governor's reception.

Nonetheless, with poor Felix's complicity they took the lead. Little, dark Cubilla advanced with the ball along the right-hand goal-line, to be confronted by Piazza. He shot from the 'impossible' angle and the ball, against all probability, bounced past Felix into the goal.

Uruguay held their lead till late in the first half, when Clodoaldo ran in on the blind side to score a fine equaliser. The sturdy, twenty-year-old right-half was now expressing the full range of his exceptional talent; a self-expression which would bear strange—and bitter—fruit in the Final.

Pelé, Clodoaldo's idol and mentor at Santos, was again in glorious form and, as in the opening match, came close to scoring a spectacular goal. Having observed Mazurkiewiecz's habit of kicking the ball out, short, to his defenders, he once whirled to intercept one of these clearances, volleyed superbly, and brought from the goalkeeper an equally superb save.

The first half was marred by a great deal of violent play by the Uruguayans; Zagalo, indeed, had feared the consequences of Uruguay scoring first, then tried to shut up shop. Though Jairzinho had too much speed and power for Mujica, Ancheta and the veteran Matosas covered well, the Uruguayan defence survived the free-kicks they ruthlessly and recklessly gave away, and it was only in injury time that Clodoaldo raced on to Tostao's fine pass to make it 1–1.

Brazil, in the second half, took hold of the game, and Uruguay's resistance became still more cynical and physical. Repeating their quarter-final ploy, they substituted Maneiro with Esparrago. This time, however, the quick sequel was a goal to Brazil. Tostao, that inspired artificer, was again behind it, serving Jairzinho under full, imposing sail. Mujica had neither the pace nor the force to hold the winger, who raced in to drive the ball past Mazurkiewiecz. Uruguay, to their credit, retaliated, and Felix now came into his own when he saved from Cubilla. Then Pelé cunningly drew the defence before rolling the ball aside to let Rivelino do proper and spectacular execution. By way of a last, bravura flourish, Pelé, fiendishly inventive, confronted Mazurkiewiecz on a through ball, ran to one side, *away* from the ball, drawing the keeper after him, then shot fractionally wide of the unguarded goal.

## Italy v. West Germany

In Mexico City, meanwhile, a thrilling, fluctuating but scarcely classic match was taking place between Italy and West Germany. This time, Germany's fortune would rebound on them; and so would Schoen's penchant for substitution.

Playing for the first time in the Azteca, and doubtless weary after their quarter-final, Germany were slow into their stride; it was Italy, through the persistent Boninsegna, who scored the only goal of the first half. Boring his way through in the eighth minute, he twice had lucky rebounds from the German defence, and finally drove the ball past Maier, left-footed, from the edge of the box.

At half-time, Italy duly took off Mazzola to bring on Rivera, but the switch was less relevant than the fact that they fell back cautiously and characteristically to defend their lead. This allowed the Germans, who had generally been making little progress, to occupy the midfield and surge forward. It is always unwise to allow space to such players as Beckenbauer and Overath, and the initiative passed to Germany; indeed, their supremacy steadily turned into a bombardment. Seeler, when the sweeper Cera allowed a ball to run past him, Grabowski, who for once played a full match, and Overath all missed very good chances. Libuda succeeded Loehr early in the second half, and twenty minutes later Schoen gambled doubly by using up his second substitute and making it Held, an attacker, for the full-back, Patzke.

It seemed, at first, another inspired alteration, for the blond Held, a star of the 1966 Final, produced just the running and finishing on the left that Germany needed. He had a tremendous drive kicked off the line, Seeler's fine header provoked a splendid save from Albertosi, and the match was in its third, breathless minute of injury time when Germany at last equalised. Grabowski crossed from the left, and the blond sweeper, Karl-Heinz Schnellinger, materialised in the goalmouth, to bang the ball home.

Now came extra time. Italy now brought on Poletti for Rosato, but the most significant sight was that of Franz Beckenbauer with his arm strapped to his side. He had been brutally chopped down, not for the first time in the game, while in full, spectacular flight towards the Italian goal, accelerating with that sudden, irresistible power and grace which are so much his own. Technically, it was not a penalty, for the foul took place, by cunning intent, a few yards outside the box. Morally, it was a hundred times a penalty. As it was, Germany did nothing with the free kick, and crime emphatically paid, for the game

was won and lost in that moment. Italian critics would later blame
Schoen for his tactics and substitutions, but the turning point was
unquestionably the foul on Beckenbauer.

Extra time began well enough for Germany. Only five minutes had
gone when Poletti clumsily and anxiously ran the ball away from
Albertosi and almost over his own goal-line, for Muller to do, inevitably
and typically, the rest.

Now the goals came thick and fast; as though it were indeed basket-
ball. Tarcisio Burgnich, switched to centre-half, took a leaf out of
Schnellinger's book by appearing in the goalmouth to score after
Rivera's free kick on the left. Then Riva sharply pivoted to beat
Schnellinger and drive home a low, left-footed cross shot from outside
the box. So the first period ended with Italy again in the lead against a
Germany now without a sweeper, and with Beckenbauer crippled.

Germany, and especially Seeler, were nevertheless far from done
for. Once more, and at the same end, Seeler had a header saved by
Albertosi. This time, however, when the corner came over, he met it
on the far, left-hand post, nodded it across goal, and Muller flung
himself to head the equaliser; his tenth goal of a tournament in which
he would finish the leading scorer.

Six minutes of the second extra period had gone when Boninsegna
got away on the left, went to the line, pulled the ball accurately back
and little Rivera thumped it past Maier for the winner.

## The Final    Brazil v. Italy

So Brazil would play Italy in the Final; a meeting of two countries
each of which had won the World Cup twice, even if the *azzurri*'s last
victory lay thirty-two years in the past. Meanwhile there was the empty
ceremony of the third-place match, in which West Germany were
lucky to beat Uruguay 1–0. Wolfgang Overath, with his phenomenal
left foot, was the star of an otherwise indifferent afternoon, and it was
appropriate that he, and it, should score the only goal.

Brazil were so strongly favoured to win the Final that it was almost
a burden for them. True—despite the indications of that strange semi-
final—Italy had a strong, *catenaccio* defence. True, Burgnich and
Facchetti, the Inter full-backs, were veterans of innumerable hard
international matches for both club and country, even if the giant
Facchetti was hardly the overlapping force he had been, and might
find himself in trouble against Jairzinho. (Indeed he did; but not, as
we shall see, quite as was expected.)

What was perfectly plain was that the Italians could hope to win
only by playing as the Dr Jekyll of the quarter- and semi-finals, rather
than as the destructive Mr Hyde of the eliminators. There was talent

enough in midfield and up front. Riva had recovered his goal-scoring
flair, Boninsegna was in splendidly incisive form, and how many teams
in the world could afford the luxury of choosing between two such
marvellous inside-forwards as Mazzola and Rivera?

The Brazilian defence was there to be attacked; even if Peru, the
only team which had so far done so, had too porous a defence of their
own to succeed. Felix's deficiencies were manifest. Carlos Alberto, the
captain and right-back, was a great force when he was coming forward,
but very much less impressive when he was against a winger who would
take him on. Brito and Piazza could well be troubled by the thrust of
Boninsegna and Riva, backed up by the sinuous dribbling of Mazzola
or the winged passes of Rivera. As against that, Italy could scarcely
expect to have again the advantage of such inept and permissive
refereeing as one had seen from Señor Yamasaki, of Mexico and once
of Peru, in the semi-final.

No one put the realities of the situation more succinctly than Francis
Lee, who observed in Guadalajara: 'Against the Brazilians, you've got
to push up and play. If you let them come at you, you're asking for
trouble.'

Italy did let the Brazilians come at them, and trouble was inevitably what they got. For the game at large, however, the World Cup
Final was a marvellous affirmation of what could still be done with
attacking football, a splendid reassurance that cynicism, caution and
negativity had not, after all, gained a stranglehold on football. The
Brazilians won by playing beautifully, imaginatively and adven-
turously.

Pelé, who had sworn, after 1966, that he would never play in a
future World Cup, and had changed his mind, would soon announce
his retirement from all international football; but in this final he excelled himself. One might also call this match his apotheosis, such was
his skill, audacity and sheer effectiveness. He scored a magnificent goal,
he created two, evoking and fulfilling, in his second World Cup Final,
all the immense promise of his first, twelve years before.

Italy's tactics were not only drearily negative but also strangely
ineffectual; even in defence. They quickly switched Burgnich to centre-
back, but never began to get to grips with Gerson, or with Carlos
Alberto. Gerson, bewilderingly, was allowed infinite space and time in
midfield, which he used with grateful and devastating mastery.
Jairzinho, drawing Facchetti cunningly into the middle—Italy's man-
to-man marking was inflexible—thus gave Carlos Alberto equal scope
and leisure to advance down the empty right wing, for Italy were not
playing with a left-winger.

After eighteen minutes Brazil took the lead. Rivelino crossed a long,
high, unexceptional centre from the left; Pelé, being an exceptional

player, got up above the Italian defence with a spectacular jump, and headed in as powerfully as he had done in Stockholm.

Though Mazzola was running and dribbling superbly, the very soul of Italy's resistance, and Boninsegna was responding vigorously to his clever passes, Italy's tactics made it seem most unlikely they could save the game. They needed a gift; and suddenly, seven minutes from half-time, they got it. Clodoaldo, intoxicated, perhaps, by his new-found freedom of expression, stupidly back-heeled the ball deep in his own half, at once putting Boninsegna clear through and the rest of his defence on the wrong foot. As Boninsegna swept in from the right of the goal, Felix dashed out, in futile desperation, was passed in his turn, and Boninsegna put the ball into the unguarded net.

That was the moment at which Italy might well, had they only had the character and courage, have turned the game. Pelé, visiting Rome a couple of years later, expressed his astonishment and relief that they had not pressed home their psychological advantage against a Brazilian team momentarily demoralised. But they did not. In the second half Brazil, despite Mazzola's continued excellence, steadily regained the advantage, until, after sixty-six minutes, Gerson, the artificer turned bombardier, pivoted to hit a tremendous low, left-footed cross shot from outside the penalty box, to make it 2–1.

That was the end of Italy. Five minutes later, Gerson took a free kick, Pelé touched it skilfully to Jairzinho, and he, pelting into the goalmouth, ran the ball in on the left-hand post. Italy brought on Juliano for Bertini; then, six absurd minutes from the end, Rivera for . . . Boninsegna, surely the most mindless substitution of the tournament.

With so little time left, it was clearly all but impossible to save the game. Equally clearly, Valcareggi had been caught in a cleft stick over the Rivera-Mazzola duality. On this occasion it was quite unthinkable to take off Mazzola at the interval, so splendidly was he playing; at the same time, the non-appearance of Rivera would certainly inspire more sound and fury. Valcareggi's 'solution' was to put Rivera on in place of Boninsegna, the one Italian forward who, given the ineffectuality of Riva, seemed capable of scoring goals. So Brazil, three minutes from time, scored a fourth goal, in the way they had so often threatened. Jairzinho found Pelé, who laid the ball off immaculately to his right for Carlos Alberto to thunder on to it, and drive it past Albertosi.

The Brazilian jubilation afterwards was as spectacular and memorable as anything one had seen on the field: a joyful, dancing invasion of fans milling around their victorious players, pulling off their bright yellow shirts and hoisting them, bare to the waist, on to their shoulders. In this exuberance, this unconfined delight, one seemed to see a reflection of the way Brazil had played; and played was, indeed, the word. For all their dedication, all their passion, they and their country had somehow managed to remain aware that football was, after all, a game; something to be enjoyed.

So the Jules Rimet Trophy, won by them for the third time, went permanently to Brazil, who had shown that enterprise, fantasy, attacking play were still compatible with success; provided you had the talent. There could be no comparison with England's brave but ultimately sterile victory of 1966, a victory which had led only to myths of 'athletic football', 'work rate', the elevation of the labourer above the artist. It would take a couple of years for the new lesson to sink home in Europe, but sink it finally would.

Overall, despite the abominable conditions, the 1970 World Cup had been a marvellous triumph of the positive over the negative, the creative over the destructive. The Final itself took on the dimensions almost of an allegory.

# RESULTS: Mexico 1970

## Group I

Mexico 0, Russia 0 (HT 0/0)
Belgium 3, El Salvador 0 (HT 1/0)
Russia 4, Belgium 1 (HT 1/0)
Mexico 4, El Salvador 0 (HT 1/0)
Russia 2, El Salvador 0 (HT 0/0)
Mexico 1, Belgium 0 (HT 1/0)

|  | P | W | D | L | GOALS F | GOALS A | Pts |
|---|---|---|---|---|---|---|---|
| Russia | 3 | 2 | 1 | 0 | 6 | 1 | 5 |
| Mexico | 3 | 2 | 1 | 0 | 5 | 0 | 5 |
| Belgium | 3 | 1 | 0 | 2 | 4 | 5 | 2 |
| El Salvador | 3 | 0 | 0 | 3 | 0 | 9 | 0 |

## Group II

Uruguay 2, Israel 0 (HT 1/0)
Italy 1, Sweden 0 (HT 1/0)
Uruguay 0, Italy 0 (HT 0/0)
Sweden 1, Israel 1 (HT 0/0)
Sweden 1, Uruguay 0 (HT 0/0)
Italy 0, Israel 0 (HT 0/0)

|  | P | W | D | L | GOALS F | GOALS A | Pts |
|---|---|---|---|---|---|---|---|
| Italy | 3 | 1 | 2 | 0 | 1 | 0 | 4 |
| Uruguay | 3 | 1 | 1 | 1 | 2 | 1 | 3 |
| Sweden | 3 | 1 | 1 | 1 | 2 | 2 | 3 |
| Israel | 3 | 0 | 2 | 1 | 1 | 3 | 2 |

## Group III

England 1, Romania 0 (HT 0/0)
Brazil 4, Czechoslovakia 1 (HT 1/1)
Romania 2, Czechoslovakia 1 (HT 0/1)
Brazil 1, England 0 (HT 0/0)
Brazil 3, Romania 2 (HT 2/1)
England 1, Czechoslovakia 0 (HT 0/0)

|  | P | W | D | L | GOALS F | GOALS A | Pts |
|---|---|---|---|---|---|---|---|
| Brazil | 3 | 3 | 0 | 0 | 8 | 3 | 6 |
| England | 3 | 2 | 0 | 1 | 2 | 1 | 4 |
| Romania | 3 | 1 | 0 | 2 | 4 | 5 | 2 |
| Czechoslovakia | 3 | 0 | 0 | 3 | 2 | 7 | 0 |

## Group IV

Peru 3, Bulgaria 2 (HT 0/1)
West Germany 2, Morocco 1 (HT 0/1)
Peru 3, Morocco 0 (HT 0/0)
West Germany 5, Bulgaria 2 (HT 2/1)
West Germany 3, Peru 1 (HT 3/1)
Morocco 1, Bulgaria 1 (HT 1/0)

|  | P | W | D | L | GOALS F | GOALS A | Pts |
|---|---|---|---|---|---|---|---|
| West Germany | 3 | 3 | 0 | 0 | 10 | 4 | 6 |
| Peru | 3 | 2 | 0 | 1 | 7 | 5 | 4 |
| Bulgaria | 3 | 0 | 1 | 2 | 5 | 9 | 1 |
| Morocco | 3 | 0 | 1 | 2 | 2 | 6 | 1 |

## Quarter-finals

*Leon*

| **West Germany 3** | **England 2** |
|---|---|
| (after extra time) | |
| Maier; Schnellinger, | Bonetti; Newton; |
| Vogts, Hottges | Cooper; Mullery, |
| (Schulz); | Labone, Moore; Lee, |
| Beckenbauer, Overath, | Ball, Hurst, Charlton |
| Seeler; Libuda | (Bell), Peters (Hunter). |
| (Grabowski), Muller, | |
| Loehr. | |

SCORERS
Beckenbauer, Seeler, Muller for West Germany
Mullery, Peters for England
HT 0/1

*Guadalajara*

| **Brazil 4** | **Peru 2** |
|---|---|
| Felix; Carlos Alberto, | Rubiños; Campos, |
| Brito, Piazza, Marco | Fernandez, Chumpitaz, |
| Antonio; Clodoaldo, | Fuentes; Mifflin, Challe; |
| Gerson (Paulo Cesar); | Baylon (Sotil), Perico |
| Jairzinho (Roberto), | Leon (Eladio Reyes), |
| Tostao, Pelé, Rivelino. | Cubillas, Gallardo. |

SCORERS
Rivelino, Tostao (2), Jairzinho for Brazil
Gallardo, Cubillas for Peru
HT 2/1

| **Italy 4** | **Mexico 1** |
|---|---|
| Albertosi; Burgnich, | Calderon; Vantolra, |
| Cera, Rosato, | Pena, Guzman, Perez; |
| Facchetti; Bertini, | Gonzalez (Borja), |
| Mazzola (Rivera), | Pulido, Munguia |
| De Sisti; Domenghini | (Diaz); Valdivia, |
| (Gori), Boninsegna, | Fragoso, Padilla. |
| Riva. | |

SCORERS
Domenghini, Riva (2), Rivera for Italy
Gonzalez for Mexico
HT 1/1

| **Uruguay 1** | **Russia 0** |
|---|---|
| (after extra time) | |
| Mazurkiewicz; | Kavazashvili; |
| Ubinas, Ancheta, | Dzodzuashvili, Afonin, |
| Matosas, Mujica; | Khurtsilava (Logofet), |
| Maneiro, Cortes, | Chesternijev; Muntijan, |
| Montero Castillo; | Asatiani (Kiselev), |
| Cubilla, Fontes | Kaplichni; |
| (Gomez), Morales | Evriuzhkinzin, |
| (Esparrago). | Bychevetz, Khmelnitzki. |

SCORER
Esparrago for Uruguay
HT 0/0

## Semi-finals

| **Italy 4** | **West Germany 3** |
|---|---|
| (after extra time) | |
| Albertosi; Cera, | Maier; Schnellinger; |
| Burgnich, Rosato | Vogts, Schulz, |
| (Poletti), Facchetti; | Beckenbauer, Patzke |
| Domenghini, Mazzola | (Held); Seeler, Overath; |
| (Rivera), De Sisti; | Grabowski, Muller, |
| Boninsegna, Riva. | Loehr (Libuda). |

SCORERS
Boninsegna, Burgnich, Riva, Rivera for Italy
Schnellinger, Muller (2) for West Germany
HT 1/0

| **Brazil 3** | **Uruguay 1** |
|---|---|
| Felix; Carlos Alberto, | Mazurkiewicz; Ubinas, |
| Brito, Piazza, | Ancheta, Matosas, |
| Everaldo; Clodoaldo, | Mujica; Montero |
| Gerson; Jairzinho, | Castillo, Cortes, Fontes; |
| Tostao, Pelé, | Cubilla, Mancio |
| Rivelino. | (Esparrago), Morales. |

SCORERS
Clodoaldo, Jairzinho, Rivelino for Brazil
Cubilla for Uruguay
HT 1/1

## Third place match

| **West Germany 1** | **Uruguay 0** |
|---|---|
| Wolter; Schnellinger | Mazurkiewicz; Ubinas, |
| (Lorenz); Patzke, | Ancheta, Matosas, |
| Fichtel, Weber, Vogts; | Mujica; Montero |
| Seeler, Overath; | Castillo, Cortes, |
| Libuda (Loehr), | Fontes (Sandoval); |
| Muller, Held. | Cubilla, Maneiro |
| | (Esparrago), Morales. |

SCORER
Overath for West Germany
HT 1/0

## Final

| **Brazil 4** | **Italy 1** |
|---|---|
| Felix; Carlos Alberto, | Albertosi; Cera; |
| Brito, Piazza, | Burgnich, Bertini |
| Everaldo; Clodoaldo, | (Juliano), Rosato, |
| Gerson; Jairzinho, | Facchetti; Domenghini, |
| Tostao, Pelé, | Mazzola, De Sisti; |
| Rivelino. | Boninsegna (Rivera), |
| | Riva. |

SCORERS
Pelé, Gerson, Jairzinho, Carlos Alberto for Brazil
Boninsegna for Italy
HT 1/1

# West Germany
## 1974

## Introduction to West Germany

After twenty years, West Germany regained the World Cup and history further repeated itself in that they lost a game dramatically on the way. Dazzling in 1972, when they won the European Nations Cup with glorious panache, the West Germany of 1974 had passed their peak with the loss of Gunter Netzer. A sparkling star in Brussels, blond hair flying as he made his thrilling runs, huge boots distributing great, sweeping passes, curling diabolic free kicks, he had since gone to Madrid and lost his form.

Poland were the surprise. Having first—surprisingly—eliminated England, despite the loss of the brilliant Lubanski from their attack they grew in stature in the intervening months, and in the tournament itself. By the end of it, Lato, Deyna and Gadocha were recognised as three of the finest players in the world, and many thought that had their match against West Germany in Frankfurt been played in decent conditions, they would have reached the Final. As it was, they took a richly merited third place. These three teams showed, triumphantly, that attacking football still lived, still worked, could still prevail.

## The Contenders

Ironically, it was the Brazilians, always in the past the banner bearers of adventurous football, who now lived, precariously on their defence, to take a fourth place which flattered them. Predictably, Zagalo was bitterly blamed, just as he'd been eulogised in 1970, yet to an outsider it seemed once more essentially a question of personnel.

For a start, there was no Pelé; or rather, there was Pelé, but a Pelé who criticised, shook people's hands, and advanced the cause of Pepsi Cola, adamantly loyal to his decision not to play in another World Cup. All might have been well had not the loss of Pelé been compounded by that of three other splendid players. Tostao, whose recovery from a damaged retina to play in the 1970 World Cup had been a small miracle, was hurt again, and this time no miracle supervened. Gerson, of the sublime left foot, the forty-yard passes, the tremendous shots, was injured too and was to be found only on the periphery of the competition, smoking of course, wryly critical. As if this was not enough, on the very eve of the competition, the dynamic young Clodoaldo, who had grown and grown throughout the 1970 tournament, broke down on the preliminary tour of Switzerland and had to be withdrawn. João Saldanha, fearsome critic of Zagalo, blamed him for this as well, saying that *he*, when manager, had been aware of Clodoaldo's fragility, and had behaved accordingly. Such criticism seemed unfair, but Saldanha and the rest were on firmer ground when they blamed Zagalo—who after all was ultimately responsible—for the Brazilians' harsh defensive methods, methods which reached their peak, or their nadir, in the match in Dortmund against Holland.

It was the first World Cup England had entered and failed to reach the Finals. In retrospect, to be eliminated by so fine a side as Poland seems no disgrace, but this is *a posteriori* reasoning. I doubt if England could have made so dazzling a contribution as Poland to the tournament, yet it should be remembered that the Poland which beat England and the Poland which took their place were two very different propositions.

Had Poland not eliminated England, it seems doubtful that they would have taken wing. That they did so at all after losing Lubanski in the first match against England, in Katowice, was extraordinary for Lubanski had been recognised till then as their one player of undoubted world class. Yet with a more adventurous, flexible manager than Sir Alf Ramsey, eventually and somewhat clumsily dismissed the following April, England might have prevailed. He had badly misread the first Polish game. After promising to field an attacking team, he inexplicably left out his best front-running forward, Southampton's graceful Mike Channon, played a 4-4-2 formation which gave the initiative to Poland, and would not bring Channon on even when the Poles scored their second goal.

The following September, the Poles had their revenge on Wales in a bloodthirsty match in which old Cardiff scores were paid off, and things might have been a little different had the Welsh not had a perfectly valid-looking goal by Wyn Davies disallowed.

So England, who had lamentably failed to beat Wales at Wembley, had to beat Poland to survive. A misleading 7–0 win against an uncommitted Austrian team raised false hopes. In the event, England pressed for most of the evening but hadn't the wit to make many clear chances. The game was drawn 1–1, England were out; and so, after his one splendid success and eight years of anticlimax, was Ramsey.

## Total Football

This World Cup was the World Cup of Total Football; both finalists were famous for it. For a couple of years, the more sophisticated European critics had been saying that Total Football was the new reality, as persuasive and historically irresistible a phenomenon as, in turn, the W formation, 4-2-4 and 4-3-3.

The term itself was confusing and imprecise. What it meant, and means, was the kind of football played by the West German team which won the Nations Cup, and the Ajax team which had won the European Cup three times in a row, and would assuredly have made it four or five times had not Cruyff, the outstanding Dutch player, insisted on a transfer to Barcelona in the autumn of 1973. If one was briefly to describe it, one might call it *Dynamic Catenaccio*.

*Catenaccio* itself had been borrowed by the Italians from the Swiss and turned into something deeply negative, however effective. On the brink of the World Cup, the Italians themselves were among the favourites. Their *catenaccio* defence with its resolutely negative sweeper and with Dino Zoff an astonishing goalkeeper, unbeaten for almost 1,100 minutes, had given them a long, impressive and unbeaten run; and there was Riva to snap up goals, Rivera and Mazzola to construct them.

But the new football made the *libero*, or sweeper, no longer a defensive figure; he was a man who used his deep role as a kind of springboard or, if you wish, a secluded lair whence he could foray upfield. If any one player invented the new role of the new sweeper, it was unquestionably Franz Beckenbauer, who had persuaded first his club, Bayern Munich, then Helmut Schoen, manager of West Germany, to let him implement it. How wonderfully it had worked in the 1972 Nations Cup. Giacinto Facchetti of Inter had inspired Beckenbauer with his attacking full-back play. If a full-back could do it, thought Beckenbauer, then why not a central defender? So the attacking sweeper was born!

The implicit theory of Total Football was that anyone could do anything: forwards become defenders, defenders become forwards. In fact—ideally—there is no such thing as either; there are merely footballers, totally versatile, totally interchangeable. Ajax, under the Romanian coach, Stefan Kovacs, and West Germany had approached this aim, though an aim it remained. Holland's chances of encompassing it had plainly been limited by the loss of two key Ajax men— the powerful centre-half, Barry Hulshoff, always ready for a run upfield, and the vigorous left-side midfield player, Gerry Muhren. In the latter's place would play a footballer who, for all his talents, seemed the very embodiment of the older school; Wim Van Hanegem of Feyenoord, powerful and tall, a lovely striker of the ball with his left foot whether at goal or in passing, hard in the tackle, a fine creative forward, but unhurried, sometimes to the point of appearing static. In the event, he would emerge as one of the outstanding players of the World Cup.

### The Groups    Holland

Holland had qualified with extreme difficulty, held both at home and away by their traditional rivals, Belgium, to a goalless draw. Their players seemed mercenary and unintegrated; Ajax men just did not get on with Feyenoord men. Despite the excellence of both these clubs, each a European Cup winner, Holland had failed to reach the Nations Cup finals, and had not qualified for the World Cup Finals since 1938. In addition, their players seemed thoroughly mercenary, for ever agitating for more money, until at one point the forceful Rinus Michels, now manager of Barcelona, had apparently said that those not satisfied with the terms could stay behind.

Nevertheless, the Dutch players had obtained the promise of a king's ransom, and even then had threatened up to the last moments to strike. For all that, their performance had improved immensely and a fine 4–1 win over Argentina in May caused many, myself among them, to favour them. In terms of talent—Cruyff, Van Hanegem, the irrepressible Johan Neeskens, the dashing full-backs Suurbier and Krol—there was none to surpass them. Only in goal did there seem a lacuna, and this surprisingly, would be made good.

When the 34-year-old veteran Jan Jongbloed was called to the colours, he assumed he would be going to Germany merely as a reserve. But with the costly Van Beveren injured and Schrijvers, the second choice, in turn getting hurt, Jongbloed got his chance. Once again, Rinus Michels was proved wonderfully shrewd, for Jongbloed was just the goalkeeper Holland needed.

The lack of Hulshoff turned their defence into an alarmingly flimsy affair, with Aarie Haan, another highly gifted midfield player, pulled into defence as a putative sweeper, though if anything more of a centre-back, ever eager to go forward. In these circumstances, Holland brought Rijsbergen, the blond young Feyenoord stopper, into the back four, relied heavily and dangerously on offside, and were lucky to have in Jongbloed an adventurous keeper in the traditions of Grosics, ever ready to dash out of his area and save the day when the offside trap broke down.

## Scotland

If England were not present, Scotland were, for the first time since 1954. They had qualified thanks to an inspired evening at Hampden against Czechoslovakia the previous September, when their little manager Willie Ormond, himself once Scotland's left-winger, had brought Coventry's clever Tommy Hutchinson into the team for his first cap at outside-left and the long legged Hutchinson had taken wing. Goals headed by the big, controversially rugged, Manchester United centre-half Jim Holton, and the young Leeds centre-forward Joe Jordan, had wiped out a soft, potentially demoralising goal by Nehoda, to give Scotland victory and put them through. The Czechs paid very dearly for having lost a point to Denmark.

Billy Bremner, the galvanic little Leeds right-half and captain, a player whose temperament did not belie his red hair, had played superbly that night but he was now thirty-two, had an infinite number of hard matches under his belt and had been very much in the wars on Scotland's ill-fated tour before the competition. Deputed to conduct the team's commercial negotiations, a job he never did for Leeds, he had been involved in a series of squabbles and was concerned with Celtic's wayward celebrated winger Jimmy Johnstone, who had drifted out to sea in a boat at Largs after the win against Czechoslovakia, in an incident in Oslo.

Both turned up late in the bar of the Panorama Hotel—not so much a hotel as a mere students' complex—and were eventually ordered to their rooms by Ormond. It was not the first nor the worst such incident that season. Some of the Scottish officials wanted to pack both men home, but Ormond pleaded successfully for them; and Bremner rewarded him by becoming one of the outstanding figures of the World Cup, winning the praise of Pelé himself.

Scotland had fallen in the same tough group as Brazil and Yugoslavia, skilfully managed by Miljan Miljanic but disappointing in their recent 2–2 draw at home to England. The team that day had tired and Dragan Dzajic, its left-winger and most celebrated star, had still to regain full form after more than a year in the Army. Nevertheless, with inside-forwards such as the sturdy little pair of Karasi and Acimovic, backed by the muscular Oblak and the dashes of the tall Bogicevic from defence, the Yugoslavs looked formidable, and they had an exceptional goalkeeper in Maric.

## The Outsiders

The fourth team was Zaire, with Australia and Haiti, the remotest outsiders of the competition. Like Morocco, their predecessors as winners of the African group, they were coached by the tall Yugoslav Vidinic, himself once his country's goalkeeper. They had fine individualists, had done well in Africa, but it was already clear from their performance in the recent African Nations Cup and from a mediocre tour of Europe that little was to be expected from them.

The Haitians, who figured in the Munich group with Italy, Argentina and Poland, were lucky to be there at all. Benefiting enormously as it was from being able to stage the whole of their CONCACAF qualifying competition, they had benefited in a still more particular way in their match with Trinidad when no fewer than four goals were disallowed to the visitors by the subsequently suspended El Salvadorian referee, Enriquez.

### Argentina

For Argentina, still more than for West Germany, whom they had impressively beaten the previous season, the World Cup had not come at the right time. On that European tour, Argentina had played some splendid football in their most classical style, and had shocked the Germans by defeating them in Munich itself. But since then Omar Sivori, as volatile a manager as he was a player, had been dismissed. His successor was the much milder, amiable, red-headed Cap, nick-named *el Polaco* for his Polish origin—less explosive, but also less inspiring.

Talent was not lacking. The thick-thighed, heavily moustached Ayala, hair hanging almost to his waist, had had a fine season with Atletico Madrid, and established himself as one of the most dangerous forwards in Europe, much faster than the traditional Argentinian attacker, possessed of fabulous control at speed and great incisiveness. But Miguel Brindisi, the midfield inside-right and supposed star of the team, whom Peron had given a medal for staying at home despite the blandishments of foreign clubs, had been a disappointment.

Fortunately there was time to call up Carlos Babington, Brindisi's fair-haired partner in the Huracan midfield. Surprisingly omitted from the original party, Babington—who had nearly joined Stoke on the basis of his English ancestry—was so pleased that he slept in his international shirt. He was to play stupendously against the Italians.

For the first time, the competition had adopted a new debatable formula, abolishing the system of quarter- and semi-finals. Now, the first- and second-placed teams in the four original qualifying groups would enter two final pools of four teams each, whose winners would contest the Final, while the second in each group would play what again transpired to be the dull and quite meaningless Third Place Match.

In the event, the plan worked better than one might have expected. This time it would not lead to any increase of defensive football in the second stage.

### Opening Stages

The chief criticism of the way the World Cup was organised lay rather in its preliminary phases. Failure to de-zone the qualifying competition allowed teams from the weaker areas a relatively easy passage, and the decision to make one South American and one European group winner play-off for a place in the finals was bitterly unfair to both. Eventually, it was Russia and Chile who were obliged to meet, and they met only once, drawing 0–0 in Moscow.

At this, the Russians suddenly developed an attack of principle, refusing on political grounds to play the return in the national stadium at Santiago, where left-wing prisoners had been shot. Their protest would have looked better had it been made before the initial match. FIFA sent a committee of inquiry to Chile and would have been prepared to have the match elsewhere in Chile, but the Russians refused and there was no alternative but to rule them out.

The tournament began with its customary anticlimax: a goalless draw in Frankfurt between Brazil and Yugoslavia. But at least there were no violent incidents. Nor would there be throughout the tournament. Forewarned by the brutal terrorist murders of the Israeli athletes at the Olympic Games, West German security this time was of a military thoroughness with tanks on the tarmac of the airports, endless searches of the passengers and armed police around and within the stadia.

Yugoslavia had the better of the argument in Frankfurt. Free kicks by the inevitable Rivelino and a newcomer, the blond, attacking left-back Francisco Marinho, proper successor to Nilton Santos, were Brazil's chief threat. Acimovic, when Oblak pulled the ball back from the goal line, and Katalinski, with a muscular header, very nearly scored for the Slavs. What was sharply apparent was Brazil's lack of a centre-forward, a Tostao, a Vavà. Jairzinho, forced to play there, would clearly have been happier on the wing.

And so we were off, with the competition starting in earnest the next day. In Berlin, where the Chilean left-wingers demonstrated on the terraces, West Germany made terribly hard work of beating Chile. A tremendous long shot by Paul Breitner, their long-legged, woolly-haired full-back, that paradox, a rich Bavarian Maoist, won them the day against a clever, compact team. Figueroa and Quintano were like rocks in the middle, Caszely—most disputably sent off—and Reinoso fiery in attack. The German defence, especially Schwarzenbeck, looked oddly vulnerable at times. It was an unimpressive start and Wolfgang Overath, recalled to play in his third World Cup, hardly looked a fit substitute for Netzer.

In Hamburg the East Germans were scarcely more impressive, finding Australia a tough nut to crack. Australia's team, made up almost entirely of immigrants, well coached by the Yugoslav Rale Rasic, would prove far the best of the three outsiders.

Not that the Haitians began badly; they surpassed themselves against Italy in Munich, where Sanon, their centre-forward, soon after half-time, made monkeys of the Italian defenders and became the first man to beat Zoff in the Italy goal for 1,147 minutes of international football. Painfully the Italians pulled themselves together to win the match 3–1, but the happy Haitians were the heroes of the day and next morning in the sunshine they strolled about the Munich zoo beaming their satisfaction, none more than their fine goalkeeper, Francillon. Alas, there were clouds on the horizon.

Scarcely had the Haitians ceased rejoicing than a thunderbolt struck them. A dope test on Ernst Jean-Joseph, their red-haired, mulatto centre-half had proved positive. Jean-Joseph protested that he had to take pills for his asthma. The team's French doctor, with ruthless impartiality, told a Press conference that this was nonsense—that Jean-Joseph was not intelligent enough to know what he was doing.

For a day or two the melancholy Jean-Joseph was to be found hanging wretchedly around the lobby of the Penta Hotel. Then Haitian officials dragged him, tearful, out of the Grunwald Sports School where the team was staying, beat him, shoved him into a car and kept him incommunicado in a room at the Sheraton Hotel, flying him back to Haiti the next morning.

The terrified Jean-Joseph made several telephone calls to a sympathetic Polish Press hostess. The plump and humane Herr Kurt Renner, attaché to the Haitian team, was unable to sleep all night and told the whole grim story to the Press. Significantly, the World Cup Organising Committee was incensed not with the Haitians but with these two, removing Herr Renner from his post, threatening to dismiss the hostess. Small wonder that Haiti should in the meantime be thrashed by Poland, then comfortably beaten by Argentina.

Argentina needed those points and the four goals they scored to qualify. They, too, had had a troubled time in camp: a player accused of assaulting a chambermaid, journalists sharply critical of the officials. They had lost their opening match, in Stuttgart, to Poland, partly thanks to a couple of sad errors by the otherwise good goalkeeper, Carnevali, and to a bizarre defensive formation. Perfumo played as sweeper behind a line of three backs, risky enough in itself and positively suicidal given the vulnerability of Perfumo, who needed Bargas playing bang in front of him, rather than in an indeterminate role in midfield.

Had the tall, nineteen-year-old centre-forward, Kempes, scored when admirably sent through by Brindisi in the opening minutes, all might have been different. But he missed, Poland scored twice in the seventh minute, and the die was cast. First Gadocha, Poland's devastatingly fast and incisive left-winger, took a corner. Carnevali dropped it, Lato put it in. Then Lato utterly split Argentina's square defence with a through pass and Poland's latest ace in the hole, the 22-year-old Szarmach, ran on to score.

In the second half Argentina took off Brindisi, ill at ease as a striker, and introduced a player who at once transformed them and who was to become one of the toasts of the tournament: René Houseman, a tiny winger, brave, serpentine and fast; socks worn scornfully round his ankles. Heredia scored after fifty-five minutes but when Carnevali's careless throw went straight to Lato, who tore through to score, that was clearly that, though Babington did score, after hitting the post of an open goal.

Next, on the same ground, Argentina and Italy; a match that was a nightmare and a humiliation for the Italians in everything but the score. Quite what possessed Valcareggi, the Italian manager, to assume that Houseman, of all people, was going to play in midfield, and to set his own creative inside-forward, Fabio Capello, to mark him, heaven knows.

At all events Capello, turned by this error into a full-back, was run ragged by Houseman, who scored a lovely goal from a pass by Babington, who bestrode the field, calmly impeccable. Too late Valcareggi understood what was happening, pushed Capello upfield and set the ruthless Benetti to mark Houseman, who ran him ragged as well, unintimidated by his brutal tackling. Alas for Argentina, moral victors on the day, Italy equalised when Perfumo turned Benetti's cross past his own goalkeeper, but it had been inspiriting to see Argentina, in both matches, throw off the over-compensatory chains of defensive football and play as they can and should.

Italy now had to play the Poles and draw with them to survive. Changes were made. Rivera had been played out of the game with contemptuous facility by the cool, experienced Telch. He was dropped, claiming he had been made scapegoat. Mazzola, the best and bravest Italian forward, stayed. Riva, as inept as Rivera, went too. If he had been a disappointment in his first World Cup, he had been a disaster in his second; and who would score goals for Italy if not he?

## Poland

Poland won 2–1, again in Stuttgart, but though Italy might have had a penalty, they were in fact overwhelmed. Fine crosses by Kasperczak, a splendid foil to Deyna in midfield, gave spectacular goals first to Szarmach with a header then to Deyna himself with a superb volley. Capello's late goal for Italy was no consolation. The Italians donned their customary sackcloth and ashes, swore to play with dynamic rather than static sweepers, to make their players run harder in training and, as always, did nothing, the wish substituting for the deed.

## West Germany

In Group I, the West Germans' wheels still would not go round. They made very heavy weather of beating the brave Australians at Hamburg, where the crowd exchanged insults with Beckenbauer and Australia might have scored twice. Rasic, with justice, said he thought little of the German defence. In West Berlin, the resourceful Chileans, though without Caszely, whose goals had taken them to the Finals, held East Germany to a draw.

So in Hamburg, on June 22, the summit encounter took place: the first meeting ever between the two Germanies. Security was all enveloping; guns to be seen everywhere, a helicopter circling the ground. Had there not been a threat that a SAM rocket would be launched at it?

None was; the only, cataclysmic, surprise came in the shape of the result, and the goal by Jurgen Sparwasser eight minutes from time. Reversing their policy of the first two matches, East Germany abandoned attack for their more accustomed counter-attack, with Bransch a resourceful sweeper, Sparwasser moving from midfield into a two-man attack with the young Hoffmann.

Twice in the first half West Germany might have scored when Gerd Muller, that astonishing opportunist, twisted past Weise, once making a chance for Grabowski, once hitting the post. But Kreische of East Germany missed a sitter. Lauck too had a chance and though West Germany dominated second-half play, it was East Germany who scored. Hamann sent Sparwasser down the right; the dark, powerful Magdeburg forward thrust his way past Vogts, shot past Maier, and the game was won.

In retrospect, there is no doubt that it was a blessing in disguise for West Germany. Defeat meant that they played in an easier group, avoiding Holland, and caused them to remodel their team, bringing the driving Rainer Bonhof of Munchengladbach into midfield.

Meanwhile, poor Helmut Schoen became the butt of a sour and disappointed public. Schoen, one heard, was no manager, an opinion quite happily advanced with another: that Beckenbauer was running the team. Certainly there had been dissidence. The West Germany players, like the Dutch, had made intransigent demands before the tournaments, so much so that their Federation had threatened to pack them off home and play the reserves in their place.

## Holland

The Dutch, meanwhile, were enchanting everybody, not only with their play but with the free-and-easy atmosphere of their training camp at Hiltrup, where wives and girl friends were allowed for one sunlit, cheerful day.

In their first match, at Hanover, they easily dispatched the Uruguayans, who were astonishingly poor, having little to offer but ruthlessness. Even this was ineffectual: they failed to kick the tormentingly elusive Cruyff, they had Montero Castillo sent off for punching Rensenbrink in the stomach, though Forlan was a much more serious offender.

Yet the Swedes, who had beaten Austria in a play-off to qualify, surprised the Dutch by holding them 0–0 in their next game. With nothing to lose, Sweden approached the tournament in a spirit at once relaxed, generous and determined. In Sandberg and the tall, slender Ralf Edstroem, they had a fine pair of forwards who had scored thirty-two goals between them for Atvidaberg the season before they left Sweden for pastures new, and in Nordqvist a resilient veteran at centre-half. In goal the blond Ronnie Hellstroem excelled himself, so much so as to regret the unexceptional contract he had signed with the Bundesliga's Kaiserslautern before the tournament.

The draw with Sweden illustrated Holland's lack of a finisher to exploit the amazing virtuosity of Cruyff and the fact that his old colleague and rival of Ajax days, Piet Keizer, was now over the hill as a left-winger. The lively Rensenbrink displaced him in their third match, against Bulgaria, who simply had no answer to the galvanic Cruyff, whirling past them at will, his pace, his passing and his finishing alike irresistible. Neeskens, breaking frequently and furiously into attack, scored twice from penalties.

## Early Matches

For Scotland it was a World Cup of anticlimax; unbeaten alone among the sixteen teams, they yet failed to qualify for the second round.

Much of this was their own fault. Bravely though they played against Brazil, resourcefully against Yugoslavia, they were absurdly cautious in their first match against the chopping block, Zaire, against whom they needed an avalanche of goals. They got only two. 'Let's face it,' said their centre-half, Jim Holton, 'we underestimated them. For fifteen minutes I wondered what the hell was going on, where the devil had this lot come from, playing stuff like that.' At last Scotland got hold of the game, Lorimer's mighty right foot shot a spectacular goal from Jordan's header, Jordan headed another from Bremner's free kick. But in the last twenty minutes, Scotland unwisely relaxed, troubled by the heat, a mistake which would cost them qualification.

Bremner himself never stopped in the next game, at Frankfurt, against Brazil. For the first twenty minutes, Brazil played probably their best football of the tournament, football for which Scotland's defence did not seem tactically briefed. But Bremner was able, with his example and his encouragement, to revive the Scots, who finished the better team and three times might have scored in the second half through Bremner and his club mates, Jordan and Lorimer.

This left Scotland on three points, Brazil on two, but since Brazil were bound to beat Zaire, who had crashed 9–0 to Yugoslavia, Scotland knew they had to beat the Slavs. Alas, they hadn't the attack to do so. Indeed, lack of commitment to attack was their undoing. Not enough was risked, while in the midfield, Kenny Dalglish, of Celtic, greatly disappointing, survived when he should have been replaced.

Permissive refereeing by a Turk did not help Scotland in the heat of Frankfurt, and they fell a goal behind when Dzajic, on the right, cleverly spun past his man and centred, for Karasi to head past the resilient David Harvey. Scotland vigorously fought back, a corkscrew run by Hutchinson, who had belatedly substituted for Dalglish, brought the equaliser for Joe Jordan, but it was not enough. Brazil beat Zaire 3–0, the third and deciding goal by Valdomiro rolling under the goalkeeper's body; and the Scots were out, though with considerable credit.

## The Surviving Groups

The two surviving groups were composed, respectively, of Holland, Brazil, Argentina and East Germany, and West Germany, Poland, Yugoslavia and Sweden.

It was quickly clear that the East Germans had shot their bolt. In Hanover they lost their opening match against Brazil to a second-half goal by Rivelino, inevitably from a free kick. Jairzinho stood on the end of the East German 'wall' and ducked as Rivelino's shot swerved wickedly in.

Argentina, alas, had to play Holland without Babington, who had mindlessly handled the ball deliberately not once but twice in the Italian game. He thus acquired three cautions and was rendered ineligible. Any chance Argentina might have had of containing the brilliant Dutch was lost. They were simply overrun; a dreadful foul by Perfumo on Neeskens was the measure of his and his team's frustration. Heavy rain in the second half was the saviour of Argentina, who would probably have lost still more heavily than 4–0. The electric Cruyff scored two of the goals himself, and made a headed goal for Johnny Rep.

In their next game—again at Gelsenkirchen—Cruyff found himself diligently marked by Weise, but Rensenbrink made a left-footed goal for Neeskens after nine minutes, scored a second himself, and Holland now faced Brazil, the holders, in the decisive match.

The Brazilians had beaten Argentina 2–1 in an all-South-American match at Hanover, the first time these famous rivals had ever met in the World Cup. Their decisive match, at Dortmund, was a sorry affair, redeemed by Holland's two marvellous winning goals in the second half. The Brazilian defence kicked, chopped and hacked from the first; and it must be said that the Dutch, thus provoked, returned the treatment with interest. Twice Brazil should have scored when the Dutch offside trap broke down, but first Paulo Cesar, then Jairzinho, missed palpable chances.

In the first half, Neeskens was knocked cold by Mario Marinho. In the second, he was scythed down by Luis Pereira, who was sent off by the unimpressive West German referee, Herr Tschenscher. Pereira could have no complaints, yet he had undeniably been one of the best defenders in the tournament; a tall, strong, mobile Negro of impressive authority.

Holland's goals redeemed the game, marvellous in their lightning simplicity. First Neeskens dashed down the middle, found Cruyff on the right and lobbed the swift, immaculate return over Leao's head, then Cruyff superbly volleyed home Krol's left-wing centre. Holland were in the Final.

The West Germans made heavier weather of it; and weather, indeed, was at the root of their victory over Poland. The weather was bad, though not as bad, in their exciting match against Sweden in Dusseldorf when Edstroem—a gorgeous volley—and Sandberg scored splendid goals, but West Germany's power, Bonhof rampant, eventually wore down the Swedish defence.

In their opening game West Germany, in Dusseldorf, had resumed their long World Cup dialogue with Yugoslavia. Dzajic, it was said, was displeased with Miljanic's defensive tactics. West Germany dominated play. Another of Paul Breitner's fulminating drives gave them the lead, after thirty-eight minutes and Muller scored the second after the blond, 22-year-old Uli Hoeness, at last showing his true ability, had got to the line and crossed. Franz Beckenbauer, at last, was in majestic form.

The Poles also won their first two games, but with little to spare. They were very lucky to get the better of Sweden, who overplayed them in the opening stages, shrewdly prompted by Grahn and Larsson in midfield, when Tapper and Grahn missed easy chances. In the second half, Tapper also missed a penalty, though Tomaszewski probably moved before the kick. So it was that Lato in the first half got the only goal; a cross by Gadocha, goal maker now rather than scorer, a header by Szarmach, another by Lato.

Then Poland beat Yugoslavia in Frankfurt, but might not have done so had Karasi not lost his head and felled Szarmach, who had been shoving him. Deyna opened the score from the penalty spot, Karasi atoned by whirling through the Polish defence to equalise, but the Lato–Gadocha combination again brought victory—Gadocha's corner, Lato's near-post header. Yugoslavia, though were without Dzajic.

Thus the decisive game was that between the Poles and West Germans in Frankfurt. A rainstorm made the pitch unplayable, but the Germans drew off the water as best they could, postponed the start and played. They won thanks to their superior strength. Yet only a staggering double save by Maier in the first half from—inevitably— first Lato, then Gadocha kept the German goal intact. In the second half, Tomaszewski saved another penalty, from Hoeness. The winning goal came when Hoeness's shot was deflected to 'The Bomber', Gerd Muller, who does not miss such chances.

## The Final   West Germany v. Holland

So the Final, very properly as it seemed, would be between West Germany and Holland. West Germany had home advantage, Holland had the more imagination. It was hard not to polarise the contest into one of personalities; Beckenbauer against Cruyff, unquestionably the game's greatest players now Pelé had gone.

So far, Cruyff had plainly surpassed Beckenbauer on the field. Though he himself denied that he was particularly fast, insisting that it was a matter of *when* he accelerated, what fascinated the observer was not only his originality, but his amazing speed of thought and execution. Muller might be the goal-scoring machine *par excellence*, still deadly, despite those who felt he had passed his peak, but Cruyff was immensely more versatile, capable of roaming the field like his idol, Di Stefano, now goal maker, now scorer, slim, long legged, almost gawky, yet superbly elegant in motion.

Who would mark him? Udo Lattek, Bayern's manager, said, 'I know that Bonhof will kill Cruyff.' The general view, however, was that he would be marked (as he was) by Berti Vogts, the tenacious blond full-back, who had once, long ago, played him out of the game in a youth tournament.

What seemed clear to some of us was that the Dutch would need to score a minimum of three goals since their inadequate defence seemed almost certain to concede a couple. Could they get them? The answer to that seemed implicit in another question: could the Germans stop Cruyff?

On the previous day, Poland won a deadly dull Third Place Match against Brazil, jeered by a justifiably disappointed crowd; Lato, predictably, was the scorer. Ademir Da Guia, the blond mulatto, son of Domingas Da Guia who had played in the 1938 tournament, at last got a World Cup game and strolled shrewdly about before he was substituted, personifying a Brazilian school which was now hopelessly outmoded, as Deyna's immensely quicker, more effective, performance in the Polish midfield showed.

No World Cup Final has had such a sensational beginning as this: a penalty awarded, a goal scored, virtually before a German player had touched the ball. Holland kicked off and played almost insolent possession football, to the incensed whistling of the crowd, then suddenly and convulsively broke away. Cruyff, who had dropped behind the forward line, began a long, almost breathtakingly ambitious run, swerved round Vogts as though he wasn't there, raced on into the penalty area and there was tripped by the desperate leg of Hoeness. Penalty.

Neeskens, of course, took it, banging his right-footed shot between Maier and the right-hand post as Maier moved to the left.

It was a vibrantly dramatic moment and one which seemed so sure to decide the match, whatever one may now say with hindsight, that the Dutch were tempted to relax, moved to play cat and mouse with an opponent which, for historical reasons, they longed to humiliate. For twenty-five minutes the Dutch did as they pleased against a stunned German team, rolling the ball about, making pretty patterns, but creating no real opportunities. Dangerous indulgence against a host team; and so it was that West Germany got off the hook—with another penalty.

Young Holzenbein, a left-winger who, like Bonhof, had come into the team only with the second stage, took chief credit for the goal. Taking a neat pass from Overath, he set off up the wing, Breitner running inside him, scorned the easy option, cut into the penalty area, beat his man and was tripped by Jansen. Breitner, full of confidence, scored from the penalty and the tide had turned.

West Germany now exultantly carried the fight to Holland; even Vogts left Cruyff, whom he was now playing so effectively, to put in a searing shot, which Jongbloed saved one-handed. Then Hoeness, devastating in his long controlled runs and sudden bursts, had beaten Suurbier and rolled the ball past Jongbloed for the excellent Rijsbergen to kick out of the goalmouth. Beckenbauer's was the next attempt, a cunning lob from a free kick, which Jongbloed clawed over the bar.

Yet the decisive moment surely came when Holland broke away and caught the West German defence hopelessly undermanned, so much so that Cruyff and Rep together descended on Beckenbauer. Cruyff did everything he should, drawing his famous rival, then giving the ball sweetly to Rep. But Rep hadn't the skill to score; Maier saved boldly at his feet and, were we to know it, Holland had lost the Cup.

After forty-three minutes, the Dutch defence wilted again and Gerd Muller scored his sixty-eighth goal for West Germany; the most important of them all.

Grabowski began the movement with a pass up the right to Bonhof, whose speed and power took him past Haan on the outside. Hulshoff would no doubt have stopped him, but Hulshoff wasn't there and when the ball came over, Muller contrived to drag it back into his path with one foot and sweep it past Jongbloed with the other.

In the second half Holland had to substitute Rensenbrink, whose pulled muscle had made him doubtful initially and had clearly handi-capped him and his team. Van de Kerkhof, the tall young forward who replaced him, would almost give Holland the equaliser when his long, straightforward cross from the left looped over all the German defence, and was ferociously met on the volley by Neeskens on the far post. Somehow Maier managed to block it.

Rijsbergen, too, hurt in a tackle by Muller in the first half, had to go off, giving way to De Jong, little Jansen dropping into the back four to look after Muller. When he brought down Holzenbein for the second time in the game, there might have been another penalty, while film has seemed to show that Muller was not offside when he ran through the Dutch defence to beat Jongbloed. For all that, Jack Taylor, the English referee, made a fine fist of the match and was very brave to give that first-minute penalty while Holland themselves scarcely deserved to lose more heavily.

So West Germany won the Cup in one of the most enigmatic of all Finals. Was Holland's penalty a poisoned gift? Would they have done better without it? Was Rensenbrink's injury decisive? All one could say with certainty was that it had been an immeasurably more drama-tic Final than 1970's and that if West Germany had taken the Cup then Holland, surely had been the most attractive and talented of all losers.

# RESULTS: West Germany 1974

## Group I

West Germany 1, Chile 0 (HT 0/0)
East Germany 2, Australia 0 (HT 0/0)
West Germany 3, Australia 0 (HT 2/0)
East Germany 1, Chile 1 (HT 0/0)
East Germany 1, West Germany 0 (HT 1/0)
Chile 0, Australia 0 (HT 0/0)

|  | P | W | D | L | GOALS F | GOALS A | Pts |
|---|---|---|---|---|---|---|---|
| East Germany | 3 | 2 | 1 | 0 | 4 | 1 | 5 |
| West Germany | 3 | 2 | 0 | 1 | 4 | 1 | 4 |
| Chile | 3 | 0 | 2 | 1 | 1 | 2 | 1 |
| Australia | 3 | 0 | 1 | 2 | 0 | 5 | 1 |

## Group II

Brazil 0, Yugoslavia 0 (HT 0/0)
Scotland 2, Zaire 0 (HT 2/0)
Brazil 0, Scotland 0 (HT 0/0)
Yugoslavia 9, Zaire 0 (HT 6/0)
Scotland 1, Yugoslavia 1 (HT 0/0)
Brazil 3, Zaire 0 (HT 1/0)

|  | P | W | D | L | GOALS F | GOALS A | Pts |
|---|---|---|---|---|---|---|---|
| Yugoslavia | 3 | 1 | 2 | 0 | 10 | 1 | 4 |
| Brazil | 3 | 1 | 2 | 0 | 3 | 0 | 4 |
| Scotland | 3 | 1 | 2 | 0 | 3 | 1 | 4 |
| Zaire | 3 | 0 | 0 | 3 | 0 | 14 | 0 |

## Group III

Holland 2, Uruguay 0 (HT 1/0)
Sweden 0, Bulgaria 0 (HT 0/0)
Holland 0, Sweden 0 (HT 0/0)
Bulgaria 1, Uruguay 1 (HT 0/0)
Holland 4, Bulgaria 1 (HT 2/0)
Sweden 3, Uruguay 0 (HT 0/0)

|  | P | W | D | L | GOALS F | GOALS A | Pts |
|---|---|---|---|---|---|---|---|
| Holland | 3 | 2 | 1 | 0 | 6 | 1 | 5 |
| Sweden | 3 | 1 | 2 | 0 | 3 | 0 | 4 |
| Bulgaria | 3 | 0 | 2 | 1 | 2 | 5 | 2 |
| Uruguay | 3 | 0 | 1 | 2 | 1 | 6 | 1 |

## Group IV

Italy 3, Haiti 1 (HT 0/0)
Poland 3, Argentina 2 (HT 2/0)
Italy 1, Argentina 1 (HT 1/1)
Poland 7, Haiti 0 (HT 5/0)
Argentina 4, Haiti 1 (HT 2/0)
Poland 2, Italy 1 (HT 2/0)

|  | P | W | D | L | GOALS F | GOALS A | Pts |
|---|---|---|---|---|---|---|---|
| Poland | 3 | 3 | 0 | 0 | 12 | 3 | 6 |
| Argentina | 3 | 1 | 1 | 1 | 7 | 5 | 3 |
| Italy | 3 | 1 | 1 | 1 | 5 | 4 | 3 |
| Haiti | 3 | 0 | 0 | 3 | 2 | 14 | 0 |

## Group A

Brazil 1, East Germany 0 (HT 0/0)
Holland 4, Argentina 0 (HT 2/0)
Holland 2, East Germany 0 (HT 1/0)
Brazil 2, Argentina 1 (HT 1/1)
Holland 2, Brazil 0 (HT 0/0)
Argentina 1, East Germany 1 (HT 1/1)

|  | P | W | D | L | GOALS F | GOALS A | Pts |
|---|---|---|---|---|---|---|---|
| Holland | 3 | 3 | 0 | 0 | 8 | 0 | 6 |
| Brazil | 3 | 2 | 0 | 1 | 3 | 3 | 4 |
| East Germany | 3 | 0 | 1 | 2 | 1 | 4 | 1 |
| Argentina | 3 | 0 | 1 | 2 | 2 | 7 | 1 |

## Group B

Poland 1, Sweden 0 (HT 1/0)
West Germany 2, Yugoslavia 0 (HT 1/0)
Poland 2, Yugoslavia 1 (HT 1/1)
West Germany 4, Sweden 2 (HT 0/1)
Sweden 2, Yugoslavia 1 (HT 0/0)
West Germany 1, Poland 0 (HT 0/0)

|  | P | W | D | L | GOALS F | GOALS A | Pts |
|---|---|---|---|---|---|---|---|
| West Germany | 3 | 3 | 0 | 0 | 7 | 2 | 6 |
| Poland | 3 | 2 | 0 | 1 | 3 | 2 | 4 |
| Sweden | 3 | 1 | 0 | 2 | 4 | 6 | 2 |
| Yugoslavia | 3 | 0 | 0 | 3 | 2 | 6 | 2 |

## Third place match

*Munich*

---

**Poland 1**
Tomaszewski;
Szymanowski,
Gorgon, Zmuda,
Musial; Kasperczak
(Cmikiewicz), Deyna,
Masczyk; Lato,
Szarmach (Kapka),
Gadocha.

**Brazil 0**
Leao; Ze Maria,
Alfredo, Marinho, M.,
Marinho, F.; Paulo
Cesar Carpeggiani,
Rivelino, Ademir da
Guia (Mirandinha);
Valdomiro, Jairzinho,
Dirceu.

SCORER
Lato for Poland
HT 0/0

## Final

*Munich*

---

**West Germany 2**
Maier; Beckenbauer;
Vogts, Schwarzenbeck,
Dreitner, Bonhof,
Hoeness, Overath;
Grabowski, Muller,
Holzenbein.

**Holland 1**
Jongbloed; Suurbier,
Rijsbergen, (De Jong),
Haan, Krol; Jansen,
Neeskens, Van
Hanegem; Rep,
Cruyff, Rensenbrink
(Van de Kerkhof, R.).

SCORERS
Breitner (penalty), Muller for West Germany
Neeskens (penalty) for Holland
HT 2/1

# Argentina
## 1978

## Fears About Argentina

The 1978 World Cup, though altogether less disastrous in actuality than it was in prospect, nevertheless left behind it a sour taste and a welter of controversy. Ecstasy and euphoria greeted Argentina's triumph within Argentina itself. Elsewhere, there was less elation. As the defeated Dutch bitterly said, it's unlikely that Argentina's team could have won the tournament anywhere but at home. Giovanni Trapattoni, manager of Turin's Juventus club, who attended the tournament, went even further. He believed that elsewhere Argentina would not even have survived the first round.

There were good reasons for such scepticism, good reasons for disappointment in a tournament whose level did not remotely approach that of 1974, whose Final was an ill-tempered, abominably refereed game, and whose whole course was marred and scarred by questionable refereeing.

Such feelings were given special pungency by the nature of Argentina's regime: a military dictatorship, its junta led by General Jorge Videla. For more than a year before the World Cup matches began, great opposition was expressed, above all in Western Europe and particularly by the Amnesty International organisation, to the holding of the Cup in Argentina. Since the junta took power in 1976, thousands of people had disappeared, thousands had been murdered and tortured. The moral aspect aside, there was the question of whether the safety of players could be guaranteed. West Germany in 1974, with the threat of the Arab terrorists, had been bad enough. In Argentina the threat came from within. There were serious doubts, moreover about whether stadia and communications would be ready in time. The previous, Peronist, Government had dragged its feet. The military junta had set up a new body, the Ente Autarquico Mundial, to speed proceedings but its task was monumental. Moreover its chief, General Omar Actis, had been assassinated en route to his first Press conference.

There were rumours that the competition would be reallocated to Holland and Belgium, rumours that the Dutch would withdraw—as Johan Cruyff had already withdrawn—if it were not. Meanwhile, even the Argentinian Minister of Economics objected to the colossal cost of the affair; it was expected to lose some $750 million.

A further fear concerned the behaviour of Argentine players and crowds. In the late 1960s, Argentinian club and international teams had been notorious for their violence. Argentinian crowds were well known for their intimidatory effect on referees. True, the new Argentine team manager, the tall, lean, fair, chain-smoking Cesar Luis Menotti,

nicknamed El Flaco (the Thin One), had promised a new era. If a
team could kick its way to the World Cup, he'd said, then he would
pick such a team, but it was no longer possible. Such methods were
obsolete. The emphasis must be on skill. Fine, if not fighting, words,
but had they real substance? In June 1977, England and Scotland
played Argentina within a week of each other in the notoriously vertiginous Boca Stadium, and each game threw up an ugly incident.
Trevor Cherry of England was punched in the mouth by Argentina's
Daniel Bertoni; the Uruguayan referee, Ramon Barreto, sent *both* of
them off. The following week, Pernia, the Argentine back, knocked
Willie Johnston of Scotland down with a cruel punch to the kidneys.
Again, the referee sent off both players.

## The Contenders    Argentina

Menotti, the Argentinian manager, had great problems in building a
team. The end of the World Cup had seen a great exodus abroad,
notably to Spanish clubs. Brindisi, Carnevali, Wolff, Babington,
Kempes, Heredia and others were in Europe now. Menotti said boldly
that he'd recall no more than three players: Kempes, Piazza, the
Saint-Etienne centre-half, and Wolff. Kempes had matured into the
most dangerous goal scorer in Spain, with Valencia. Wolff was now
playing in defence—where Argentina looked weakest—with Real
Madrid. Piazza had actually been released by Saint-Etienne and was
back in Buenos Aires when his wife and child were hurt in a car
accident, and he returned to France. Wolff was lost because Menotti
insisted he be in Buenos Aires by the beginning of April. Real Madrid
could not possibly release him then.

So, without Kempes, his team—which had played a long, indifferent
series in the Boca Stadium the previous year—laboured convincingly
through a number of friendlies.

### Holland

If Argentina would be missing many stars, the two greatest stars of all
would not be there, either. Johan Cruyff of Holland, inspiration of the
1974 team, best and most versatile centre-forward in the world, had
stood firmly by his decision not to take part, despite huge offers,
endless pleading and pressure. Alas for Holland, Cruyff was not the
only absentee of renown; indeed, he had seemed to set a fashion. For
varying reasons, Van Beveren, the country's best goalkeeper, Ruud
Geels, the excellent Ajax centre-forward and Wim Van Hanegem—
as late as May 1978—dropped out, while the splendid attacking left-
back Hovenkamp was hurt. It was thus a much-diminished Dutch

team which flew to Argentina, even if such distinguished survivors as Rep, Rensenbrink, Haan and Neeskens were present. The new manager was Ernst Happel—an Austrian, once in charge of Rotterdam's Feyenoord, but now the most part-time of international managers, since he had charge of Belgium's Bruges.

## West Germany

West Germany would be without Franz Beckenbauer, a loss which would prove irreparable. In April 1977 he suddenly, and shockingly, accepted a $2,500,000 offer to join the Cosmos of New York.

Schoen had already lost several other of his 1974 players. The tournament was scarcely over when the prolific Gerd Muller, the wily Jurgen Grabowski and the inventive Wolfgang Overath announced that they would play no more international football. They had had enough of its strains, its tension and its travelling. They wanted, they said, to spend more time with their families.

Yet the 1976 West German team seemed perfectly capable of winning the World Cup again, and the 1977 team won comfortably at Boca against Argentina. The pre-World-Cup season started cheerfully enough, with a fine win against Italy in West Berlin. Manny Kaltz, the Hamburg defender, was no Beckenbauer in skill and poise, but he had done well at sweeper and was, some said, at least a better defensive player than Beckenbauer. With the New Year, however, results fell away. The 'new' system of playing the acrobatic Schalke 04 centre-forward, Klaus Fischer, between two wide wingers was no longer so successful.

## Scotland

From Britain, Scotland alone as in 1974 would make the trip, under the euphoric managership of Ally MacLeod. England, after a disastrous three years of management by Don Revie, which came to a squalid if lucrative end when he decamped to Arabia, were eliminated by the Italians. Northern Ireland found Holland too much for them. Wales went out to Scotland—controversially. The Czechs, winners of the 1976 Nations Cup with a glittering pair of performances—though they beat West Germany in the Final only on penalties—were also victims of the Scots as indeed they had been in 1974.

Of Scotland's talent, there was no doubt. They had more outstanding players, certainly, than any of the other British teams. There was some doubt, however, both about the experience and the detachment of their manager, who had left Aberdeen to take over Willie

Ormond's team little over a year before, and of the team's ability to turn its talent into results.

After qualifying for the World Cup by beating Wales at Liverpool, the euphoria of the Scots was infinite and continued to be so, even if their geographical sense was not always impeccable. WE'RE ON OUR WAY TO RIO! cried the headline of a Scottish daily newspaper, next morning. Wild plans were conceived by fans desperate to get beyond Rio, to Argentina; one even contemplated hiring a submarine. Others worked their way across the subcontinent, though ultimately the following was counted in hundreds rather than thousands.

The Scots had an abundance of fine midfield players at a time when most other countries looked for them desperately; Rioch, Masson, Hartford, Gemmill, Macari, Souness. They were severely weakened, though, by the news that Danny McGrain, the Celtic right-back, who had missed the game against Wales with a chronic foot injury, had no chance of recovering in time for the World Cup finals. McGrain, perhaps the best right-back in football, a player of power, authority, mobility and drive, by turns a stout defender and an extra forward, was without an equal.

To his unavoidable loss was added the quite avoidable loss of Andy Gray, the excellent young Aston Villa centre-forward, inexplicably left out of the final forty players, let alone the final, permitted, twenty-two, by an increasingly unpredictable MacLeod. His reasons made little sense, the less so as he preferred to Gray, in excellent form, the obscure Joe Harper, who had played for him at Aberdeen. Moreover, MacLeod decided to take to Argentina the injured Gordon McQueen, though it was all but certain that the big centre-half would be unable to play.

As the competition grew nearer, so MacLeod's statements and postures grew more extreme. 'I'm a winner!' he cried, promising great things, evidently borne along by the exultant optimism of the fans. The Scottish newspapers did nothing to restrain him; their nickname of 'supporters with typewriters', conferred on them by an English colleague, seemed amply earned.

If MacLeod was over-sanguine, he was also remarkably commercial. How much money he made in the year leading up to the World Cup is unknown, but he bought himself a public house for an estimated £70,000. (MacLeod himself said that in fact it was rented, and its cost was exaggerated.) Around the Scottish camp hung such an aura of materialism, of wheeling and dealing, that it was astonishing to read a Scottish FA report, three months after the World Cup, which blamed MacLeod for not having made clear to his players how much they stood to earn.

## Brazil

Brazil, too, were under a new manager, the 39-year-old Army captain, Claudio Coutinho, an elegant polyglot who had come into football by the roundabout route of physical training. He was an enthusiast of the Cooper Test system of assessing athletes—the emphasis was on endurance—and had been physical 'preparer' of the 1974 World Cup team, manager of the 1976 Olympic soccer team. Charming, good looking, cosmopolitan, he took over from the São Paulo veteran, Osvaldo Brandao. Coutinho at once restored the wayward overlapping full-back Francisco Marinho to the team, which showed instant improvement, successfully completed the qualifying group against Colombia and Paraguay, then himself ran into the familiar torrent of criticism.

In his case he was blamed for trying to impose on the players the concept of 'polyvalence', which, he explained, was simply another way of saying Total Football. But by early 1978, when the team was in training camp outside Rio, Coutinho's approach seemed quite another one. Now the emphasis was on fitness and what he conceived to be 'European' hardness. Touch players such as the gifted young centre-forward, Reinaldo, were encouraged to chase back and challenge. Defenders were exhorted to stop their opponents by hook or by crook.

## Italy

Enzo Bearzot, the new Italian manager at first appointed jointly with the veteran Fulvio Bernardini, had pulled his team together. A large, dark man of almost Red Indian looks, and an international half-back, he was a passionate moralist who hated much of what Italian football had become and was anxious to wean it away from negativity. This would take time, because almost every major club played with a static sweeper and attacked on the break, but Total Football was for Bearzot 'the true aim'.

The nearer the competition drew, the less impressive Italy seemed, though several new young players emerged—Cabrini, the attacking left-back, for instance—on the eve of the competition. Paolo Rossi, whose valuation by Lanerossi Vicenza at £3,000,000 in May, led to the resignation of the President of the Italian League in protest, was a centre-forward of outstanding talents. Small but marvellously adroit, he was unable, however, to win a place in the team before it left for Argentina.

Italy's task had been made no easier by some politicking which had gone badly astray. Initially, before the draw for the finals was made in

Buenos Aires in January, Italy had expected to be seeded, with all the consequent advantages. Strong objection to this was made, however, by the West Germany FIFA delegate Hermann Neudecker, with the result that Holland—the 1974 finalists—were seeded instead. Italy then urged that they be placed in the Buenos Aires group, a privilege granted to them. Bizarre classification, however, which rated feeble Mexico on the same level as Hungary, Spain and Peru led to a lop-sided grouping. In the second pool, the West German holders and the Poles were faced merely by Mexico and Tunisia, the African entrants, while Group I was composed, formidably, of Argentina, Italy, Hungary and France. The French, who possessed one of the best players in Europe in the 21-year-old Michel Platini, a midfield player from Nancy with a superb touch and a remarkable flair for scoring from free kicks, were known to be a gifted side.

## The Preliminaries

Under the impetus of EAM, Argentina made up for the slack years of Peronism and licked their stadia into shape, though there were problems till the last—just as there had been, after all, in Montevideo when the World Cup began. At the rebuilt, imposingly modern River Plate Stadium, seawater was used to sprinkle the grass, which withered and died in the sun. A new field was hastily laid. Rich and green it looked, but the bounce was often capricious. At seaside Mar del Plata, where the Brazilians were reluctantly to play, concerned about the cold weather, heavy rain had made the pitch a fiasco in which divots were kicked up in dozens.

A few weeks before the tournament was due to start, a bomb was found, despite the heavy security, in the Press Centre in Buenos Aires. It exploded as it was being taken away, killing one policeman and wounding another. Many footballers, among them Paolo Rossi and West Germany's goalkeeper, Sepp Maier, signed an Amnesty International petition protesting about the torture and treatment of political prisoners, but it was easy for Argentina's military government, controlling almost all sources of information, to represent to them that their country was the victim of a conspiracy of vilification.

It is true that the Amnesty International campaign told only part of the story. Though there was no denying that dreadful outrages had been committed by the military regime, they had taken over a country in a state of virtual civil war in which normal life in the great cities had become almost impossible and kidnapping and assassination were rife. The attitude of the ordinary bourgeois citizen in Buenos Aires during the World Cup seemed to be one of relief that he could now live and work without fear—though the solemn parade of the mothers each

Thursday afternoon in the Plaza de Mayo, where the Presidential palace stands, was a bleak reminder of what lay beneath the surface of 'normal' life.

### Early Games

Thus the World Cup did not go to the Low Countries, nor to Brazil, which had made it plain that it would be ready to accept it. Instead, it opened on June 1 in the River Plate Stadium with one more of those stupefyingly boring curtain-raisers, this time between West Germany and Poland.

It had surely become plain enough that such preludes, pulling two teams from the pack and placing such pressure on them, were self-defeating. It would grow equally clear that the clumsy new formula, initiated in 1974, whereby the first stage of four qualifying groups led not to quarter-finals but to two more league groups whose winners contested the Final, was disastrous.

For this first game, Helmut Schoen surprisingly and suddenly abandoned his policy of two wingers and a centre-forward, instead fielding only two strikers in the Schalke men, Abramczik and Fischer.

There seemed some consolation in the lively form of Hansi Muller, a tall 20-year-old from Stuttgart, more midfield fish than upfield fowl, but he was *persona non grata* to some of the senior professionals.

Though neither team deserved to win a depressingly cautious match, which was ultimately and deservedly whistled by the River Plate crowd, there might have been a Polish victory but for a couple of alert saves by Sepp Maier. The lack of Gadocha—and of their old spirit of adventure—was plain in Poland's team, but in Adam Nawalka, a 20-year-old right-half from Wisla Cracow they clearly had a new player of great energy and potential in midfield. It was characteristic of Gmoch's costive approach that the clever 22-year-old Zbigniew Boniek should come on only as a late substitute for the veteran Lubanski—who had missed the 1974 World Cup Finals with an injured knee but had found his way back into the team after moving to Belgium. Boniek would, in the event, emerge as one of the outstanding young players of the tournament, balanced, adroit, insidious and a good finisher into the bargain.

Schoen did not stick long to his 4-4-2 formation. Protests from his players led him for the next game, against Mexico in Cordoba, to switch to yet another new strategy, a two-centre-forward attack. It was about this time that the old familiar pattern of West German participation in World Cups asserted itself, as his senior coaches were to be heard pungently criticising him for his vacillation. There was dissatisfaction, too, among the players with the lonely, boring life they led in training camp at Ascochinga outside Cordoba, though things there were enlivened by the controversial visit of the Nazi war hero, Colonel Hans-Ulrich Rudel. As a wartime fighter pilot, Rudel was said to have destroyed a thousand Russian tanks. Later, he had organised Peron's air force. An unrepentant Nazi, he had been banned from addressing any political meetings in Bavaria.

### Group I   Argentina v. Hungary

The following evening, Argentina opened their programme in Group I with a torrid match against Hungary. At Wembley Stadium ten days earlier, the elderly Hungarian manager, Lajos Baroti, had stood in the evening sunshine as his players trained and told me of his fears about the tournament. Everything, he'd said, even the air, was in favour of Argentina. He was afraid that the referees might well give them a couple of penalties: 'The success of Argentina is financially so important to the tournament.'

The Hungarians had surprisingly eliminated their old foes Russia and then put out Bolivia in two final qualifying games. Much was expected of the 22-year-old Andras Toroscik, a small, blond centre-forward with delightful ball control, superb balance and an ability to pick his way through penalty areas to score remarkable goals. The tall, lean Tibor Nyilasi, who had played with him since they were youth internationals, was an attacking midfielder of great talent, dangerous in the air.

When Argentina took the field, it was to a snowstorm of torn-up paper, swirling in the floodlights. The River Plate Stadium, its terraces set well back from the field with a track between, was a much less intimidating one than Boca's, but referees, as we would quickly see, were still alarmingly susceptible.

With so much bad faith on both sides, it would have required an immeasurably stronger referee than the feeble Portuguese, Garrido, to have brought the game smoothly into harbour. The Hungarians, who had been rough at Wembley against England, were harsher still here, pursuing a policy of ruthless challenge and quick counter-attack which seemed for some time as if it might pay. It was in fact a game which began with great promise but degenerated long before the end into sheer beastliness.

Hungary took the lead after only twelve minutes when Zombori completed a clever move with a shot which Fillol, the Argentine goal-keeper, couldn't hold, Csapo driving in the loose ball. It was not till the second half, when the busy little Osvaldo Ardiles, so soon to come to Tottenham, moved from right to left in midfield that Argentina took a grip on the game, even though Leopoldo Luque had equalised within three minutes after Gujdar couldn't hold Mario Kempes's thundering left-footed shot.

Two things were impressively evident about Argentina: first that Cesar Menotti, undaunted by the looming shadow of Juan Carlos Lorenzo, his ruthless predecessor, really had persuaded his team to attack, second, that they now had the pace which in previous years Argentinian teams so plainly lacked. Lorenzo, manager now of Boca Juniors, was reduced to a mere benign commentator. The strength of the Argentine attack, meanwhile, was the electric combination of the two big strikers, Luque, a right-footed player, and the left-footed Kempes. These two made space for one another, played off each other and in general showed a pace and power which was often splendidly exciting. Once Gujdar had to dive perilously at Luque's feet, but in the end he was beaten by Bertoni after he had brought Luque down in a fulminating Argentine attack, seven minutes from the end.

Toroscik, performing small miracles of skill against defenders who fouled him almost every time he tried to beat them, had had his name taken by Garrido in the first half merely for hurling the ball away in petulance when denied a throw-in. Given what had gone before, and would come after, it was rather like indicting and jailing a *mafioso* for income-tax evasion. When Gallego, however, yet again fouled Toroscik, something snapped. Toroscik kicked him to the ground, and off he went. A few minutes later he was followed by Nyilasi, guilty of a spiteful foul on the largely innocent left-back, Tarantini.

## Italy v. France

What brought the Italians to life, ironically, was the goal headed against them in thirty-eight seconds at Mar del Plata by the French centre-forward Lacombe. It forced them out of their customary defensive crouch and made them attack. There was also the question of piqued pride. 'We wanted to show them we weren't the imbeciles they took us for,' said Dino Zoff, the veteran goalkeeper. 'We came here with no hope,' admitted Roberto Bettega, who had a splendid game. 'Some of the Press had written us off as tourists.'

Paolo Rossi played and scored a pin-table goal in Italy's 2–1 success. His excellent form in training games against local sides had moved Bearzot finally to include him in preference to the bigger Torino striker, Francesco Graziani, who had had a lean season. Marco Tardelli, marking Platini—sometimes too aggressively—seemed a regenerated player. He owed this, he would later say, above all to the 'tranquillity' of the Hindu Club, where Italy (like France) had set up training camp. Wisely Bearzot banned all Italian newspapers from the camp and the players were gradually able to disperse the miasma of pessimism and criticism surrounding them on their arrival.

There was a new sweeper in the young Juventus player Gaetano Scirea, the 35-year-old Giacinto Facchetti having finally been forced out of the team by a bang in the ribs from the notorious Romeo Benetti during a League game between Inter and Juventus. This, too, would be a help for Scirea, uneasy in his previous appearances, would now take wing and make a much more adventurous contribution to the team than the static Facchetti could even have done.

Platini left the churned-up field of Mar del Plata complaining that he had had no decent support in midfield, where he missed the powerful, combative Bathanay. Things in the French camp had been tense, with the players painting out the Adidas stripes on their boots because they wanted more money. This distressed their idealistic manager Michel Hidalgo, already unnerved by an attempt to kidnap him shortly before the team left France.

### France v. Argentina

In their next match, however, the French surpassed themselves. Their opponents were Argentina, again in the River Plate Stadium, and now they restored both Dominique Bathenay and Dominique Rocheteau, the Saint-Etienne men. Bathenay had been suffering from injury; Rocheteau, an elegant sinuous outside-right, had only lately recovered from it. Marius Tresor, the splendid black sweeper from Guadeloupe, had been injured too and was estimated by French critics to be at no more than seventy per cent of full efficiency. For all that he was one of the most impressive, dominant defenders of the World Cup.

That Argentina eventually beat France 2–1 was largely the fruit of two abominable decisions by the referee, M. Jean Dubach of Switzerland; a penalty given (and that is the right word) to Argentina, a penalty refused to France. The French, with Bathenay now giving Platini the muscular support he needed, played much delicate, delightful football in the first half. Argentina, whose rhythm would be destroyed when Luque dislocated his elbow, relied heavily on Kempes, who hit the post with a tremendous left-footed drive after beating Trésor in the forty-second minute. The game was in injury time when another majestic burst by Kempes, always wonderfully ready to run at and commit a defence, ended with Luque dashing through, Tresor falling as he challenged him and landing on the ball with his hand. M. Dubach, well behind the play, blew his whistle, then astonishingly ran to consult his Canadian linesman, who had been even farther from the incident. This done he pointed for a penalty which Daniel Passarella, the Argentine centre-back and captain, drove left-footed into goal.

It was a monstrous decision, which looks no better in retrospect now that Winsemann, the Canadian linesman, has revealed what Dubach asked. 'Inside or outside?' he enquired in German. If he needed to ask that, then his eyesight was scarcely sufficient for a football referee. The only point at issue was whether or not the handling was intentional.

Though the goal had come so cruelly, and at so delicate a moment, the French fought back well, They equalised seventeen minutes into the second half after a splendid run and cross from the right by Battison found the Argentine defence adrift. When Lacombe's attempt came back from the bar, Platini scored easily. Didier Six, who had a mixed game indeed, should have put France in the lead after twenty-seven minutes after a glorious run and pass by Platini, but he shot wide with Fillol alone to beat. Thus Argentina were allowed to win the game with a goal quite out of the blue by Luque, a tremendous right-footed shot from outside the box as the defence momentarily stood off. Eleven minutes from time, Platini put Six through again, but when he was manifestly pulled down, M. Dubach did nothing. France were out, but with honour.

### Argentina v. Italy

Now Argentina met Italy, again by night. Both teams had already qualified. It was a question of which would win the group and thus stay in Buenos Aires, a consummation devoutly to be wished, it seemed, by Argentina. The second-placed team would have to play in Rosario.

Bearzot at first decided to use several reserves, but Paolo Rossi and others who would have been left out protested. Rossi said that he felt perfectly fit; if there was any reason for excluding him, he would like to be told. So it was the full Italian team which met an Argentine side now without Kempes.

It was in this game that Menotti made his one tactical error. He decided to play Kempes as an orthodox centre-forward between two wingers. Before the tournament began, there had been sustained discussion in the Argentine Press about how Kempes should be used: should he play as a striker or just behind the front three of Bertoni, Luque and Houseman. This was the role he had often filled in Spain for Valencia, the one in which he would eventually play here. Now he was a fish out of water, denied the invaluable support of the injured Luque in the middle, denied the room and space he would find by dropping farther back.

This time there would be no nonsense about the refereeing. The choice had fallen on the little Israeli, Abraham Klein, who made it clear from the first that he would not be influenced or frightened.

Though their pattern of play had been disjointed, Argentina still might have scored twice in the first half, were it not for glorious saves by Zoff from Kempes and Passarella—always ready to go up into attack. Gradually the Argentine fire was extinguished by Italy's tight, man-to-man defence and after sixty-seven minutes Bettega scored the only goal of the game. Rossi, with a fine determined burst on the left, began the move, winning the ball and crossing it. He then moved on into the middle to play an elegant one-two with Bettega, who ran on easily to shoot past Fillol. Italy would play in Buenos Aires, Argentina in Rosario. Later, disappointed Italian players said it was a pity it had not worked out the other way.

## Group II

In Group II, the West Germans and Poles qualified, as everyone expected, but they were given a surprisingly hard time of it by an admirable Tunisian side. Opening the new stadium at Rosario, Tunisia, their midfield cleverly organised by Dhiab, seemed inferior to Mexico at first, fell behind to a penalty kick, but dominated the second half with their superior speed and stamina to win 3–1.

Poland were next, again at Rosario, and Tunisia gave them a hectic run for their money. They set Khaled Dasmi, rude but efficacious, to dog the steps of Deyna and were helped by the fact that the Poles again did not bring Boniek on till the closing stages. It was an unfortunate mistake by Amar Jebali which enabled Lato to score the game's only goal three minutes from half-time. Thereafter Tunisia were on top and surprised the critics by their technical superiority—to all but Lubanski. They deserved to equalise.

With West Germany they drew 0–0, and might have won. The left-footed Dhiab, slight but adroit, looked better than any of the West German midfielders, Flohe and Bonhof included. Dieter Muller and Klaus Fischer were easily snuffed out up front. The German team, according to *La Nacion* of Buenos Aires, was fragile and without imagination. But it had qualified to play in Pool A, the Buenos Aires group.

## Group IV

In the Cordoba-Mendoza group, Peru astonished, Scotland succumbed and the Dutch made few friends. Iran, who had already lost at home to Wales before the competition began, had done well to knock out the Australians, but looked an uninspired, untalented lot in Argentina where they failed to win a game. Holland beat them quite comfortably, all three goals going to Rob Rensenbrink, two from the penalty spot, though an Argentine critic said the Dutch team resembled a superb machine which lacked the man who invented it. That man, clearly enough, was Johan Cruyff.

Scotland, the players restless at their hotel in Alta Cracia, maligned by the local Press as fervent drinkers, came out to play Peru at Cordoba absurdly unprepared. Quite simply, Ally MacLeod had failed to do his homework; otherwise Scotland could scarcely have given Teofilo Cubillas the untramelled freedom of midfield.

Cubillas, a black player of great virtuosity, had been one of the revelations of 1970, a rapid striker. Now, at twenty-nine, after experience in Portugal, he was back in Lima and had dropped into midfield. Peru's form in 1978 had been so poor that MacLeod had plainly decided they were not worth taking seriously; indeed, his whole approach by now seemed to be the old, hubristic British one of 'let them worry about *us*'.

## Scotland's Departure

Surprisingly, he decided to persevere in midfield with Don Masson and Bruce Rioch, each a half-back rather than an inside-forward, despite the fact that both had been in such poor form, so disaffected, that Derby County had put them on the transfer list. True neither had played badly against England at Hampden, where Asa Hartford had been ebullient in midfield, but to leave out the tall, adroit Graeme Souness after he had run into such splendid form with Liverpool, playing such a large part in their conquest of the European Cup, seemed absurd. Not till the last game, against Holland, did he come into the side and then his impact was immediate. After the Peruvian debacle, Martin Buchan, played out of position at left-back since Donachie was suspended, complained that he had not known Munante was so fast. It had long been an open secret throughout Latin America.

Ironically Scotland began quite well and scored a good goal after fourteen minutes. Dalglish and Hartford gave Rioch the chance of a shot, Quiroga, the eccentric Peruvian goalkeeper, who would cross the halfway line when the spirit moved him, couldn't hold the ball; Joe Jordan put it in.

Gradually, however, the virtue began to ebb out of Scotland. Cubillas, pacing his game beautifully, showing great skill both on the ball and in his use of it, was growing more and more apparent. Two minutes before half-time—a traumatising moment—he was involved in a quick, clever exchange of passes which let Cueto through to equalise.

Scotland's chance to win the game, and perhaps acquit themselves adequately in the tournament, arose and was thrown away after seventeen minutes of the second half. Diaz brought down Rioch and

Masson took the penalty. He had scored coolly against Wales; surely he must do so now. But his shot was a poor one and Quiroga, who almost certainly moved before the ball was kicked, turned it round the left-hand post.

That was the end of Scotland, who had no answer to Cubillas. Two splendidly-struck right-footed goals in the seventy-second and seventy-ninth minutes cooked their goose. For the first, he was left unmarked. For the second, he thumped a swerving free kick high into the left-hand corner, after himself starting the move which led to it with a superb long crossfield pass—the kind which once was accounted a British speciality. Afterwards he remarked modestly that he didn't know why everybody had been writing him off as too old; after all, he was only 29.

Still worse was to follow for Scotland. Willie Johnston, the little 31-year-old outside-left, in tremendous form against Peru, was one of two players singled out for a dope test; and the test proved positive. He had taken two Fencamfamin pills. Shades of poor Jean-Joseph of Haiti (by now in Chicago with Godocha) in 1974. Johnston at first protested that he had taken them for his hay fever, but it soon transpired that it was something that he'd often done in club games. 'Pep pills?' said a sceptical Glaswegian fan. 'I thought they were tranquillisers.' Johnston was packed off home in disgrace, suspended from international football for a year, told by Scotland he would never play for them again and consoled only by the rustle of bank notes as a Sunday newspaper paid him a large sum for his 'story'.

Scotland's morale lay in ruins. There were complaints about the poor training facilities, complaints about the hotel, complaints about MacLeod. It was a demoralised team which laboured in its next match to an embarrassing draw against Iran. Scotland's goal was farcical, scored by Eskandarian against his own team as he and his goalkeeper fell to the ground and he thrust out a desperate foot.

Holland, meanwhile, were proving as enigmatic as they had looked before battle began. There was, to begin with, a manifest conflict in approach and temperament between their managers, Ernst Happel, the dour Austrian, and Jan Zwartkruis, an Air Force Officer who had managed the team before Happel and who had known most of the players for years, having run the Army team. In a remarkable outburst at Holland's training camp—where the Dutch players were restless, too—he criticised Happel for treating his men 'as footballers, rather than as human beings'. He may have had a point in so far as Happel's treatment of Jan Jongbloed, the 37-year-old goalkeeper, was concerned. Jongbloed, furious when Happel almost casually told him he'd been dropped after the game against Scotland, had to dissuade his wife from coming to beard Happel in his den.

Initially, it was supposed that Happel would experiment with a new system which placed five men in midfield, roughly in the shape of an X with the key player in the centre. This had been tried in May against Austria in Vienna with Wim Van Hanegem in the middle. Afterwards, however, the big, 34-year-old inside-left had been told by Happel that he could not guarantee him a place in Argentina and he had therefore become the last Dutch player to withdraw.

Held to a goalless draw by Peru, Happel dropped Aarie Haan, restored to midfield for this World Cup, from the team to play Scotland and chose Johan Neeskens though he was known not to be fit. Indeed, he did not last many minutes. The Scots at last brought Graeme Souness into the side. Asked whether he thought Scotland could score the three goals they needed against Holland Jongbloed replied, 'Yes, but not in ninety minutes.'

Score them, however, they did, including what many considered the finest goal of the competition; it took a desperate rally by the Dutch to pull the score back to 2–3 and stay in the competition. Scotland at last, and too late, had cast off their complexes to play splendid football. The Dutch, by contrast, played a sour, negative game, with much harsh tackling and excessive emphasis on the offside trap.

They owed much to the splendid play at sweeper of Ruud Krol— their 1974 left-back who rescued them time and again. His former partner at full-back, Wim Suurbier, was surprisingly put at centre-back against Jordan, though he himself had never claimed to be strong in the air, where Jordan was at his strongest.

This, in any event, was a new Scotland, driven on from midfield by Souness and the exuberant little Archie Gemmill. Rioch, too, looked far more enterprising, hitting the angle of post and bar after only five minutes. The Dutch went into the lead when Johnny Rep was brought down by Kennedy and Alan Rough the goalkeeper, and Rob Rensenbrink scored from yet another penalty. But Johan Neeskens had already left the field, after a lunging tackle on Gemmill, and the Dutch team laboured. Just before half-time, Jordan headed down Souness's clever lob and Dalglish equalised. When Souness was fouled, after half-time, Gemmill in turn scored a penalty to make it 2–1.

This, though, was as nothing to the goal with which he made it 3–1, an astonishing slalom which took him from just outside his penalty area round three bemused defenders to end with a slashing shot past Jongbloed. A twenty-five-yard shot by Johnny Rep finally beat the vulnerable Rough to give Holland their second goal and take them into Group A. In Glasgow the cruel word went round that 'Micky Mouse is wearing an Ally MacLeod wrist watch'. A characteristically crass report by the Scottish Football Association, who confirmed MacLeod in office by a casting vote, seemed to put most of the blame on the Scottish journalists.

Certainly they had been mindlessly euphoric. Certainly the London Press had done Scotland a disservice by competing for sensational revelations from the players, but the players themselves had been disaffected and greedy. There was an especially displeasing episode when Don Masson went to Ally MacLeod to say that he, too, had taken 'pep' pills, only to withdraw his story when MacLeod marched him in to the Scottish officials.

## Group III

In Mar del Plata, Brazil blundered their way into the second round, thanks chiefly to two shocking errors by their opposition. They were an unhappy ship—appropriately commanded by Admiral Heleno Nunes —from the first. Rivelino was overweight and unhappy; there were tense relations between Coutinho and another of his most gifted players, the little, attacking midfielder, Zico, unhappy at the long spell in training camp which prevented him seeing his baby son. Reinaldo, the clever, sharp mulatto centre-forward, reduced by an infinity of cartilage operations, had been under a cloud since making good-hearted if ingenuous remarks about Brazil's political prisoners. There was no Luis Pereira to play sweeper. The 1974 captain had virtually withdrawn from the team after a poor season with Atletico Madrid. He was also afraid, he said, that if he played badly against Spain he'd be accused in Brazil of 'throwing' the match.

Brazil began indifferently against Sweden in Mar del Plata, then played still worse against Spain and Austria. The Swedes running themselves to subsequent extinction, scored first. Reinaldo equalised for Brazil with delightful finesse when the first half was in injury time, but the Welsh referee, Clive Thomas, whimsically decided to blow for full time precisely as the ball was going into the net for what would have been Brazil's winning goal. The Brazilians protested. The Swedes retorted that as the corner kick sailed over they had relaxed when they heard the final whistle. Thomas incurred the disapproval of FIFA not for this, however, but for covering his face theatrically with his hands when Bo Larsson almost put through his own goal.

For the next game, against Spain, who had been beaten 2–1 in Buenos Aires by an unexpectedly lively Austria, Brazil omitted Rivelino, whose supposed unfitness would become a bone of contention, Rivelino subsequently insisting he was injured, Coutinho that he was not. Without his heavy-thighed, heavily moustached, sombre and irascible presence in midfield, Brazil were much diminished. Dirceu, who now filled the left midfield position, was much eulogised by the end of the competition, but despite abundant energy and a strong left-footed shot, he seemed prosaic by comparison with the likes of Rivelino and Gerson.

It was a stupendous mistake in the second half by Julio Cardeñosa, the little Spanish midfielder, which permitted Brazil to draw 0–0. When the tall Real Madrid centre-forward Santillana flicked a high ball on to him, Brazil's defence was left in chaos; even the greying Leao was out of goal. Perhaps if Cardeñosa had not had so much time, he would have scored, simply have put the ball into the empty net. Instead he hesitated pitifully, and was lost. By the time he shot, the black Amaral had scuttled back to clear from the line. Some players, observed a Buenos Aires paper, became famous for the goals they scored. Cardeñosa had achieved fame through the one he missed. It says something for Cardeñosa's character and skill that in Spain's final game, in Buenos Aires, he should be the inspiration of their win against Sweden.

Brazil's, and Coutinho's, bankruptcy was shown by the fact that he used a right-back, Toninho, as his outside-right. Shades of Julinho, Garrincha and Jairzinho!

Against Austria, once more at Mar del Plata, Brazil won 1–0 because a centre from that same Toninho, now at right-back was allowed to drift over his head by the tall Austrian stopper, Pezzey. Roberto, on the far post, had infinite time to control the ball and score. So Coutinho, who had been burned in effigy in the streets of Mar del Plata by enraged Brazilian fans and relieved publicly of full powers by the egregious Admiral Nunes, survived—with his team. Calm elegance had given way to a haunted anxiety. He banned foreign journalists from his Press conferences and sometimes refused to give conferences at all. He would be shamefully traduced by Nunes before the game against Poland, as a man of 'scarce technical abilities', that the team had been saved by its players and by 'wise officials'. If they were so wise, you wondered, then why had they appointed a man of 'scarce abilities' in the first place.

## The Final Groups

The two final groups would be made up by: Italy, Holland, West Germany and Austria, in Buenos Aires and Cordoba; Argentina, Peru, Poland and Brazil in Rosario and Mendoza. The second was clearly the weaker, although Argentina won it only by goal difference. The question of goal difference had already caused extreme confusion when it seemed that Brazil might finish level on points with other teams in its group for second place; and level on goal difference, too. FIFA's rules on the subject were extremely vague, but Brazil's lucky win against Austria made the matter academic, for the moment.

Goal difference rendered Holland's 5–1 win over Austria in their opening Group A game in Cordoba of colossal importance. Quite how the Austrians, who had played so well in their first two matches and would play so well in the last two, collapsed so ineptly was a mystery.

The Dutch, much happier on the Cordoba surface than Mendoza's, gave a glorious display of Total Football. They successfully introduced two young players, the midfielder Pieter Wildschut and the tall centre-back Erny Brandts, who headed the first goal after five minutes from a free kick. Resenbrink at last justified the hopes placed in him with an irresistible display, scoring another penalty, beating men at will, brilliantly making goals for Rep and Willy Van de Kerkhof. Aarie Haan returned to the midfield, though Neeskens was again absent.

By contrast, Italy and West Germany played a stultifying goalless draw. 'The Germans', remarked Franco Causio next day, 'built the Berlin Wall in Argentina.' Though Dino Zoff made a wonderful save from Bernd Holzenbein in the first half, and West Germany fashioned several chances late in the second, the German attitude was cravenly defensive, Rummenigge more full-back than winger. Only two spectacular goalmouth clearances by Manny Kaltz from Roberto Bettega—much less incisive than usual—prevented Italy from deservedly winning. Maier, moreover, was once exceedingly lucky when he completely misjudged a lob by Cabrini which came back from the post, though he atoned with a fine save from Bettega's header.

The Italians, however, were running out of steam. Their next game in the River Plate Stadium against Austria saw them begin superbly but fade embarrassingly. That lack of stamina which had bedevilled Italian football so long was all too manifest. After the disastrous Dutch game Enzo Bearzot was to complain violently of the referee, but in this game the Belgian Francis Rion's refereeing greatly favoured Italy. Towards the end, when the tired Italian defenders were going through the old repertoire of obstruction and tripping, he should have given Austria at least one penalty (Senekowitsch the blond Austrian manager, said two) and taken several Italian names.

The goal with which Italy won the game after fifteen minutes, however, was a gem. Cheekily crossing his feet, Paolo Rossi found Franco Causio on his left, outpaced Obermayer, the big blond Austrian sweeper, to the return ball and beat Koncilia to score. Other heroes, however, were evidently tired, not least Bettega and the blond Romeo Benetti.

The 'reprise' of the 1974 World Cup Final between West Germany and Holland, at Cordoba, provided one of the best games of the competition. West Germany, recalling Abramczik and so playing with two wingers, took the lead after only three minutes when the little Schalke 04 man dived bravely to head the ball past Schrijvers, after the keeper could only block one of those fierce free kicks for which Bonhof was famous, but which he so seldom produced in Argentina. Holland equalised through Haan with one of *his* specialities: a thirty-five-yard drive to which Maier did not move. Similar inattention by the Dutch defence allowed Dieter Muller to regain the lead for West Germany with a simple headed goal, twenty minutes from time, but with only seven left, René Van de Kerkhof threaded his way through the German penalty area, beat Maier with his shot, and Russmann's attempt to push it out with his hands failed.

In Rosario, Argentina defeated Poland 2–0 with difficulty. Kempes not only scored both goals but, punching off the Argentine line from Lato, enabled his team to keep their 1–0 lead.

Kempes headed the first goal from Bertoni's left-wing cross, with some complicity from the Polish defence. Jacek Gmoch remarked that Tomaszewski had been unsettled by the proximity of the crowd and, indeed, this was much more of a tight traditional soccer stadium than River Plate's. Eighteen minutes from time, Kempes scored the second goal after a spectacular, sustained run to the by-line by little Ardiles.

At Mendoza, an improved Brazil easily accounted for Peru, whom they always beat, two of the goals being scored from long range by Dirceu. The meeting of Brazil and Argentina in Rosario thus became crucial.

Luque returned for this game, greatly diminished. Not only had his shoulder been hurt, his brother had been horribly burned to death in a car accident. Within ten seconds, Luque had cruelly hacked down the Brazilian half-back Batista, who would be fouled still more brutally in the second half by Villa. Both teams, one French critic remarked, 'were finally the prisoners of their fears, and totally destroyed one another'. Palotai of Hungary was a flaccid referee.

This left Brazil, holding a goal advantage over Argentina, to play Poland at Mendoza, Argentina to play Peru (beaten by Poland) in Rosario. Brazil were scheduled to kick off in the afternoon, Argentina in the evening. Predictably, the Brazilians protested; predictably, their protest was turned down.

Brazil, beating Poland 3–1, gave their best performance of the tournament, though an Argentine critic disdainfully remarked that they won because 'they imposed a conquering temperament which allowed them to overcome their defects and lack of talent.' Poland, in fact, would have been ahead at half-time had they taken their chances. As it was, Brazil went into the lead with one of their right-back's, Nelinho's, extraordinary free kicks, Lato equalised just before half-time. After it Brazil hauled themselves up by their boot-straps, gained control, beat a tattoo on the Polish goalposts and scored twice more through Roberto. It was a game poorly refereed by the Chilean, Juan Silvagno, but then who refereed well?

Italy's Artemio Franchi presided over a Referees' Committee which largely emulated the three wise monkeys. They had given no specific instructions to referees on how to officiate, he said, each must be left to do so in his own way. Such an abdication of responsibility by the Committee led to a serious lack of control, above all in the failure to book offenders for grave fouls, and had its all too appropriate climax in the ineptitude of Sergio Gonella of Italy in the Final.

Brazil's success meant that Argentina had to beat Peru that evening by at least four goals to reach the Final. They beat them by six in a game which has left bitter memories. Before it the Peruvian captain, Hector Chumpitaz, said he realised that it was Peru's task 'to safeguard the decency of the competition'. After it, Quiroga the goalkeeper, actually born in Rosario, published an open letter defending himself and his team. It was a game in which Peru opened briskly, their right-winger Munante hitting the post, their left-winger Oblitas shooting just across the goal. Then the team collapsed and lay down abjectly before the opposition. Why? Claudio Coutinho, Brazil's disappointed manager, attacked them bitterly, said that their players would feel no pride when they heard their national anthem in the next World Cup. Argentine newspapers reported that the Brazilians had tried to offer money to Peru to play well. Some thought they were bribed, some thought they were simply frightened by the torrid atmosphere. What-ever, it was a shabby way for Argentina to reach the Final.

There, they would meet the Dutch, conquerors of Italy in Buenos Aires. Falling behind after eighteen minutes when Erny Brandts, lunging ahead of the encroaching Bettega, not only put through his own goal but disabled his goalkeeper, Schrijvers. Holland recovered in the second half to win. Brandts, remarkably, scored their traumatising equaliser, five minutes after half-time, a left-footed player, up for a free kick, swinging his right foot at the ball and sending it hurtling into the left-hand corner past Zoff. '*Che culo!*', what luck, remarked the Italian defender, Claudio Gentile, the following day. 'I'd never have believed it. He was in the middle of three of us, and the fellow shoots with his head down. He didn't even look up.'

The second goal came from a terrific, thirty-yard shot by Aarie Haan, which Zoff reached, touched but couldn't stop. Later, sunning himself on a beach in Sardinia, Haan said he thought Zoff should have stopped his own shot, but not Brandts's. The game was ill-tempered and abominably refereed by the Spaniard, Angel Martinez. Bearzot insisted that his players were intimidated, that Haan had committed the worst foul of the World Cup on Zaccarelli. Bad it unquestionably was, but it was the immediate sequel to a painful foul by Benetti on Haan himself as he went up the wing. Later, Benetti should have been sent off when he elbowed Neeskens in the face.

In Cordoba, Austria surprisingly beat a flaccid West Germany 3–2. There were rumours that certain German players did not wish to be bothered with the Third Place game. Schoen himself, at the subsequent Press conference said 'I do not want to mention any names, but I was utterly disappointed with our defence, which made things easier for our opponents to score goals.' Helmut Senekowitsch of Austria then chivalrously impugned the West German players' attitude. 'I deplore the fact that Schoen will be retiring from his professional career after seeing his team defeated in this manner.'

### The Final   Argentina v. Holland

Would Holland win, without Cruyff? Their form had been mercurial; no European team had won the World Cup in South America, but they seemed to be running into form and Argentina's defensive weaknesses remained manifest. Four years earlier, inspired by Cruyff, Holland had made the merest mouthful of the Argentinians; but that was not in Buenos Aires. Meanwhile, Brazil, with long shots by Nelinho and Dirceu, right footed and left footed, beat Italy 2–1 to take third place after falling behind to a goal headed easily by Causio.

Would Neeskens play on Kempes in the Final? Would Ardiles play at all? The answers turned out, respectively, to be no and yes though Ardiles, that fragile, sleek-haired, ebullient tango-figure, who had hurt an ankle, would not last the game. 'The Dutch,' Paolo Rossi had admiringly observed, 'change positions as easily as they'd take a cup of coffee.' They marked the Argentinian strikers man to man while the Argentine defence continued to mark zonally and, no doubt, live dangerously. Each team was capable of blood-chilling excesses. Would Gonella be strong enough to control and contain them?

He would not, so much was obvious before a ball had even been kicked. The Argentinians took the field five full minutes late, a most arrant piece of gamesmanship, then, having done so, complained about the bandage René Van de Kerkhof, the Dutch winger, was wearing on his forearm. The Dutch, especially Neeskens, a Spanish speaker, protested violently that Van de Kerkhof had worn the bandage in several preceding games, but Gonella upheld the protest. The Dutchman was obliged to leave the field, where he simply covered that bandage with another.

Subsequently Passarella explained, 'We could not allow ourselves to concede any advantage. Luque saw the danger the bandage could be and I as captain had the obligation to protest.'

'Clearly,' said René Van de Kerkhof, 'but why did they let us wear it in the other games?'

The Dutch team, thus incensed, committed in the opening minute the first of some fifty fouls, a crude one by the young defender Poortvliet. To say that Gonella favoured the Argentinians was true to the extent that he was a weak, fearful referee who quickly allowed the game to slip out of his feeble grasp, tending to penalise the away team. Thus, he twice allowed Argentina's defensive midfield player, Gallego, to handle the ball deliberately without booking him, and if there was the benefit of a doubt it usually went to Argentina. Nevertheless, the attitude of the Dutch team itself was scarcely benign.

The game was a dramatic rather than a distinguished one, turning in the end on a couple of saves by Fillol and three marvellous slaloms by Mario Kempes, distinguished not only by his skill, speed and courage but by his remarkable composure. Both defences in the first half were curiously vulnerable. Four times, at the Dutch end, Passarella came upfield and was 'forgotten', three times Jongbloed saved and once the ball whistled just above the bar. At the other end Johnny Rep pounced when Jansen's cross was headed straight out to him, only for Fillol gallantly to save: as he did again, with his legs, when Neeskens nodded the ball down to Rensenbrink. What each team manifestly lacked in midfield was a true creator. Argentina had in Gallego a defender, in Kempes an attacker, in Ardiles a busy, venturesome half-back. Holland had the muscular versatility of Willy Van de Kerkhof, Neeskens and Haan. There was no Van Hanegem or Overath, as there had been in 1974, and despite the current heresy that such 'generals' were obsolete, the effect of their absence was manifest in the quality of play.

Kempes it was, much too vaguely marked by Willy Van de Kerkhof, given room and time to run at the defence, who scored the first half's only goal. There were seven minutes left to half-time when a four-man movement on the left was concluded by Luque—who had pulled the sweeper Krol out with him—crossing to Kempes. Only Haan stood between him and Jongbloed and, riding Haan's desperate tackle, he ran on to drive the ball home with his formidable left foot. It was right on half-time that Fillol made his crucial save from Rensenbrink, served by Neeskens. From a player cast out by Menotti but restored, a goalkeeper so vulnerable to crosses in the opening games, Fillol had grown into Argentina's rescuer.

He began the second half by saving a thundering shot from Johan Neeskens, hit from far outside the box. Holland now had a grip on the game, but they were not making any clear chances; the much-maligned Argentine defence proved surprisingly resilient when at bay. After fifty-nine minutes Holland took off Johnny Rep, no favourite of Happel and replaced him with the tall Dirk Nanninga, the object plainly being to attack Argentina in the air. Seven minutes later Argentina substituted Ardiles, obviously not wholly fit, with Larrosa, who'd taken his place against Peru.

Holland pressed on. Neeskens forced his way through, to be shockingly brought down by Galvan, who was shown the yellow card; but when he fouled Rensenbrink in the box—an obstruction at the least—no whistle blew. Now Holland moved up Erny Brandts, pulling back Willy Van de Kerkhof; and at last, with two tall men hungry for crosses, the equaliser came.

Haan began the movement with a sweeping long ball from left to right. René Van de Kerkhof controlled it, slipped round Tarantini, centred; and Nanninga rose splendidly to head into the goal.

There was still time for Passarella to elbow Neeskens in the face, then, in the very last minute, for Krol perfectly to put Rob Rensenbrink through. The Argentine defence was scattered, but when Rensenbrink shot, he hit the left-hand post and, did we but know it, the Cup had passed from Holland.

In extra time it was logical and legitimate to expect the Dutch to go on dominating what looked an exhausted Argentine team, but somehow (will we ever know quite how?) Menotti roused his men, as Alf Ramsey had at Wembley. The Dutch restored Brandts to defence, and suddenly found themselves under pressure; Argentina were running and probing again. With fourteen minutes of extra time played, one to go, Kempes received from the lively Bertoni, forced his way through the defence again, almost lost the ball to the brave Jongbloed, managed to retain it and made the score 2–1.

That was that. The second period saw Holland throwing men up in desperate quest for a second equaliser, leaving great gaps in which the Argentinians frolicked. Luque, taking the ball from Krol, was once clean through, only for Jongbloed to frustrate him; but with five minutes left, another marvellous burst by Kempes and a one-two with Bertoni allowed the winger easily to score the third. The stadium now was a volcano of joy; the streets of Buenos Aires would be thronged all night by ecstatic thousands. If it had not been a famous victory, it had been a thrilling one, and if Holland deserved sympathy for losing their second consecutive World Cup Final, perhaps Argentine football deserved its honour, for the players it had given us over the years.

Kempes was not the least of them.

# RESULTS: Argentina 1978

## Group I

Argentina 2, Hungary 1 (HT 1/1)
Italy 2, France 1 (HT 1/1)
Argentina 2, France 1 (HT 1/0)
Italy 3, Hungary 1 (HT 2/0)
Italy 1, Argentina 0 (HT 2/0)
France 3, Hungary 1 (HT 3/1)

|           | P | W | D | L | GOALS F | A | Pts |
|-----------|---|---|---|---|---------|---|-----|
| Italy     | 3 | 3 | 0 | 0 | 6 | 2 | 6 |
| Argentina | 3 | 2 | 0 | 1 | 4 | 3 | 4 |
| France    | 3 | 1 | 0 | 2 | 5 | 5 | 2 |
| Hungary   | 3 | 0 | 0 | 3 | 3 | 8 | 0 |

## Group A

Peru 3, Scotland 1 (HT 1/1)
Holland 3, Iran 0 (HT 1/0)
Scotland 1, Iran 1 (HT 1/0)
Holland 0, Peru 0 (HT 0/0)
Peru 4, Iran 1 (HT 3/1)
Scotland 3, Holland 2 (HT 1/1)

|          | P | W | D | L | GOALS F | A | Pts |
|----------|---|---|---|---|---------|---|-----|
| Peru     | 3 | 2 | 1 | 0 | 7 | 2 | |
| Holland  | 3 | 1 | 1 | 1 | 5 | 3 | |
| Scotland | 3 | 1 | 1 | 1 | 5 | 6 | |
| Iran     | 3 | 0 | 1 | 2 | 2 | 8 | |

## Group II

West Germany 0, Poland 0 (HT 0/0)
Tunisia 3, Mexico 1 (HT 0/1)
Poland 1, Tunisia 0 (HT 1/0)
West Germany 6, Mexico 0 (HT 4/0)
Poland 3, Mexico 1 (HT 1/0)
West Germany 0, Tunisia 0 (HT 0/0)

|              | P | W | D | L | GOALS F | A | Pts |
|--------------|---|---|---|---|---------|---|-----|
| Poland       | 3 | 2 | 1 | 0 | 4 | 1 | 5 |
| West Germany | 3 | 1 | 2 | 0 | 6 | 0 | 4 |
| Tunisia      | 3 | 1 | 1 | 1 | 3 | 2 | 3 |
| Mexico       | 3 | 0 | 0 | 3 | 2 | 12 | 0 |

Italy 0, West Germany 0 (HT 0/0)
Holland 5, Austria 1 (HT 3/0)
Italy 1, Austria 0 (HT 1/0)
Austria 3, West Germany 2 (HT 0/1)
Holland 2, Italy 1 (HT 0/1)
Holland 2, West Germany 2 (HT 1/1)

|              | P | W | D | L | GOALS F | A | Pt |
|--------------|---|---|---|---|---------|---|----|
| Holland      | 3 | 2 | 1 | 0 | 9 | 4 | |
| Italy        | 3 | 1 | 1 | 1 | 2 | 2 | |
| West Germany | 3 | 0 | 2 | 1 | 4 | 5 | |
| Austria      | 3 | 1 | 0 | 2 | 4 | 8 | |

## Group III

Austria 2, Spain 1 (HT 1/1)
Sweden 1, Brazil 1 (HT 1/1)
Austria 1, Sweden 0 (HT 1/0)
Brazil 0, Spain 0 (HT 0/0)
Spain 1, Sweden 0 (HT 0/0)
Brazil 1, Austria 0 (HT 1/0)

|         | P | W | D | L | GOALS F | A | Pts |
|---------|---|---|---|---|---------|---|-----|
| Austria | 3 | 2 | 0 | 1 | 3 | 2 | 4 |
| Brazil  | 3 | 1 | 2 | 1 | 2 | 1 | 4 |
| Spain   | 3 | 1 | 1 | 1 | 2 | 2 | 3 |
| Sweden  | 3 | 0 | 1 | 2 | 1 | 3 | 1 |

## Group B

Argentina 2, Poland 0 (HT 1/0)
Brazil 3, Peru 0 (HT 2/0)
Argentina 0, Brazil 0 (HT 0/0)
Poland 1, Peru 0 (HT 0/0)
Brazil 3, Poland 1 (HT 1/1)
Argentina 6, Peru 0 (HT 2/0)

|           | P | W | D | L | GOALS F | A | Pt |
|-----------|---|---|---|---|---------|---|----|
| Argentina | 3 | 2 | 1 | 0 | 8 | 0 | |
| Brazil    | 3 | 2 | 1 | 0 | 6 | 1 | |
| Poland    | 3 | 1 | 0 | 2 | 2 | 5 | |
| Peru      | 3 | 0 | 0 | 3 | 0 | 10 | |

## Third place match

*Buenos Aires*

---

**Brazil 2**          **Italy 1**
Leao; Nelinho, Oscar,  Zoff; Scirea, Gentile,
Amaral, Neto; Cerezo   Cuccureddu, Cabrini;
(Rivelino), Batista,   Maldera, Antognoni
Dirceu; Gil            (Sala, C.), Sala, P.;
(Reinaldo), Mendonça,  Causio; Rossi, Bettega.
Roberto.

SCORERS
Nelinho, Dirceu for Brazil
Causio for Italy
HT 0/1

## Final

*Buenos Aires*

---

**Argentina 3**       **Holland 1**
(after extra time)
Fillol; Olguin,        Jongbloed; Krol,
Galvan, Passarella,    Poortvliet, Brandts
Tarantini; Ardiles     Jansen (Suurbier);
(Larrosa), Gallego,    Van de Kerkhof, W.,
Kempes; Bertoni,       Neeskens, Haan; Rep
Luque, Ortiz           (Nanninga),
(Houseman).            Rensenbrink,
                       Van de Kerkhof, R.

SCORERS
Kempes (2), Bertoni for Argentina
Nanninga for Holland
HT 1/0 FT 1/1

# Index